AIRBRUSH

ROCKPORT PUBLISHERS

ROCKPORT PUBLISHERS, INC.
ROCKPORT, MASSACHUSETTS

First published in the United States of America by:
Rockport Publishers, Inc.
146 Granite Street
Rockport, Massachusetts 01966
Telephone: (508) 546-9590
Fax: (508) 546-7141

Other Distribution by:
Rockport Publishers, Inc.
Rockport, Massachusetts 01966

Cover Contributors:
(Clockwise from top left)
Thomas Cain
Robert Revels
Jerry Lofaro
Ron Houghton, Jr.
Thomas Cain

ISBN 1-56496-159-1

10 9 8 7 6 5 4 3

Printed in Hong Kong

Introduction

Although the computer has taken over much of the hand manipulated design, illustration, and photo-retouching currently being produced, it will still be a long time before free-hand skills in art and design are given over to machines. Year after year the growing popularity of airbrush illustration proves this point.

A dramatic change in the perception of the airbrush as a legitimate art form has occurred just in the past decade. Airbrushing has evolved from a "hobby" medium that was not taken seriously, to one of the most acceptable and desirable forms for expressing art and design. In many design plans, the airbrush is now chosen in place of traditional methods.

As a result the applications for airbrush art and the diversity of the artists using it have expanded. From humble beginnings as a decoration technique for vans and T-shirts, airbrush art has spread into the fields of graphic design, sign design, commercial advertising, illustration, and garment design. In fact, the soft, graduated, and three-dimensional tones created by airbrushing have become design standards in almost all facets of the industry.

The growing sophistication of the airbrush medium is demonstrated in *Airbrush Action Magazine's* annual Airbrush Excellence Competition; a showcase of the most original and creative airbrush projects produced in a given year. In this volume of **Design Library: Airbrush** you will find the winners circle—a selection of the finest projects of past competition winners.

Dedicating an entire book to only the best—the best airbrush artists and their best work—may seem high-minded. However, as Cliff Stieglitz, the publisher of *Airbrush Action Magazine* wrote,"We feel artists cannot improve with mediocrity as their model." It is this dedication to striving for the best that drives the *Design Library Series,* and it is the reason that this volume exists.

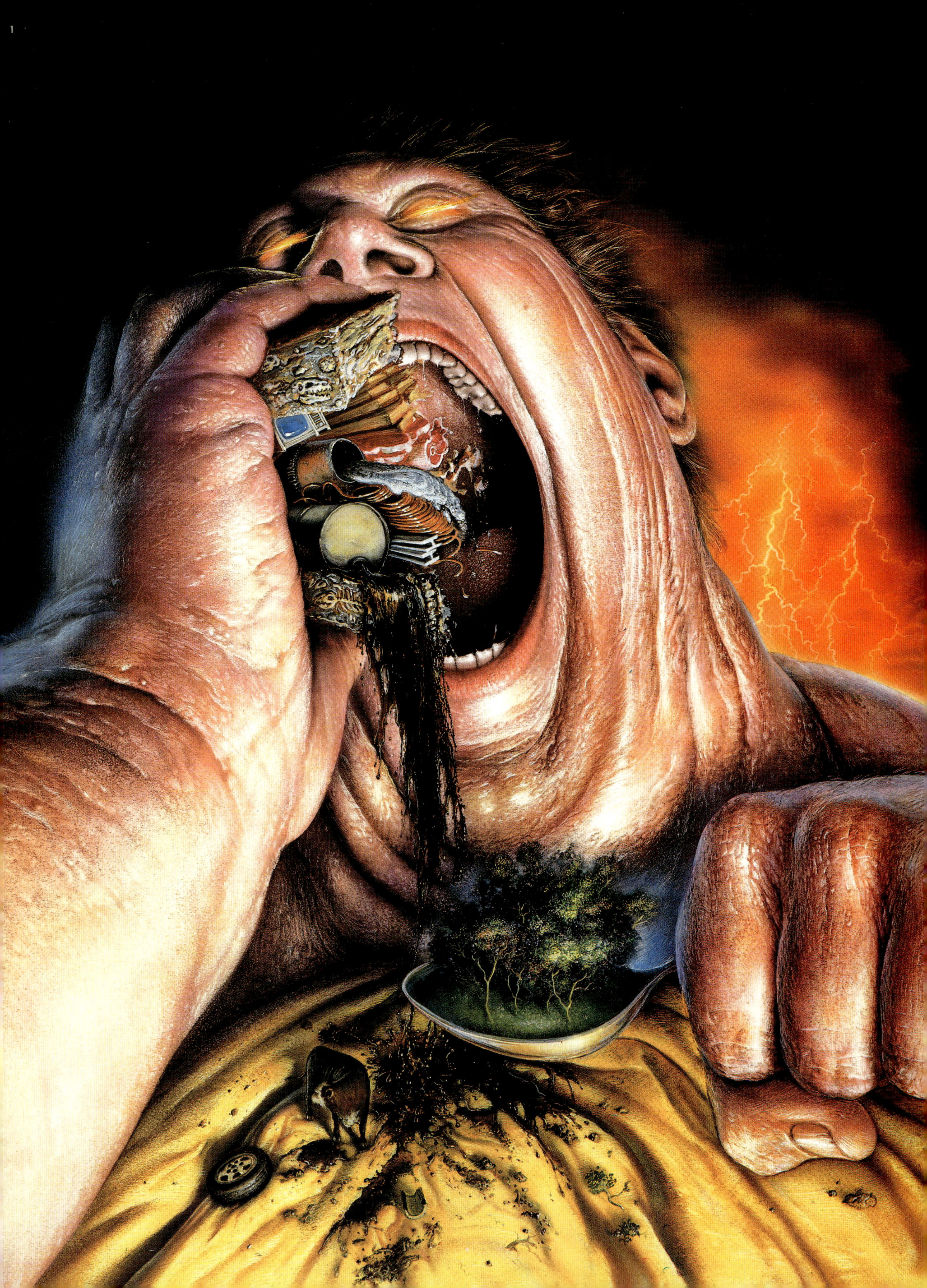

1
Illustrator **MARK A. FREDRICKSON**
Title **THE OVERCONSUMPTION OF THE EARTH'S RESOURCES**
Client **INTERNATIONAL WILDLIFE MAGAZINE**
Art Director **DAN SMITH**
Usage **EDITORIAL**
Media **ACRYLIC**

2
Illustrator **MARK A. FREDRICKSON**
Client **MEAD**
Art Director **MARNA HENLEY**
Usage **SCHOOL PORTFOLIO COVER**
Media **ACRYLIC**

3
Illustrator **MARK A. FREDRICKSON**
Client **GENESIS SEGA**
Art Director **DENI MOORE**
Usage **"QUAD CHALLENGE" VIDEO GAME PACKAGING**
Media **ACRYLIC**

4
Illustrator **MARK A. FREDRICKSON**
Title **THE EXTREMIST**
Art Director **DAVE BETT**
Usage **JOE SATRIANI ALBUM COVER**
Media **ACRYLIC**

2

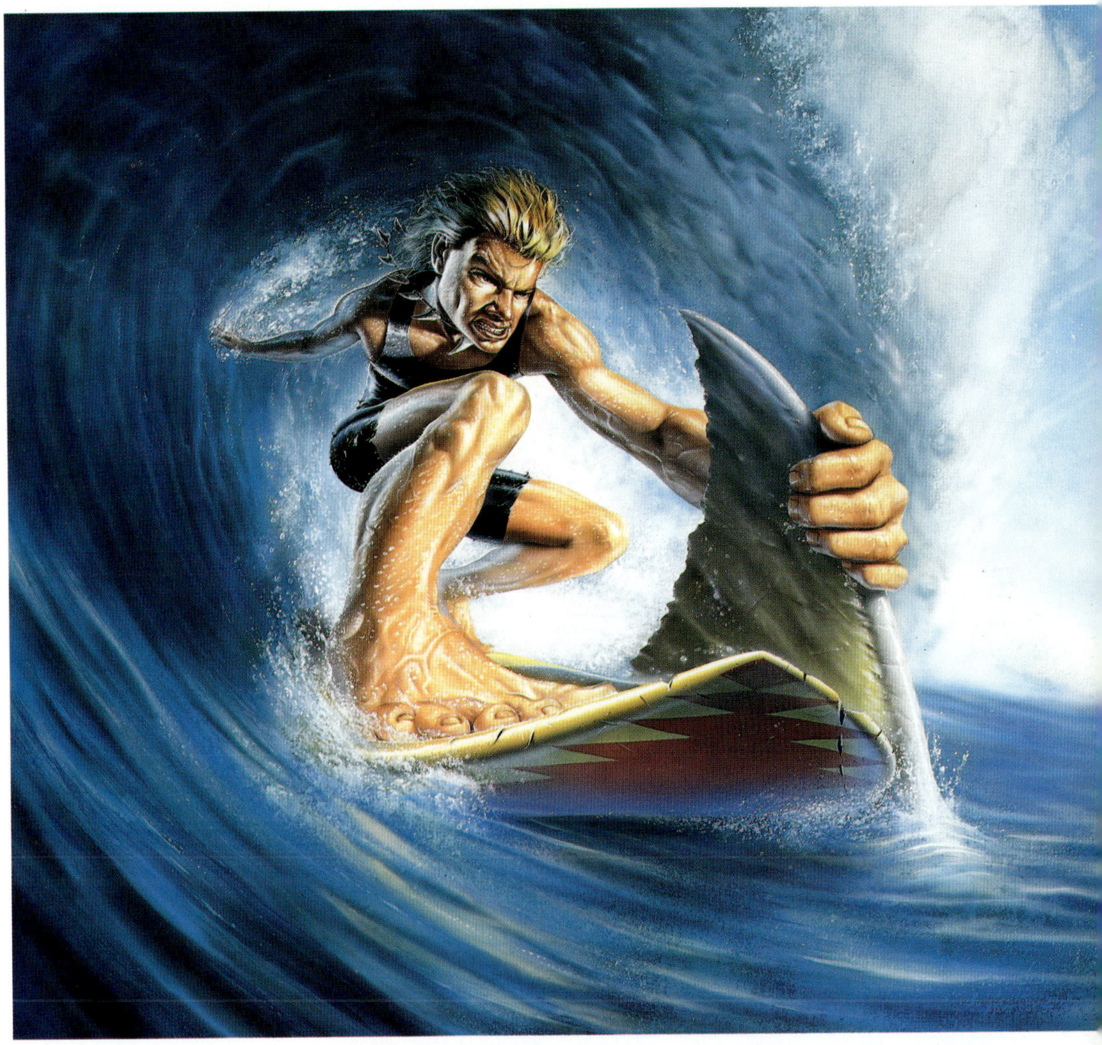

3

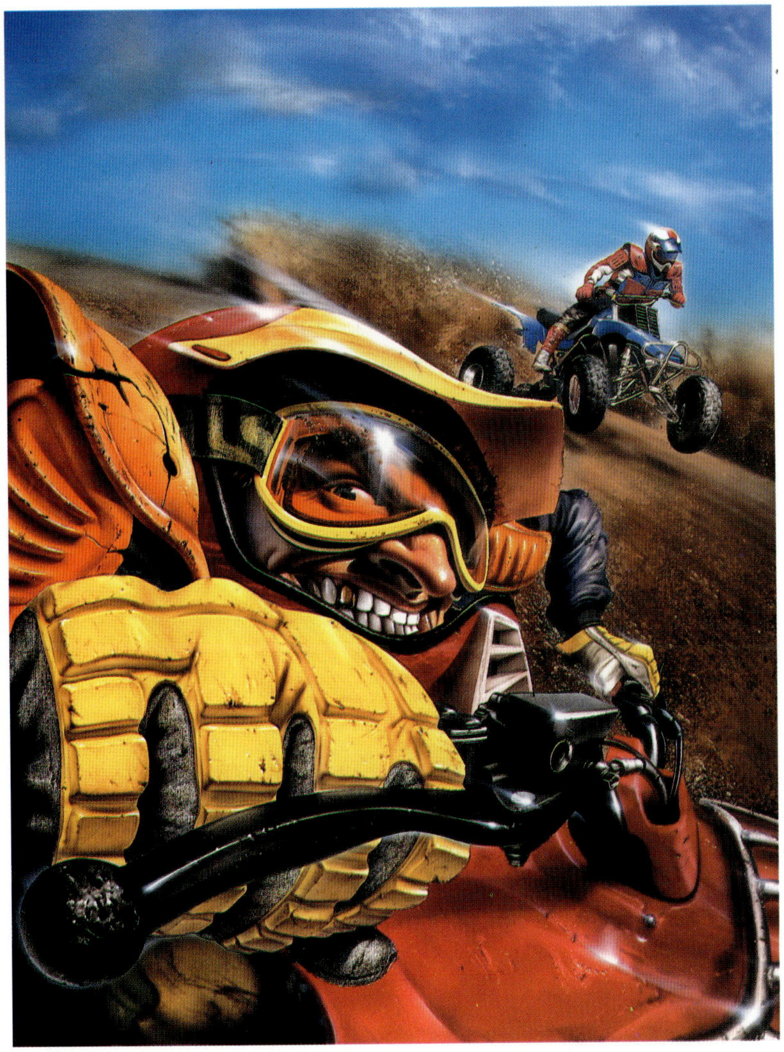

4

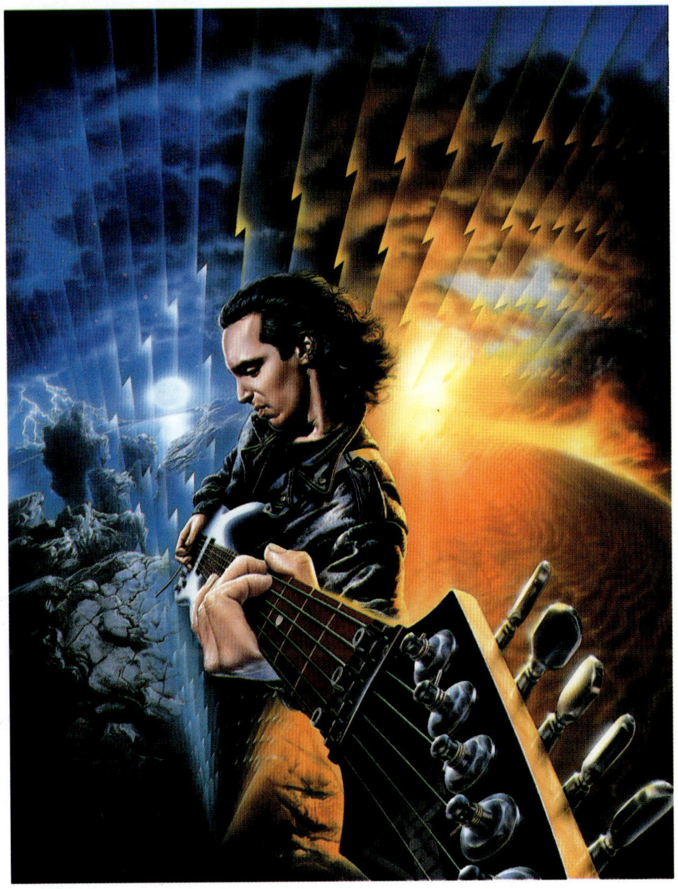

1

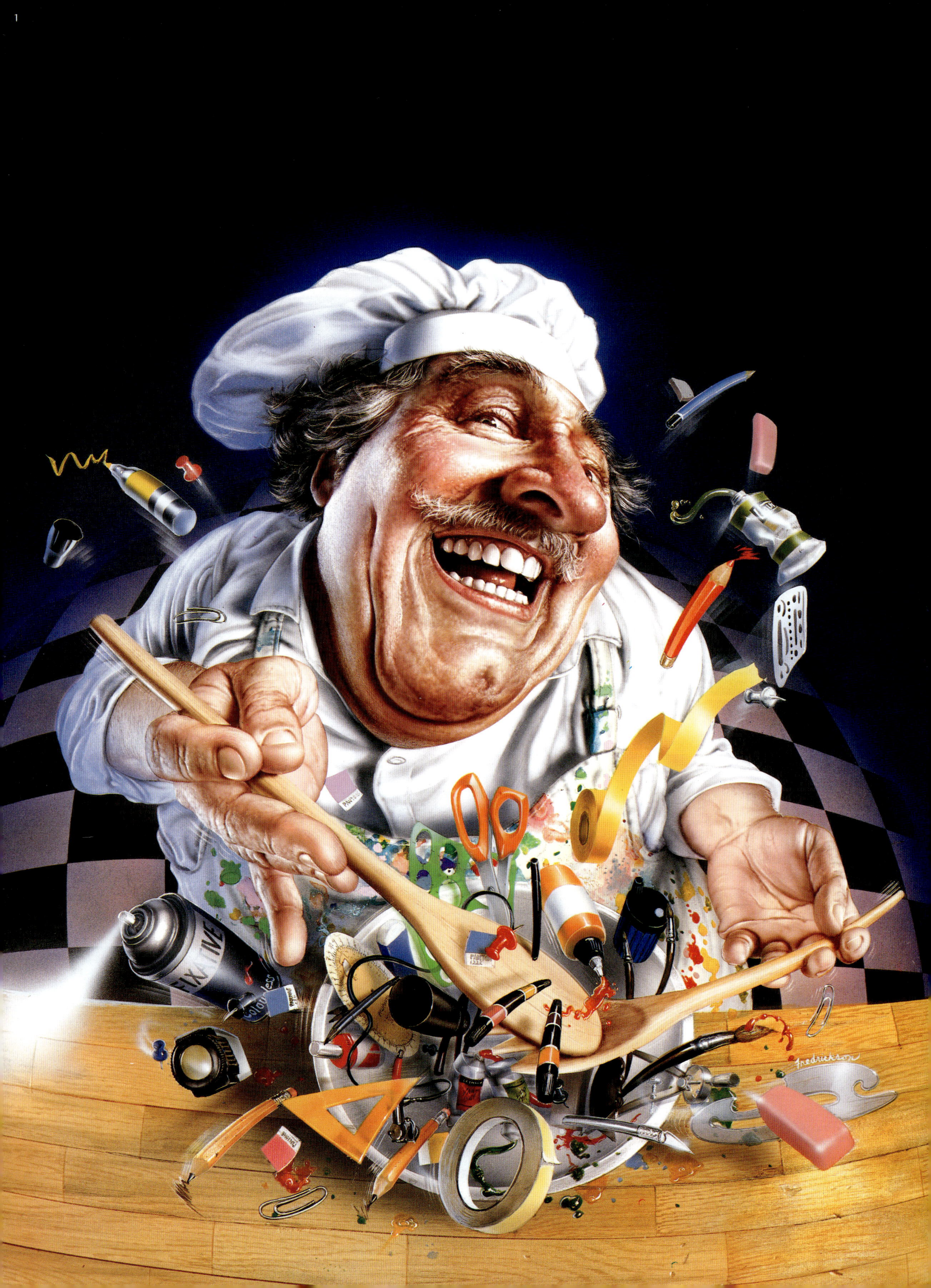

2

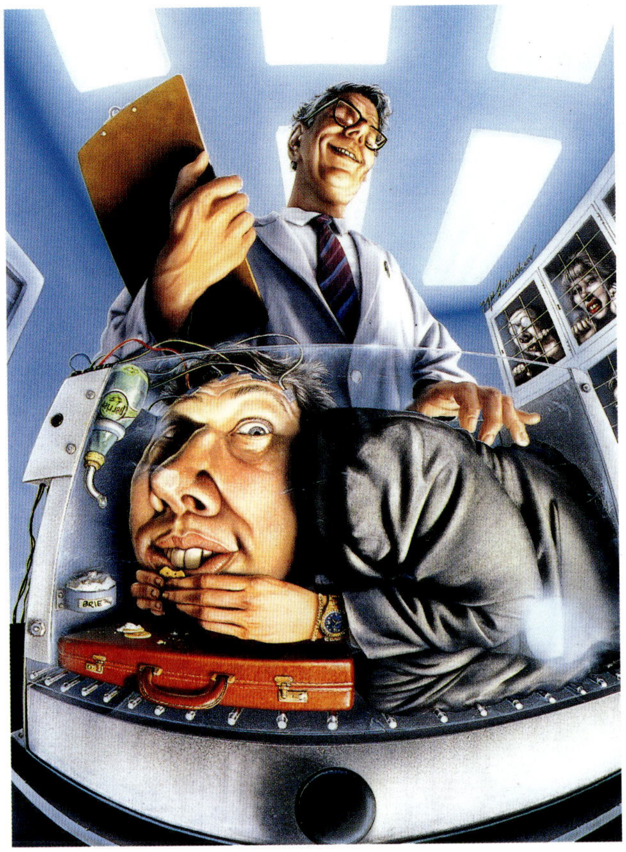

3

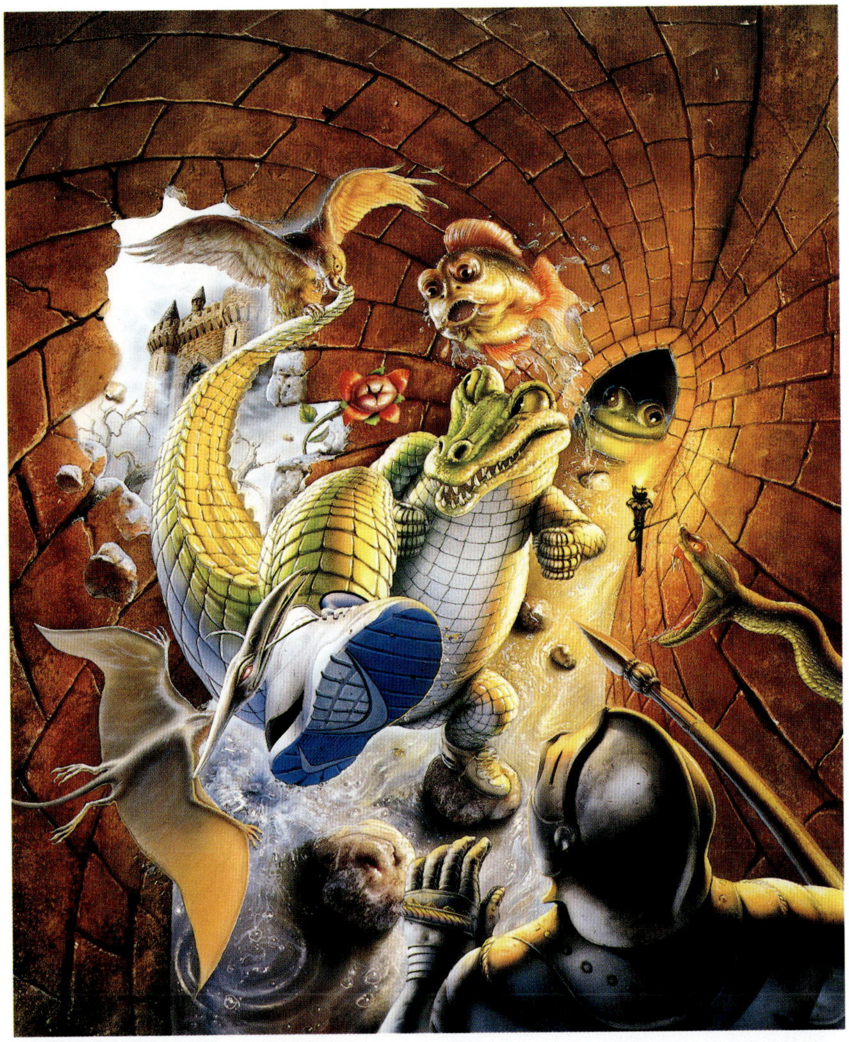

1
Illustrator **MARK A. FREDRICKSON**
Client **RSVP**
Art Director **DAVID BARTELS**
Usage **ILLUSTRATION AND DESIGN DIRECTORY COVER**
Media **ACRYLIC**

2
Illustrator **MARK A. FREDRICKSON**
Client **KSK COMMUNICATIONS**
Art Director **RAE ANNE HYTONE**
Usage **LAW FIRM BROCHURE**
Media **ACRYLIC**

3
Illustrator **MARK A. FREDRICKSON**
Client **NINTENDO GAME BOY**
Art Director **DENI MOORE**
Usage **"TAILGATOR" VIDEO GAME PACKAGING**
Media **ACRYLIC**

4
Illustrator **MARK A. FREDRICKSON**
Client **MEAD**
Art Director **MARNA HENLEY**
Usage **SCHOOL PORTFOLIO COVER**
Media **ACRYLIC**

4

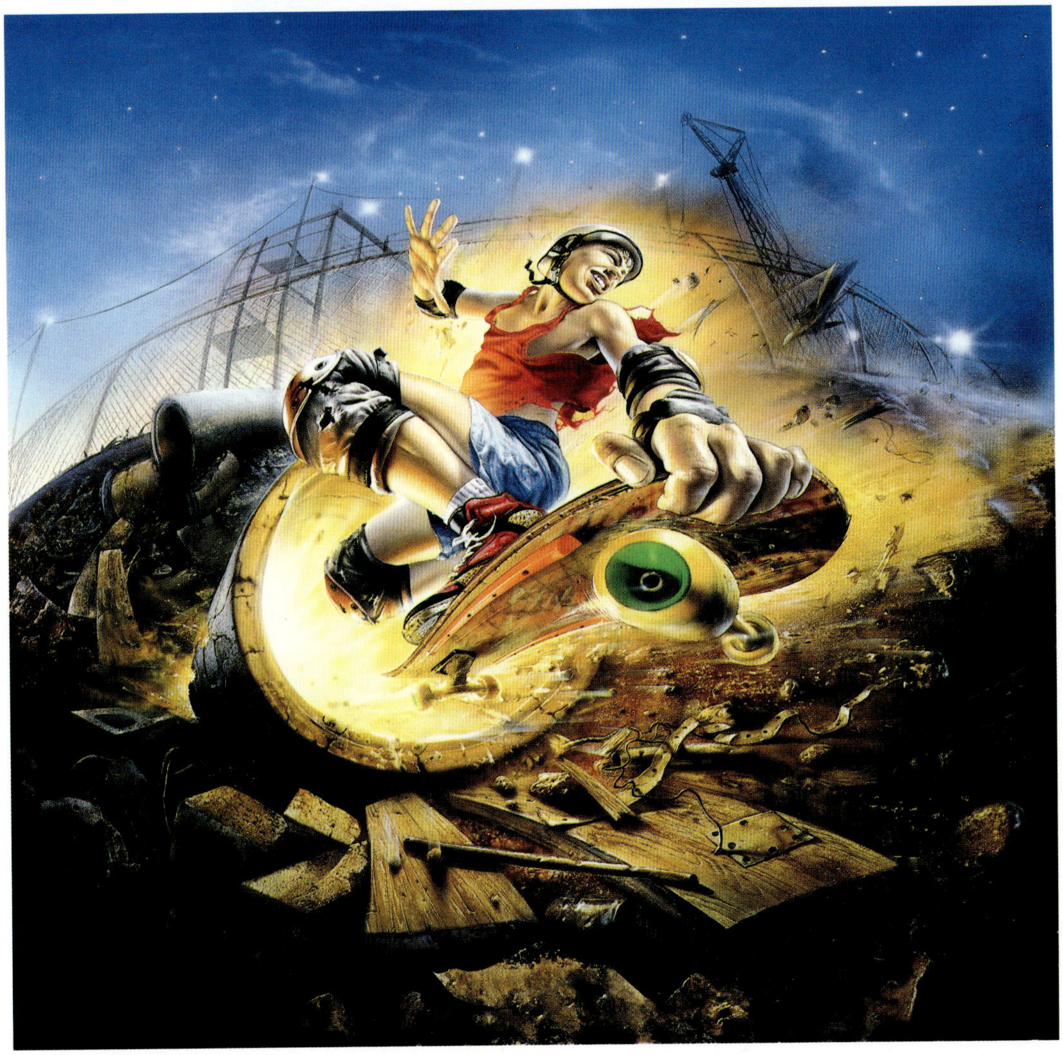

1

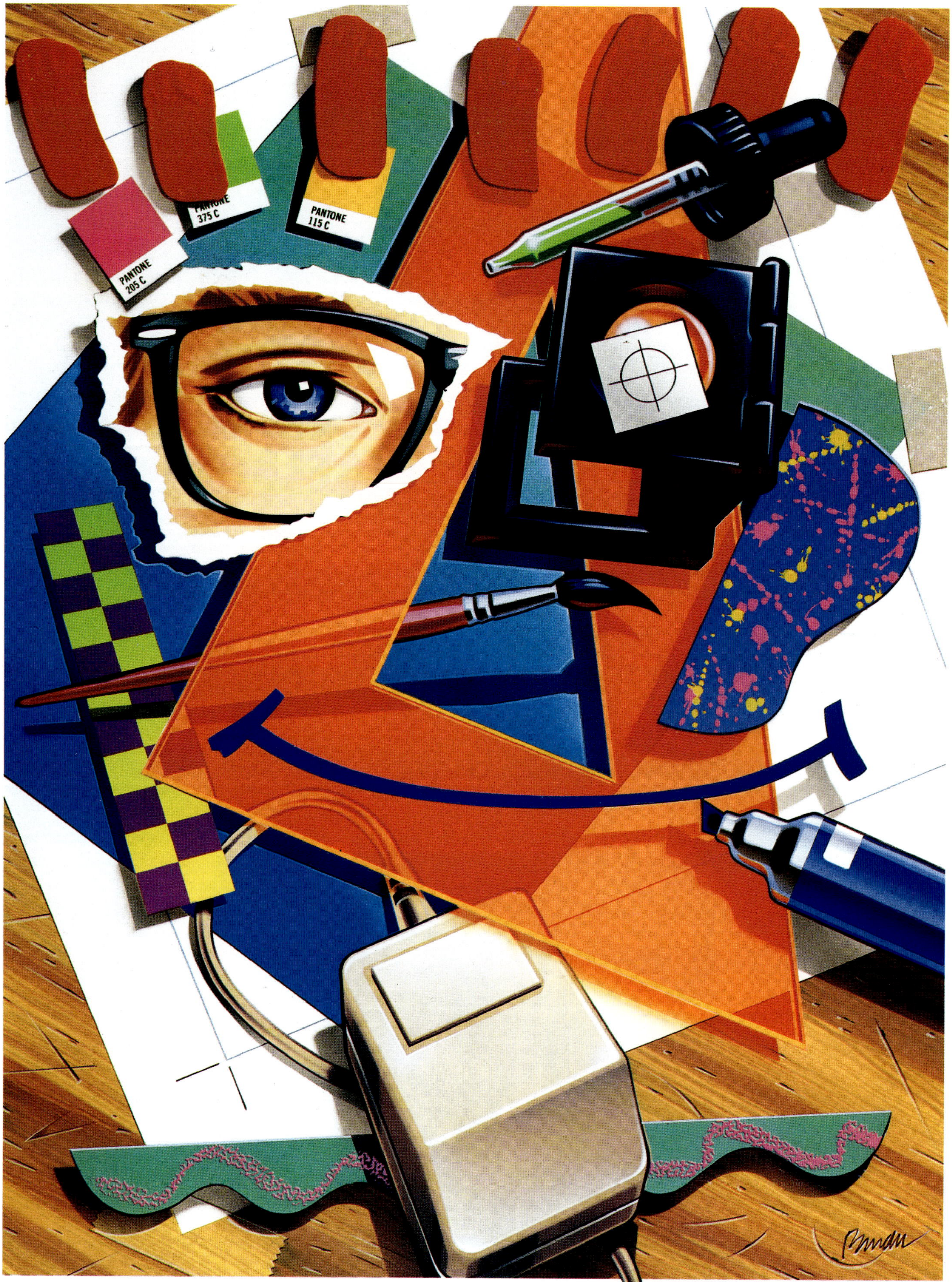

1
Illustrator **MARK BENDER**
Usage **SELF PROMOTION**
Media **GOUACHE, WATERCOLOR**

2
Illustrator **MARK BENDER**
Client **THE DETROIT LIONS/NFL**
Usage **CALENDAR COVER**
Media **GOUACHE, WATERCOLOR**

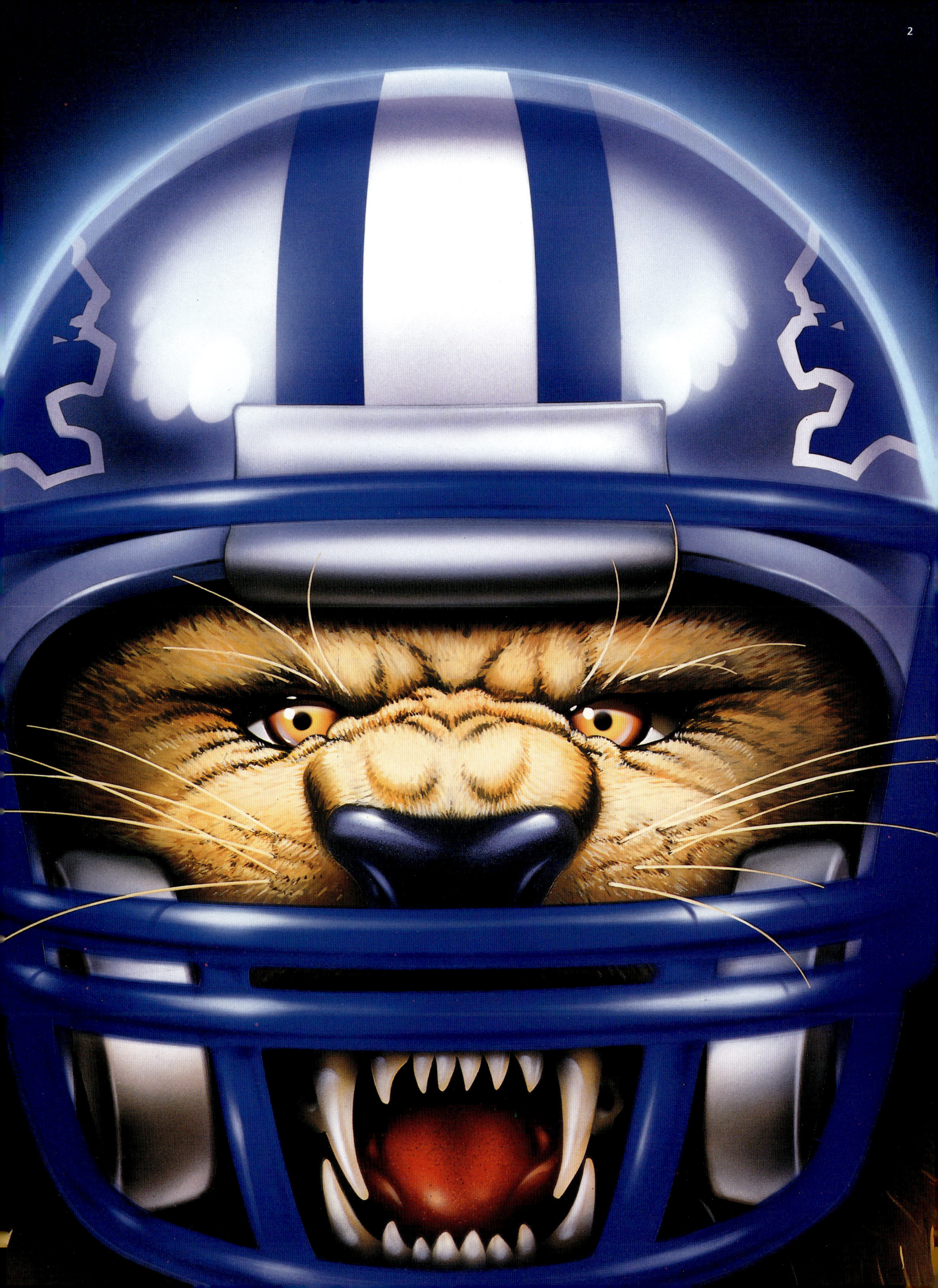

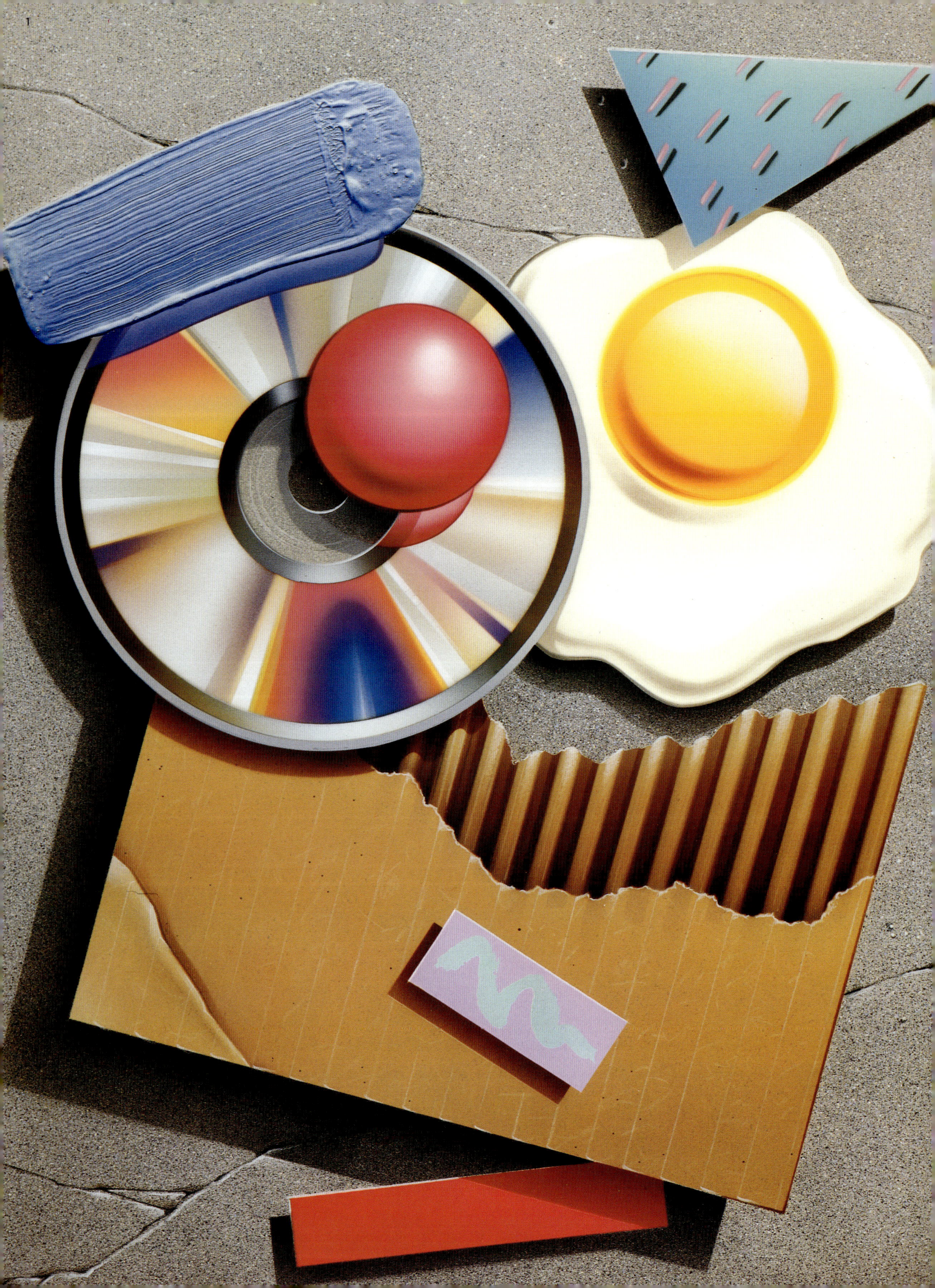

2

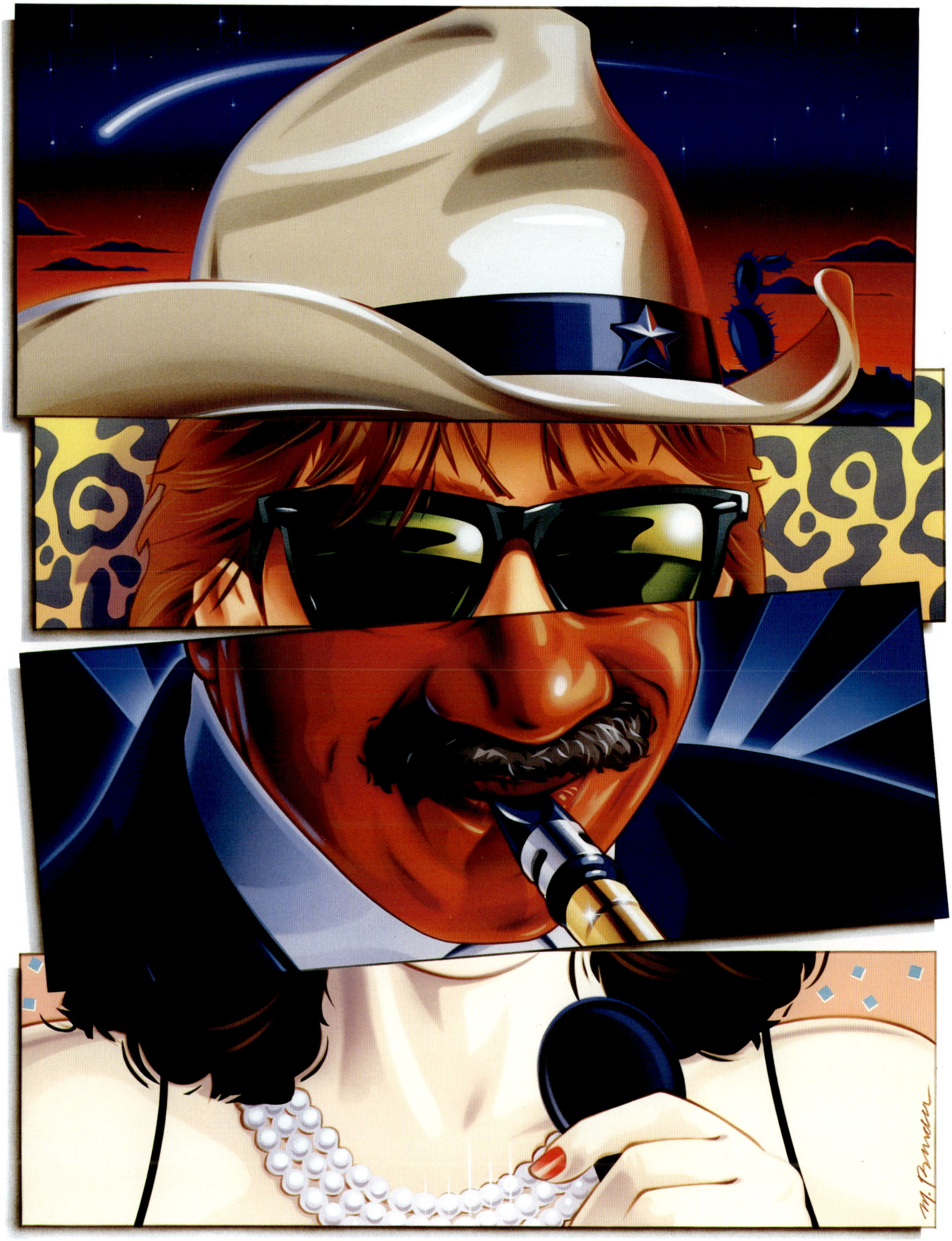

1
Illustrator **MARK BENDER**
Usage **SELF-PROMOTIONAL POSTER**
Media **GOUACHE, WATERCOLOR**

2
Illustrator **MARK BENDER**
Client **COCA-COLA STAR LAKE AMPHITHEATRE**
Art Director **CHERYL FOSTER**
Usage **PROGRAM COVER**
Media **GOUACHE, WATERCOLOR**

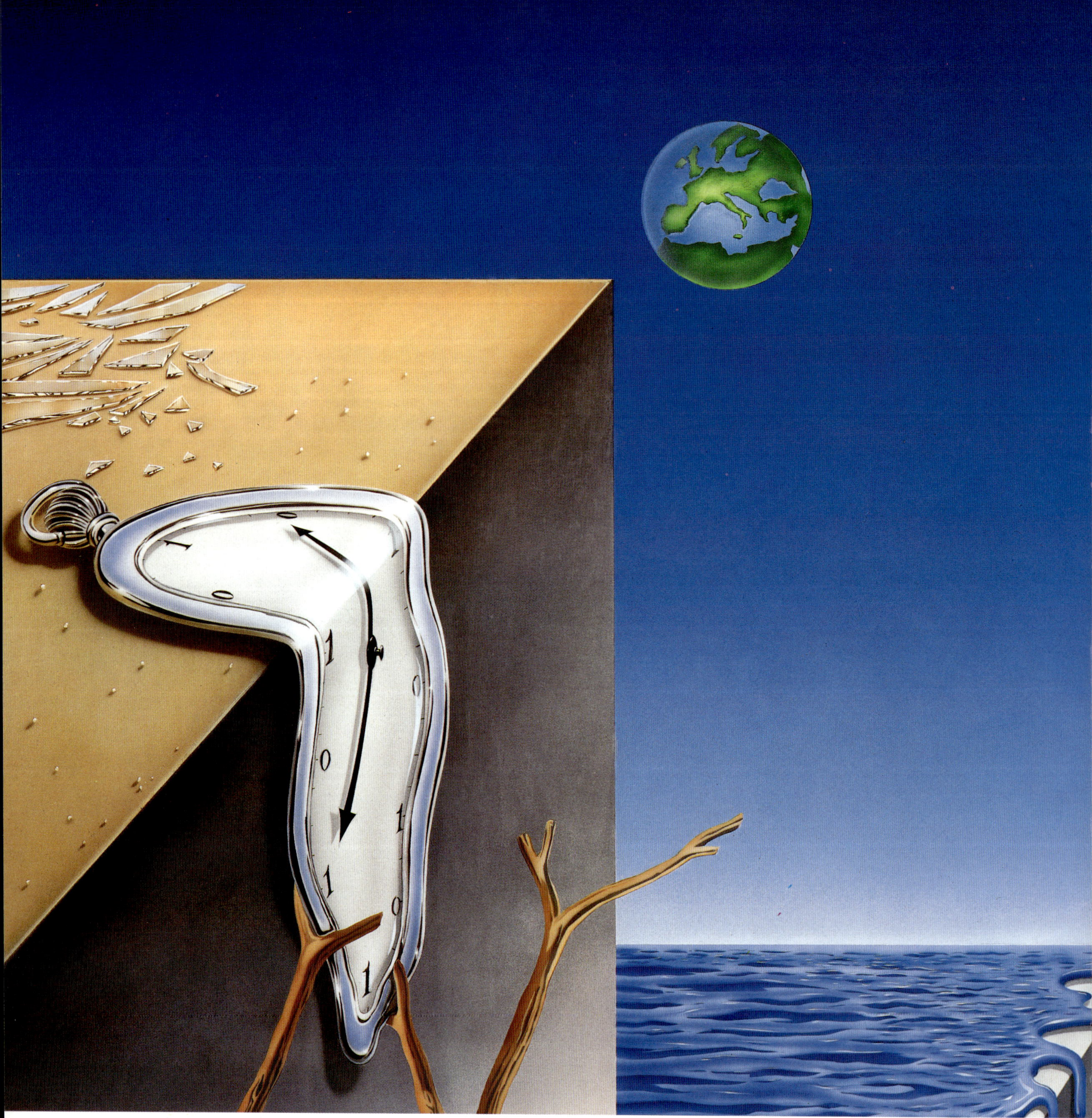

1
Illustrator **DICKRAN PALULIAN**
Client **DATA COMMUNICATIONS**
Art Director **KEN SURABIAN**
Usage **EDITORIAL**
Media **GOUACHE**

2

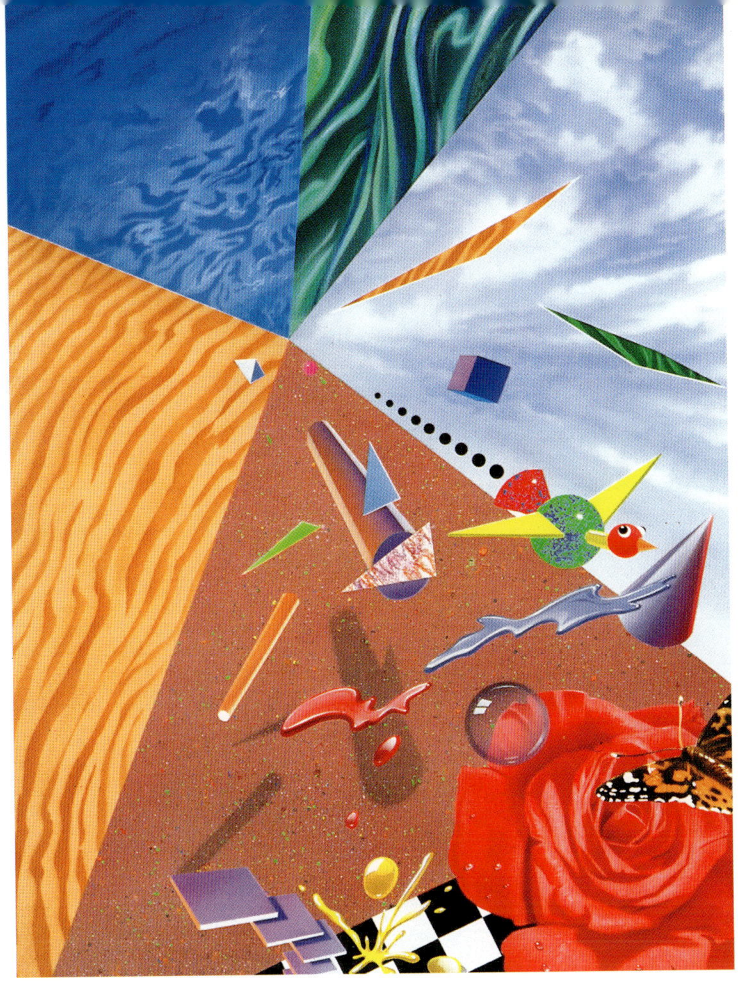

3

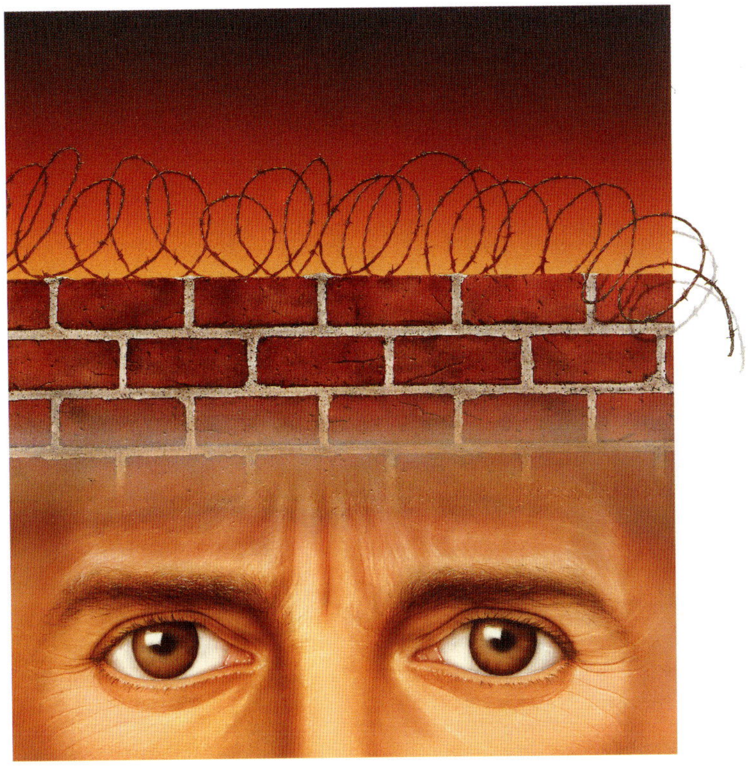

4

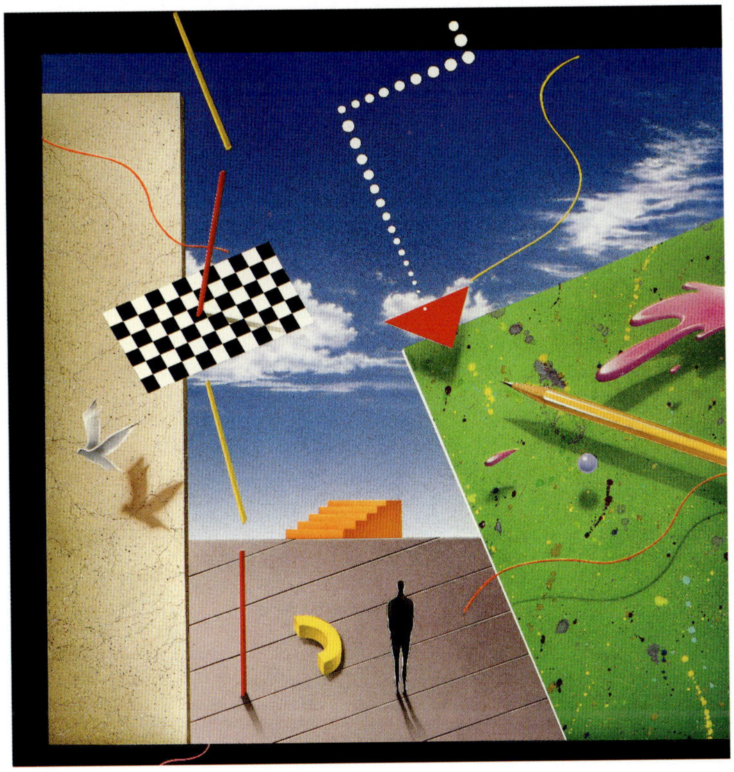

5

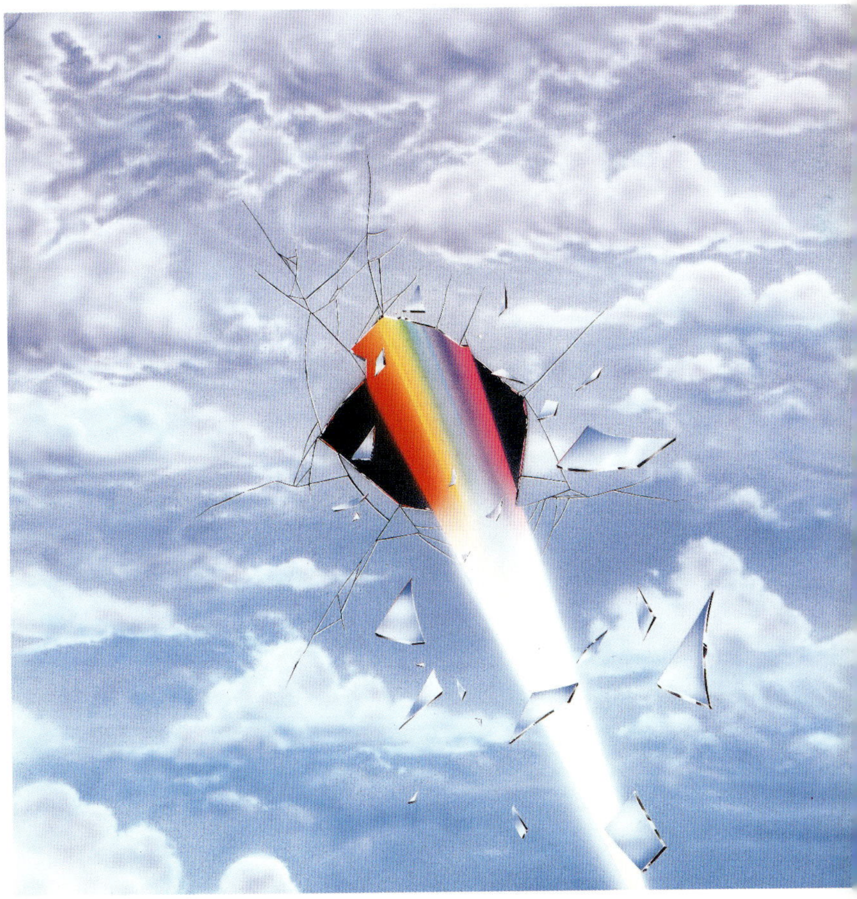

2
Illustrator **DICKRAN PALULIAN**
Client **BYTE MAGAZINE**
Art Director **NANCY RICE**
Usage **EDITORIAL**
Media **GOUACHE**

3
Illustrator **DICKRAN PALULIAN**
Client **ARCO METALS**
Media **GOUACHE**

4
Illustrator **DICKRAN PALULIAN**
Usage **COMMERCIAL**
Media **GOUACHE**

5
Illustrator **DICKRAN PALULIAN**
Client **AT&T**
Art Director **STEVE PHILLIPS**
Usage **COMMERCIAL, EDITORIAL**
Media **GOUACHE**

1
Illustrator **BUD THON**
Client **CYPRESS MICROCOMPUTER**
Art Director **JOHN MIWA**
Usage **BROCHURE**
Media **ACRYLIC**

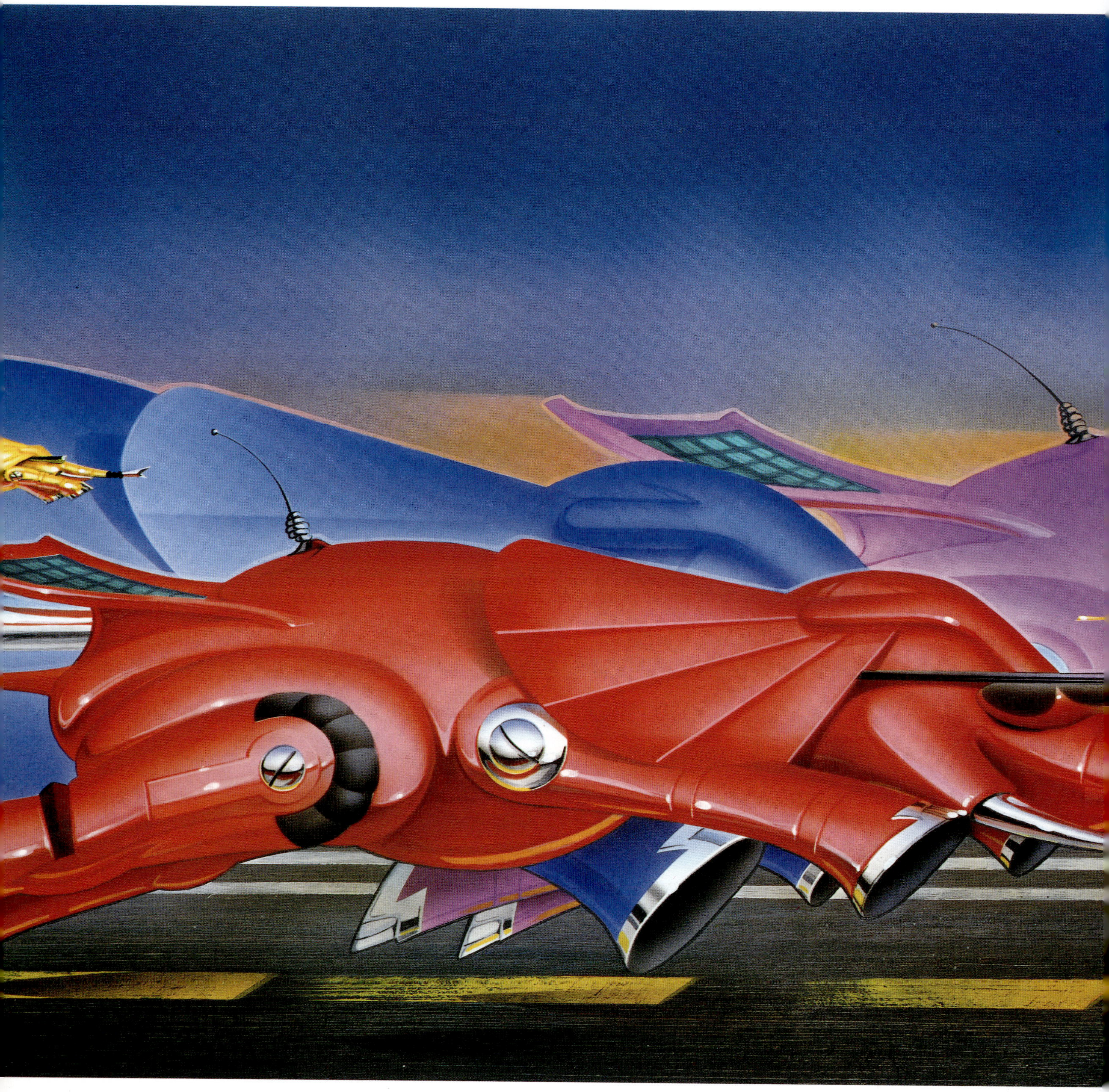

1

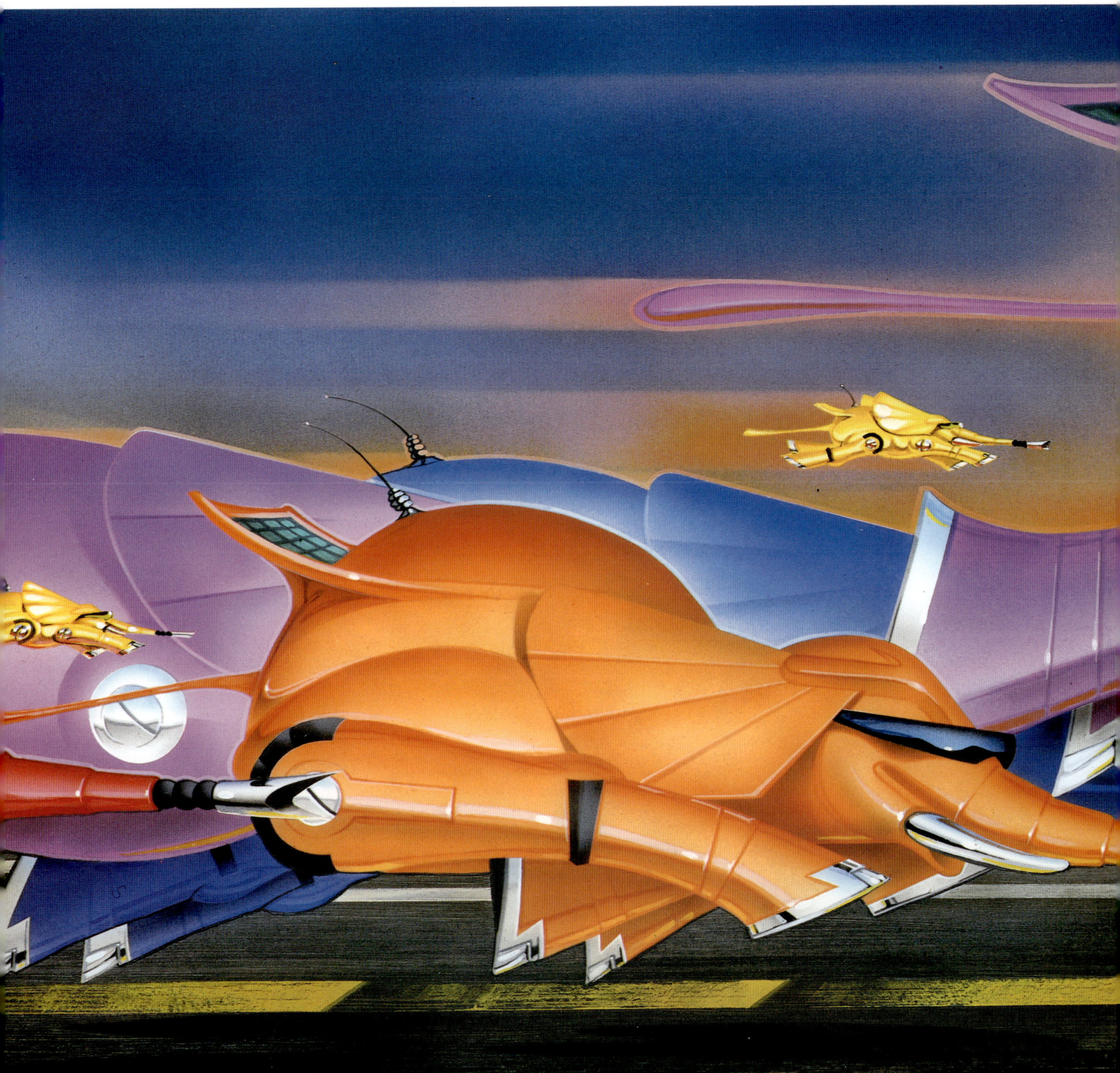

1

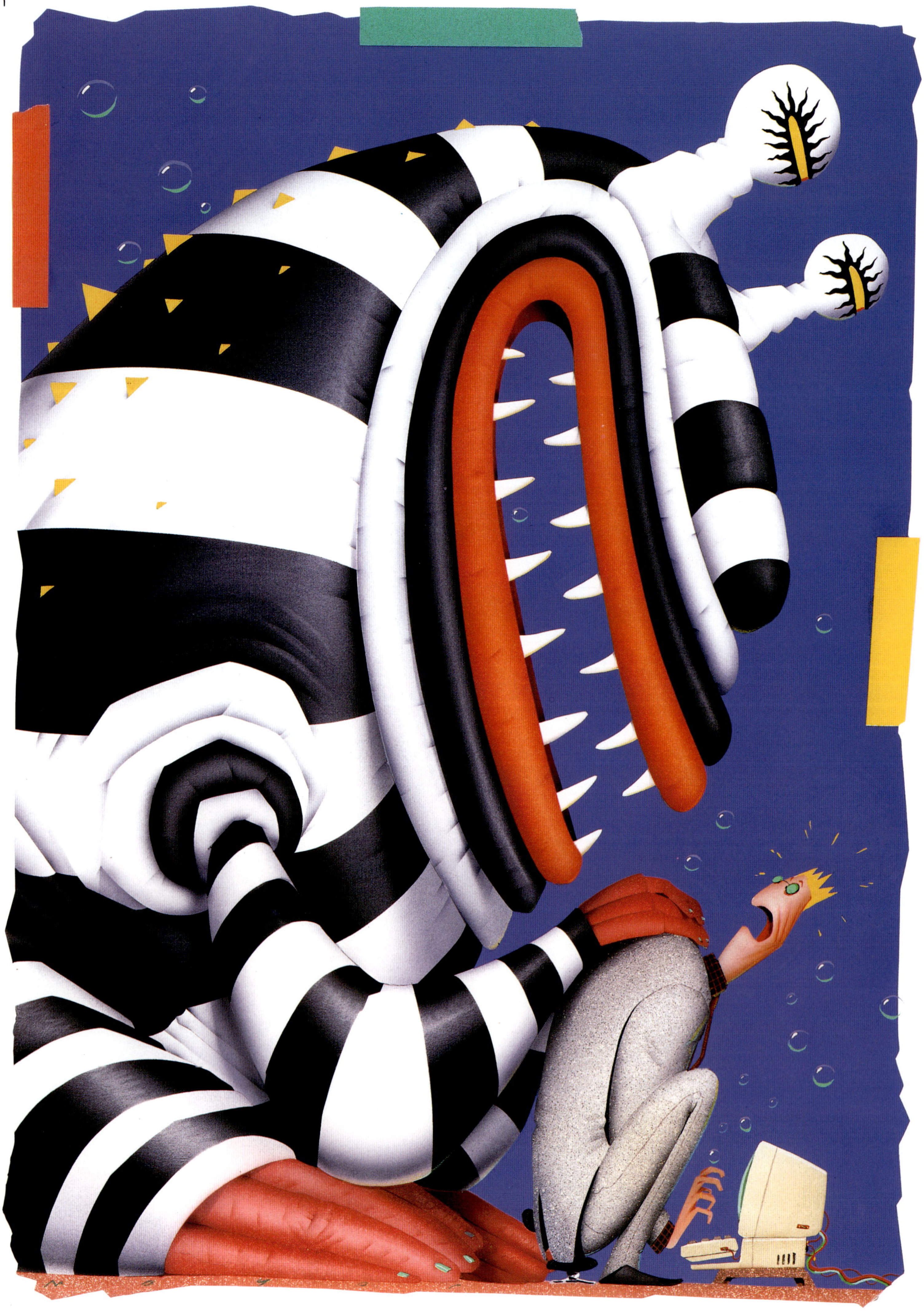

2

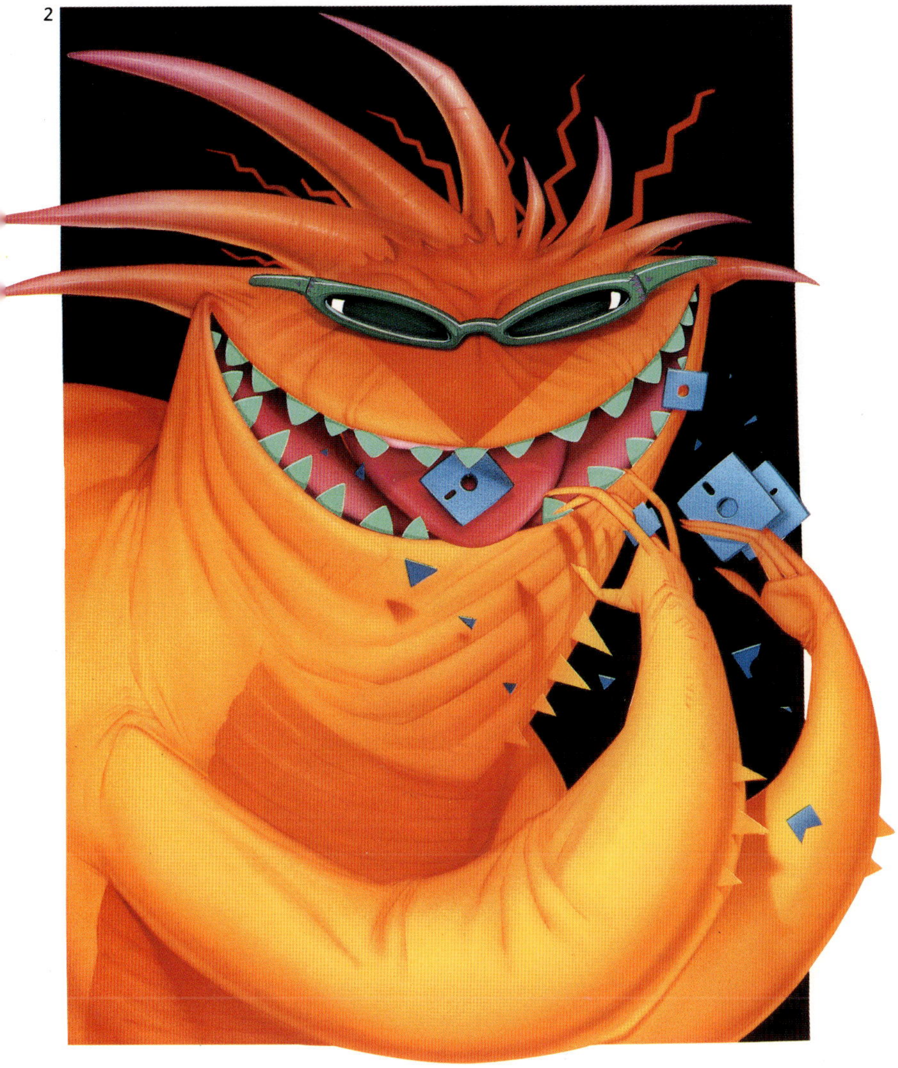

3

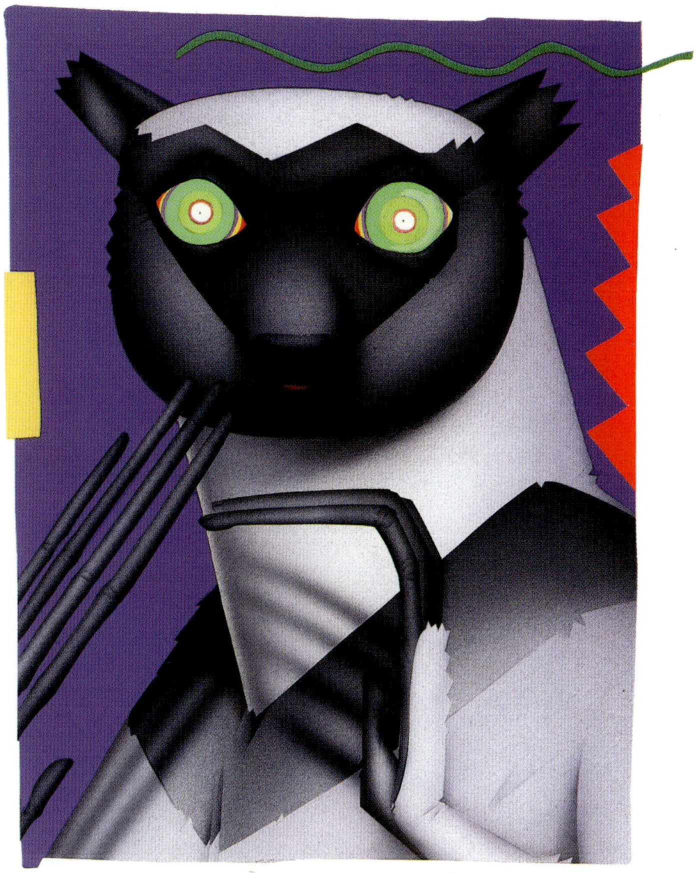

1
Illustrator **BILL MAYER**
Client **UNITED NATIONS/EARTH ISLAND INSTITUTE**
Usage **CALENDAR, POSTER**
Media **GOUACHE, DYES**

2
Illustrator **BILL MAYER**
Client **COMPUTERWORLD**
Art Director **TOM MONAHAN**
Usage **EDITORIAL**
Media **GOUACHE, DYES**

3
Illustrator **BILL MAYER**
Client **LEAR'S MAGAZINE**
Art Director **AVIA PETERSON**
Usage **EDITORIAL**
Media **GOUACHE, DYES**

4
Illustrator **BILL MAYER**
Title **IDENTITY CRISIS**
Client **GRAPHIC ADS/SULLIVAN, HAAS, COYLE**
Art Director **JERRY SULLIVAN**
Usage **POSTER**
Media **GOUACHE, DYES**

4

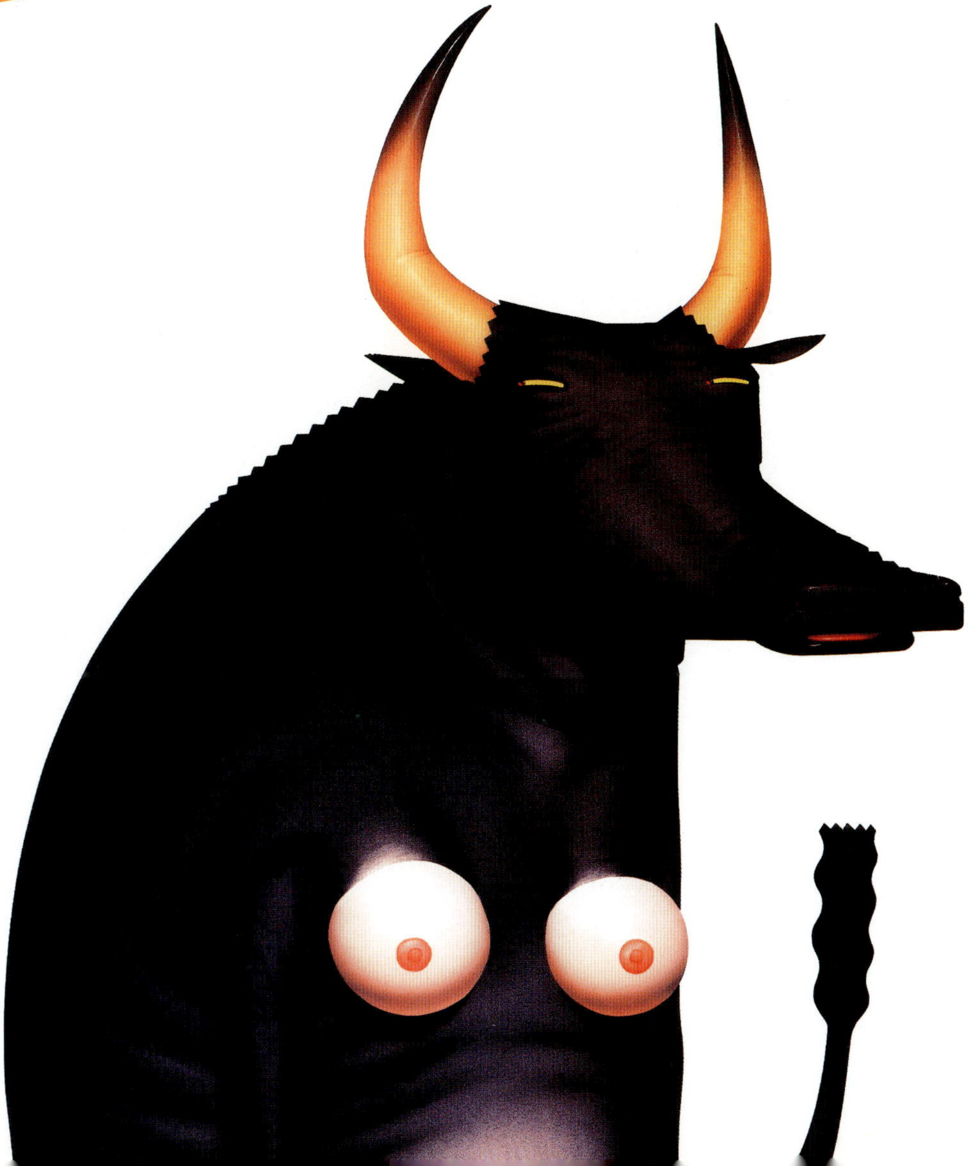

1

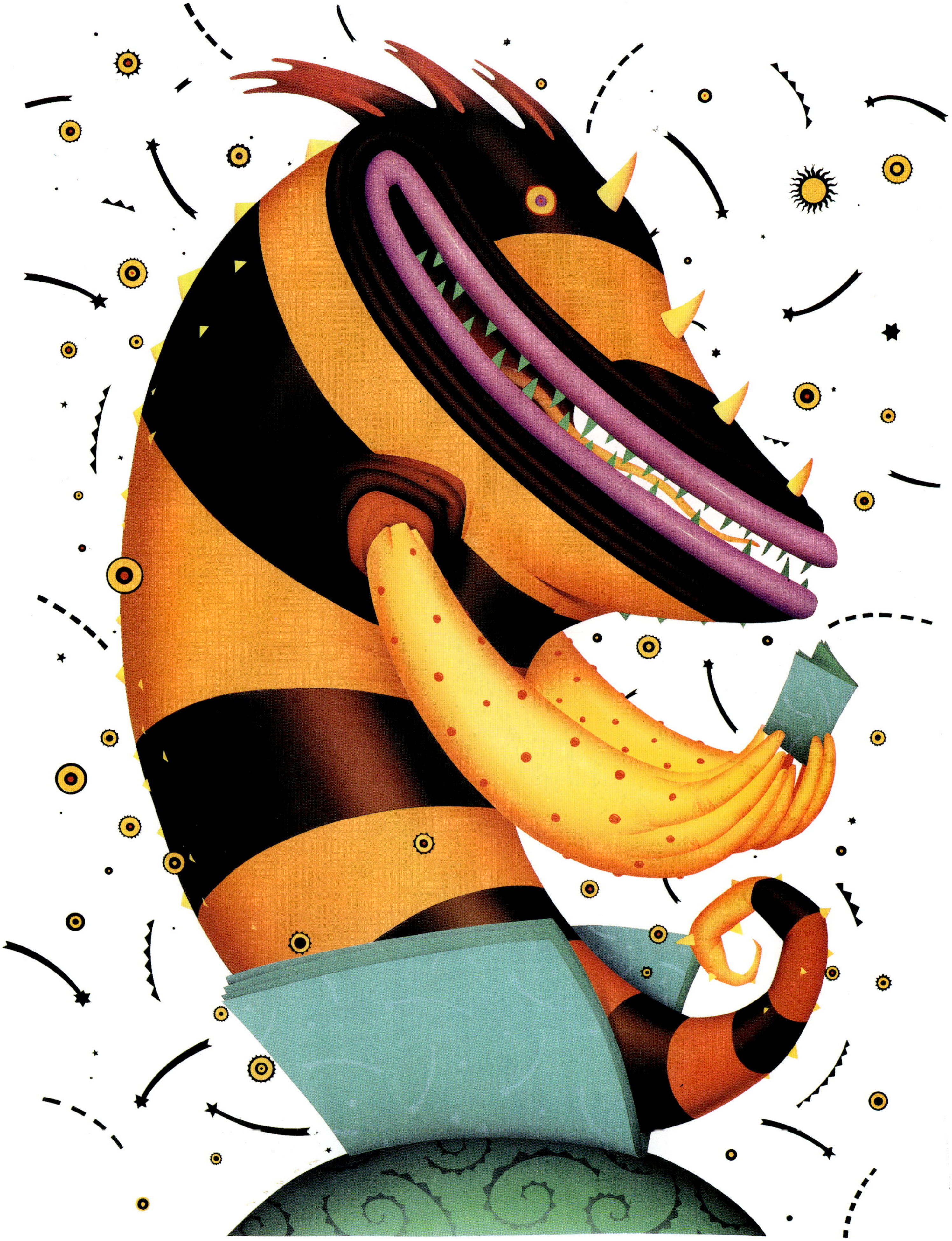

1
Illustrator **BILL MAYER**
Client **WILLIAMSON PRINTING**
Art Director **ALAN LIDJI**
Usage **ADWEEK INSERT**
Media **GOUACHE, DYES**

2

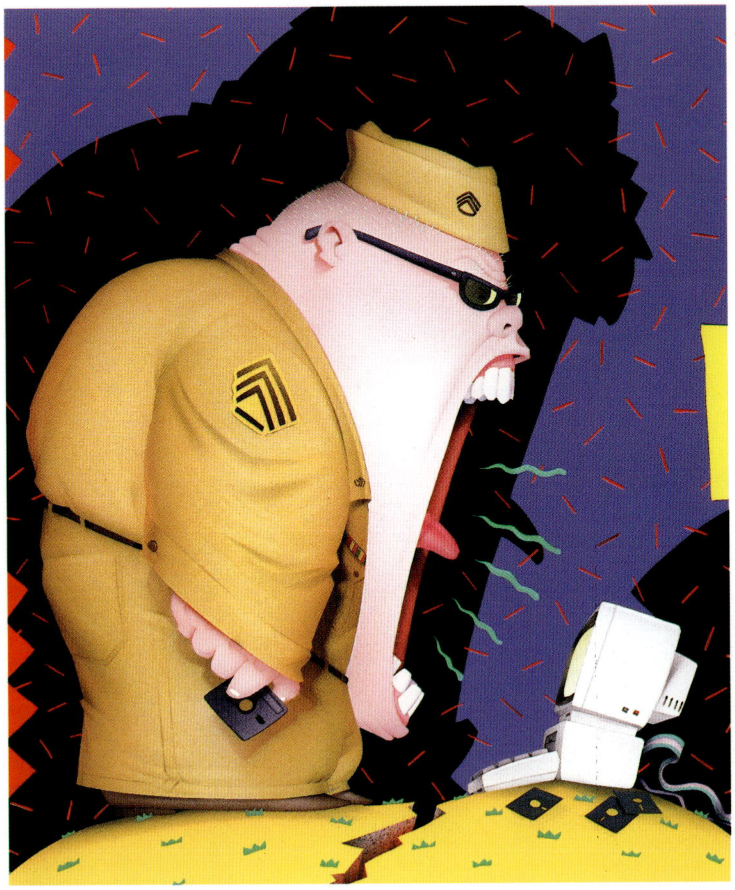

3

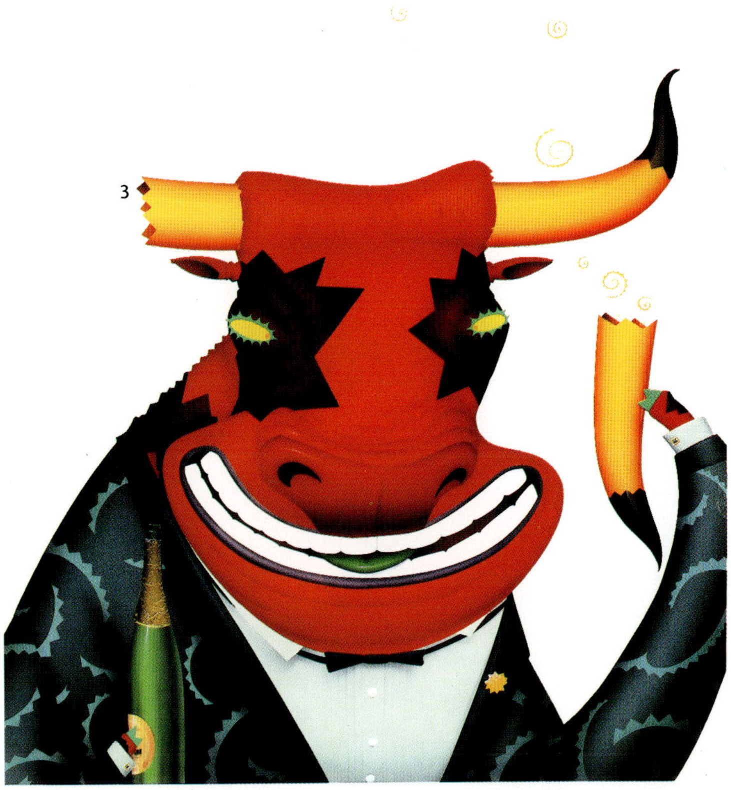

4

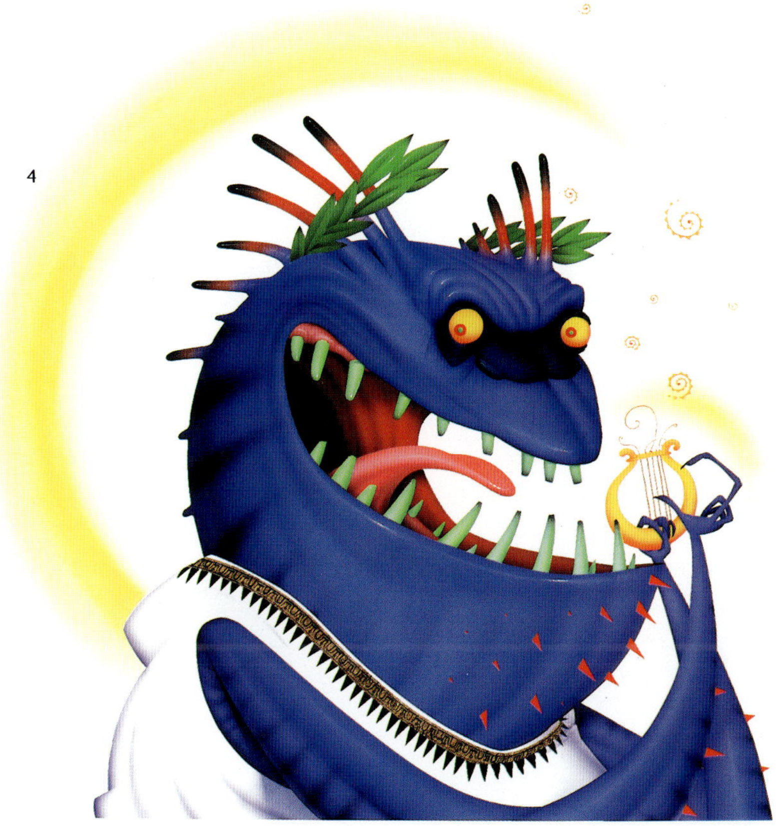

5

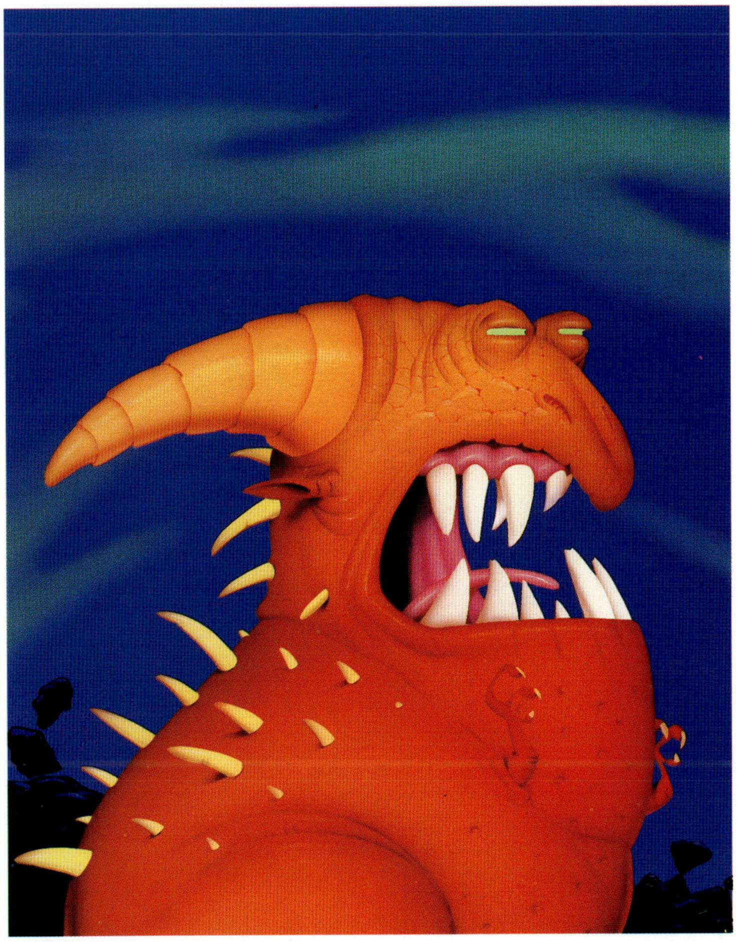

2
Illustrator **BILL MAYER**
Client **VAR BUSINESS**
Art Director **DAVID LOWEY**
Usage **EDITORIAL**
Media **GOUACHE, DYES**

3
Illustrator **BILL MAYER**
Client **TEXAS MONTHLY MAGAZINE**
Art Director **D.J. STOUT**
Usage **MAGAZINE COVER (BUM STEER AWARDS)**
Media **GOUACHE, DYES**

4
Illustrator **BILL MAYER**
Client **BANTAM BOOKS**
Art Director **JIM PLUMERI**
Usage **"CLASSIC NINTENDO" BOOK COVER**
Media **GOUACHE, GOLD FOIL, DYES**

5
Illustrator **BILL MAYER**
Client **BANTAM BOOKS**
Art Director **JIM PULMERI**
Usage **"ULTIMATE NINTENDO" BOOK COVER**
Media **GOUACHE, DYES**

1

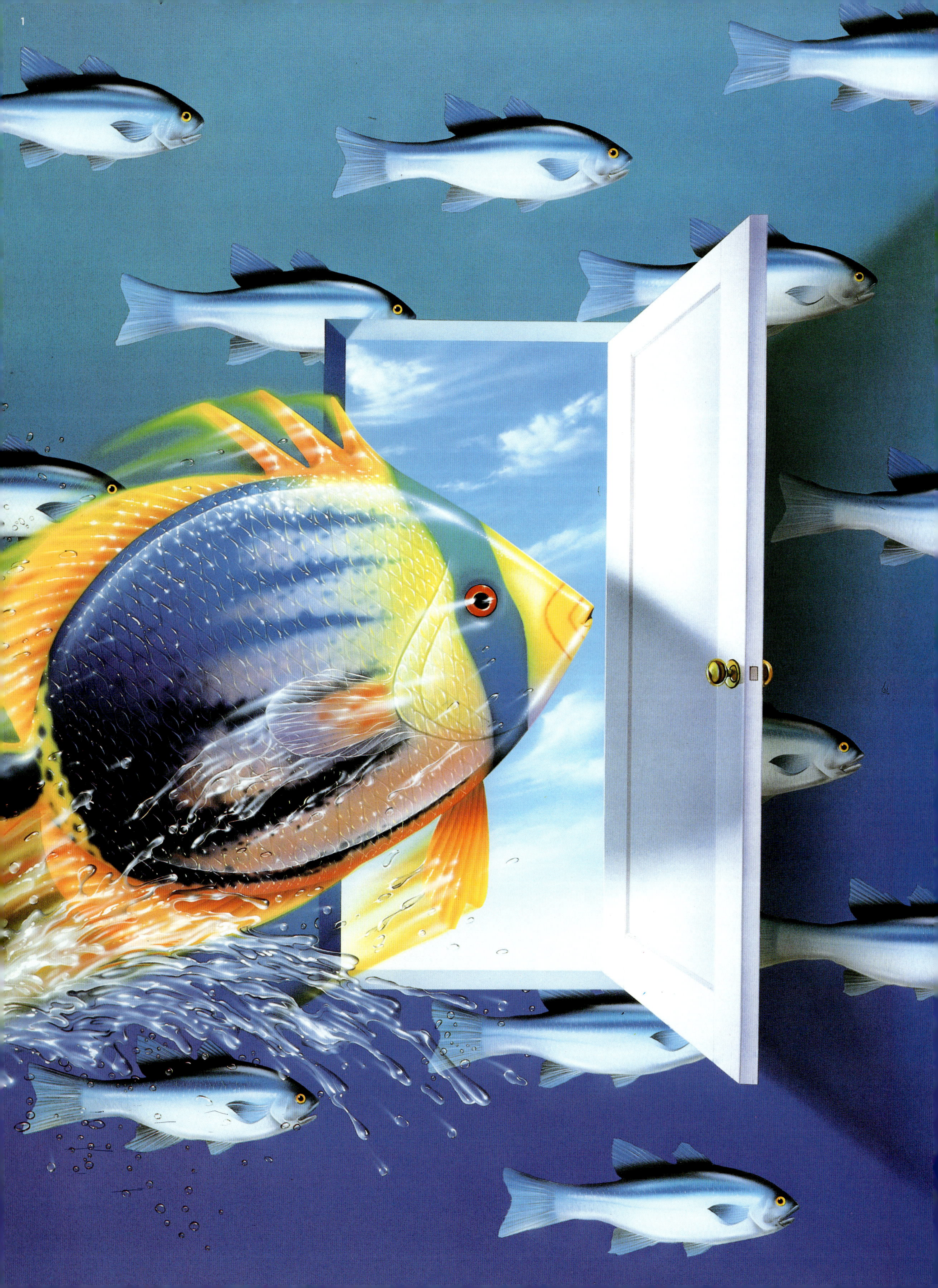

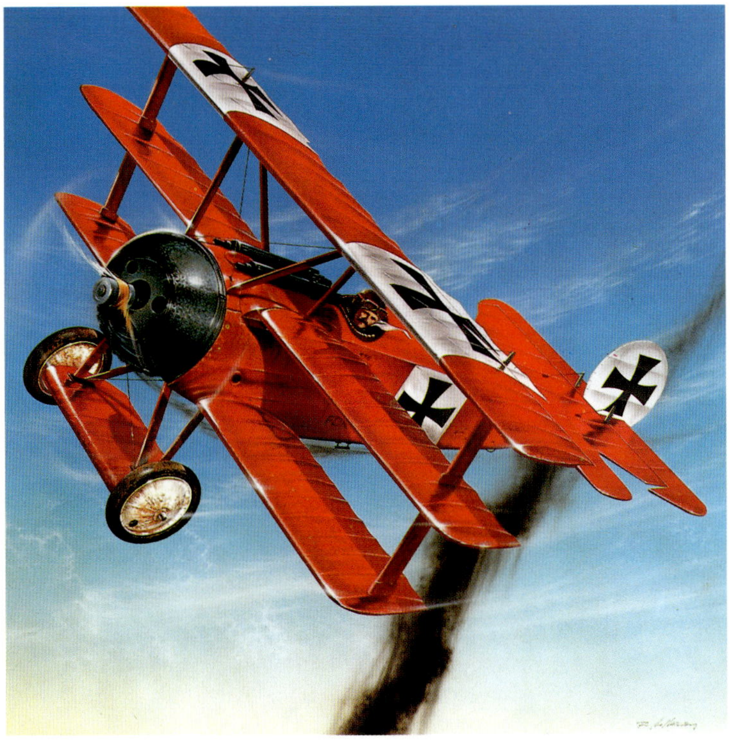

2

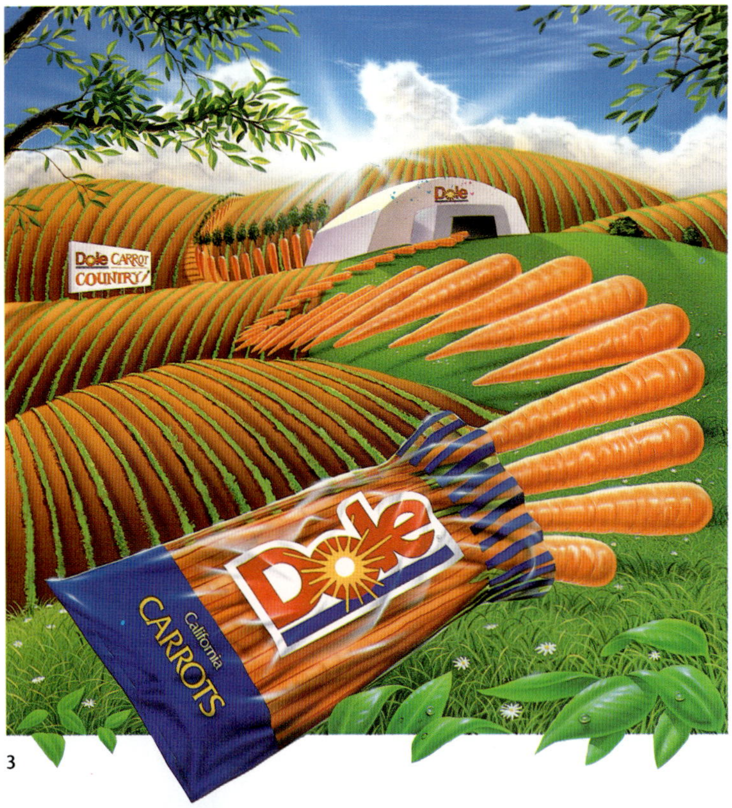

3

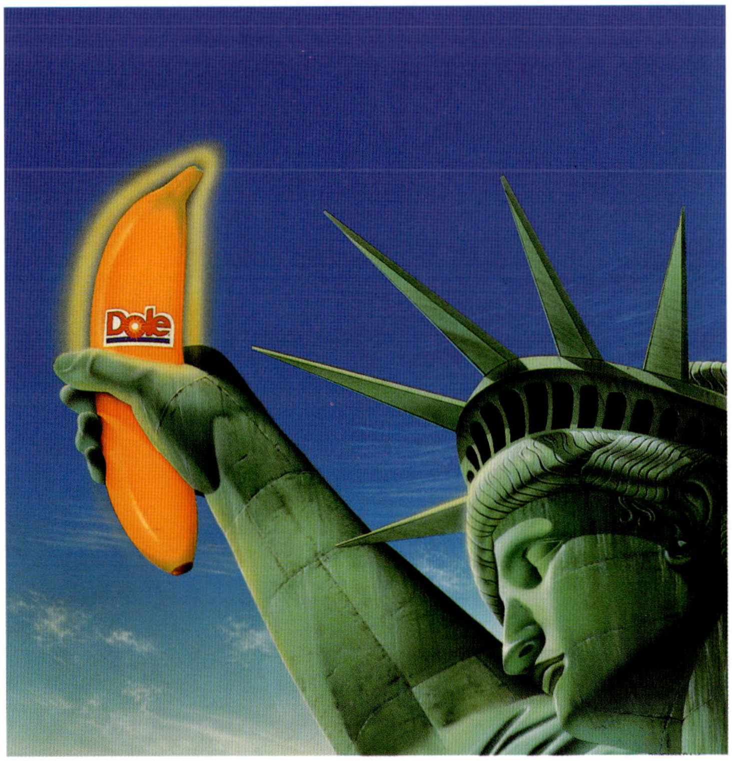

4

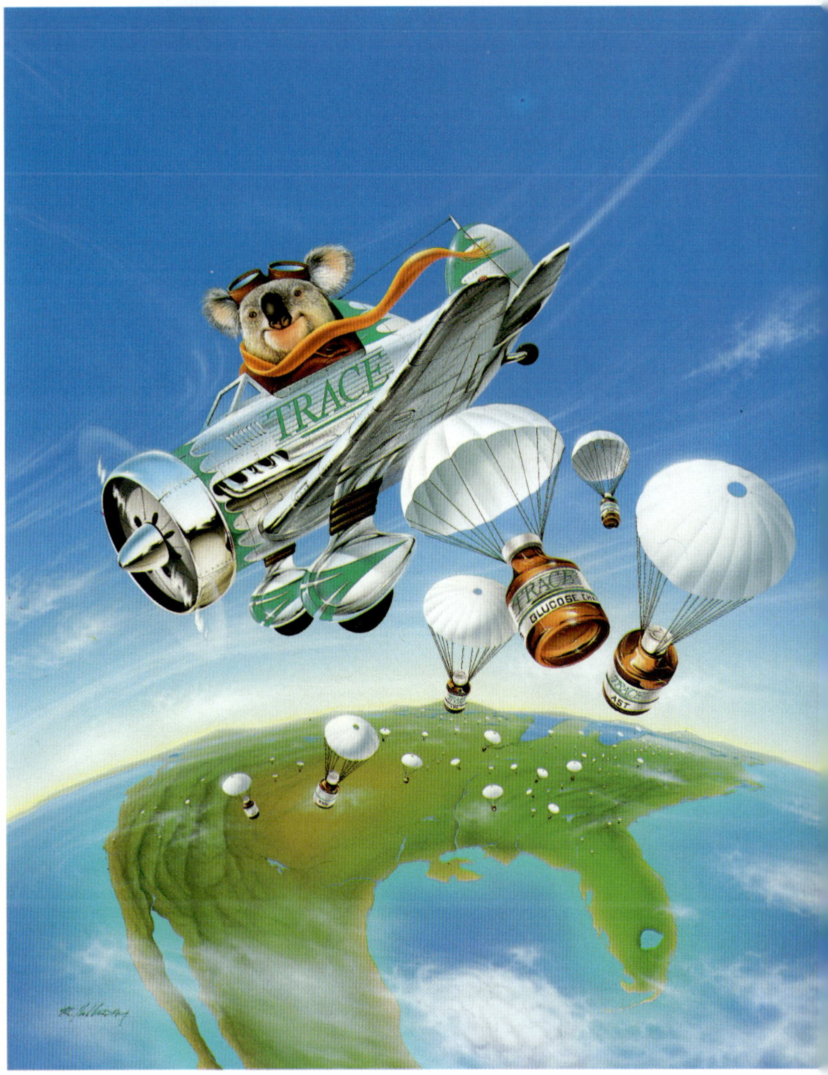

5

1
Illustrator **REGGIE HOLLADAY**
Client **AT&T**
Usage **IN-HOUSE PROMOTION**
Media **ACRYLIC**

2
Illustrator **REGGIE HOLLADAY**
Usage **SELF PROMOTION**
Media **ACRYLIC**

3, 4
Illustrator **REGGIE HOLLADAY**
Client **DOLE**
Art Director **MEAD GOODALL**
Usage **TRADE ADVERTISEMENT**
Media **ACRYLIC**

5
Illustrator **REGGIE HOLLADAY**
Client **TRACE PHARMACEUTICALS**
Usage **POSTER FOR TRADE SHOW**
Media **ACRYLIC**

1
Illustrator **MARTY BRAUN**
Title **CALIFORNIA ROAD TRIPS**
Client **SACRAMENTO BEE MAGAZINE**
Art Director **JIM CARR**
Usage **MAGAZINE COVER**
Media **ACRYLIC**

2
Illustrator **MARTY BRAUN**
Title **THE SPEEDERS CLUB**
Client **NEW ENGLAND MONTHLY**
Art Director **TIM GABOR**
Usage **EDITORIAL**
Media **ACRYLIC**

3
Illustrator **MARTY BRAUN**
Title **BAD TRIPS: THE DOWN SIDE OF TOURISM**
Client **CLEVELAND PLAIN DEALER MAGAZINE**
Art Director **JERRY SEALY**
Usage **EDITORIAL**
Media **ACRYLIC**

4
Illustrator **MARTY BRAUN**
Title **NEW YEAR'S DAY BOWL GAMES**
Client **PHILADELPHIA INQUIRER**
Art Director **BILL MARSH**
Usage **TV SECTION COVER**
Media **ACRYLIC**

1

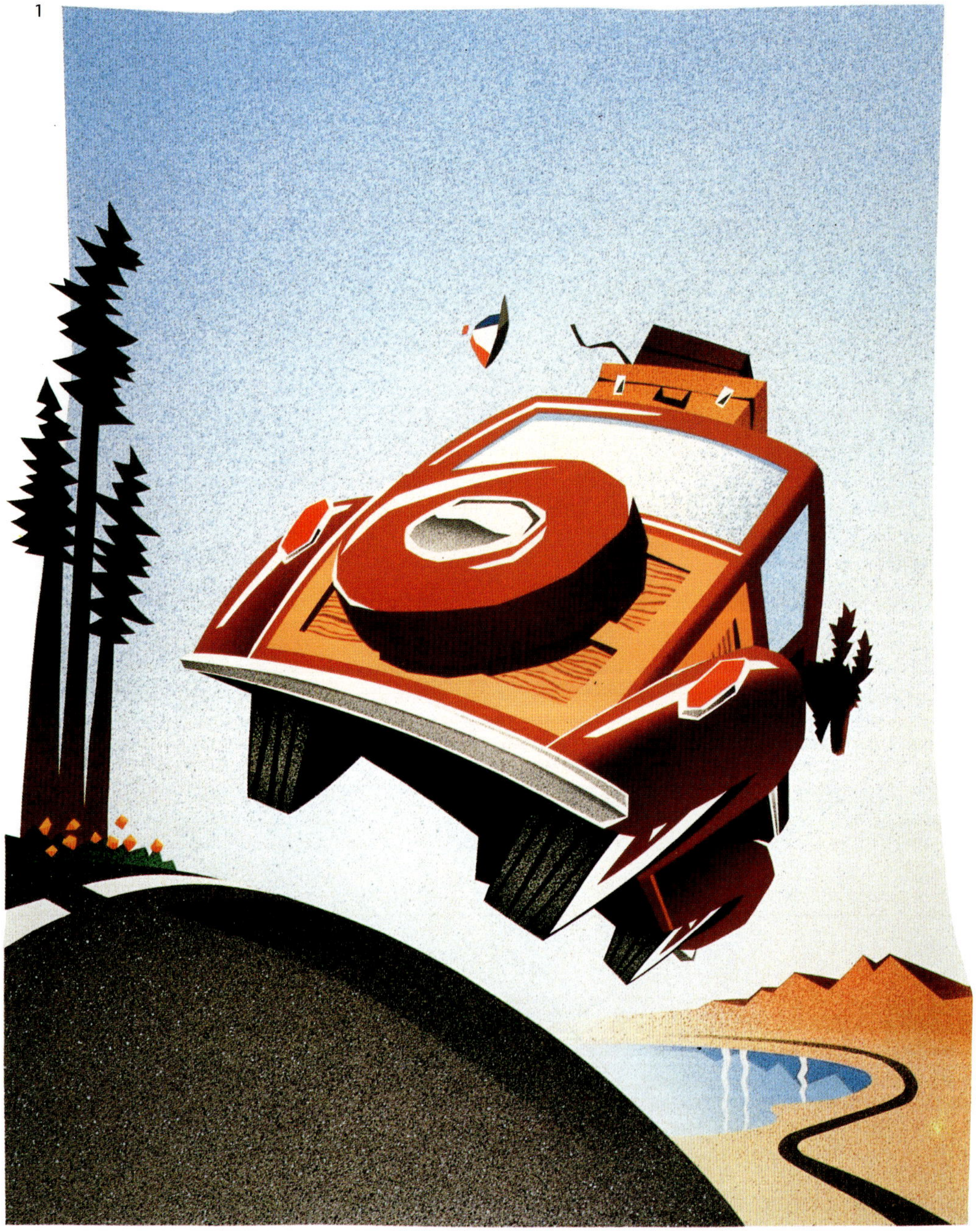

2

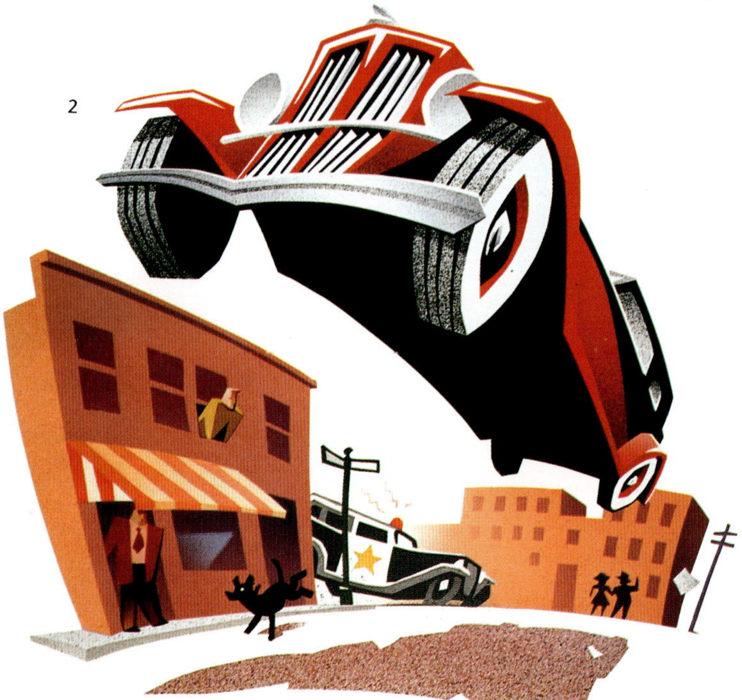

3

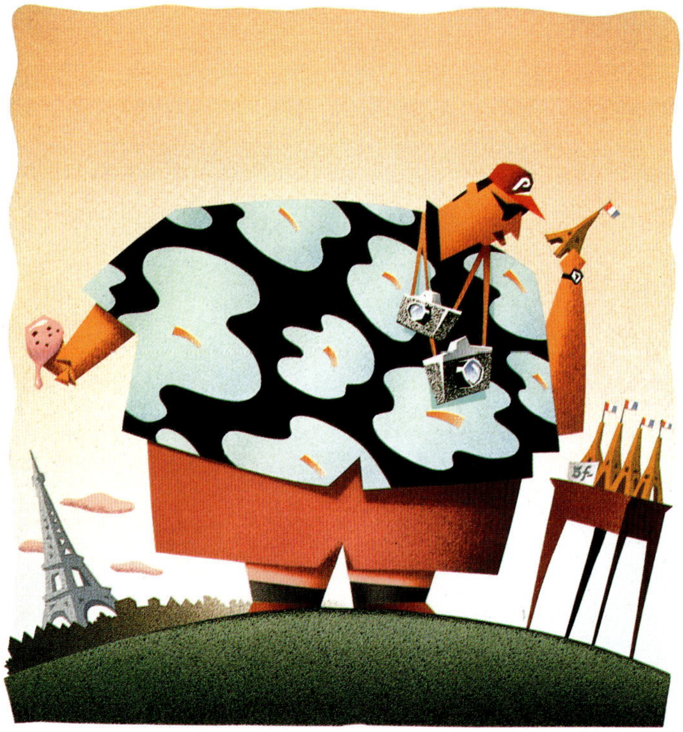

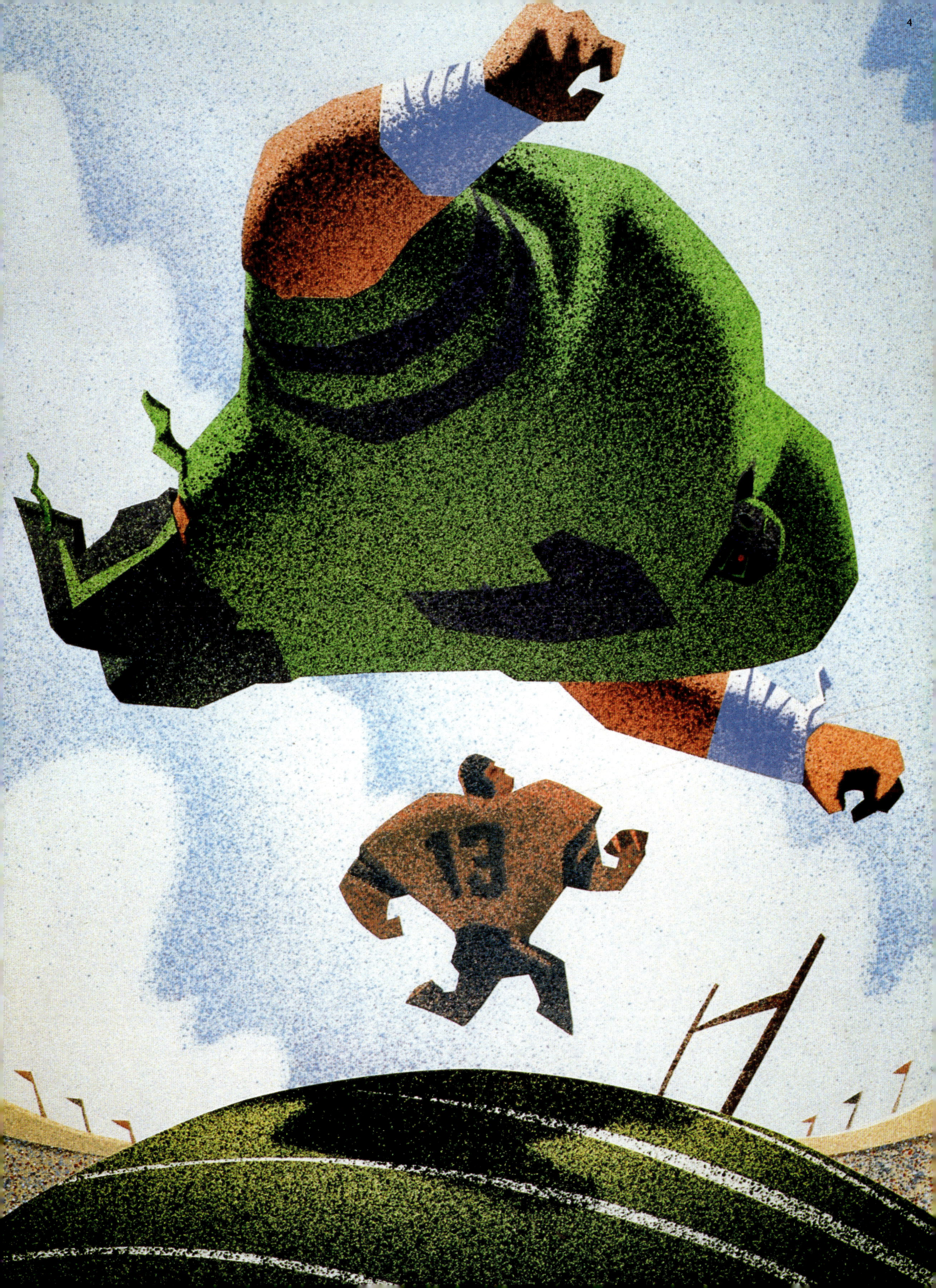
13

1
Illustrator **THOMAS CAIN**
Title **PAINTED PONY**
Usage **SELF PROMOTION**
Media **ACRYLIC**

2
Illustrator **THOMAS CAIN**
Title **JUST A CHIQUITA**
Usage **SELF PROMOTION**
Media **ACRYLIC**

3
Illustrator **THOMAS CAIN**
Title **JET FUEL DRAGSTER**
Usage **SELF PROMOTION**
Media **ACRYLIC**

1

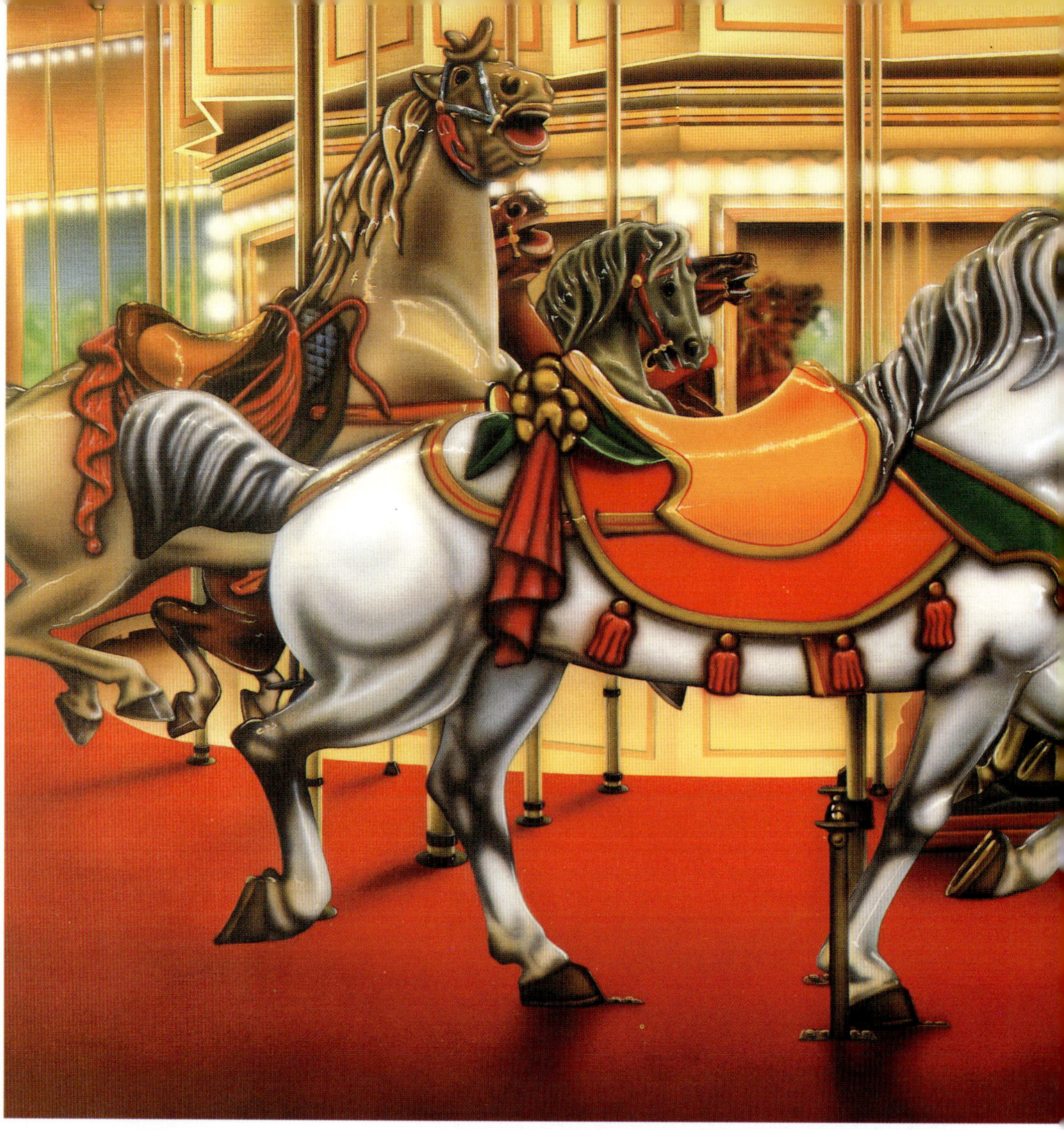

2

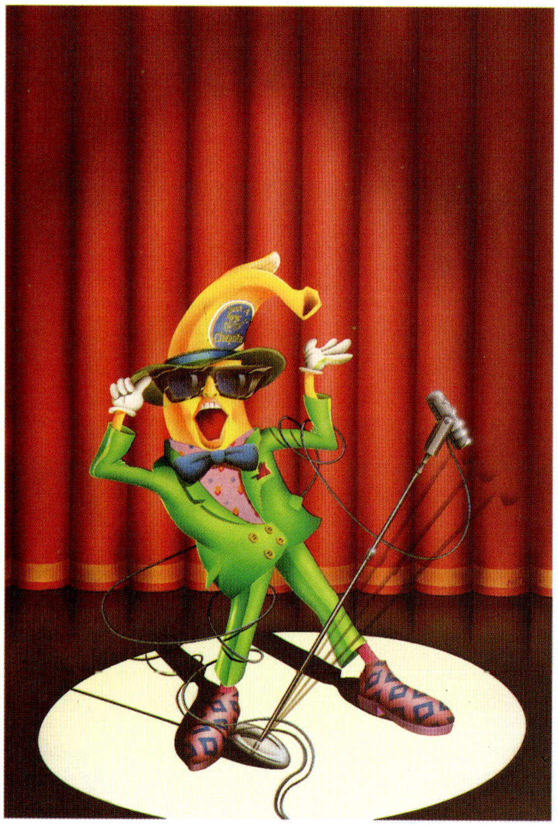

3

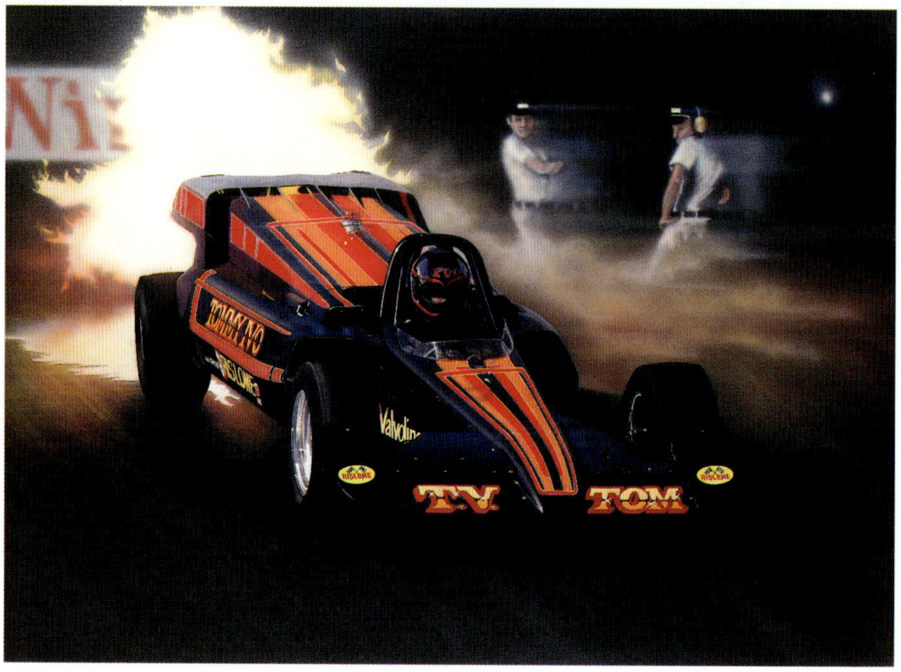

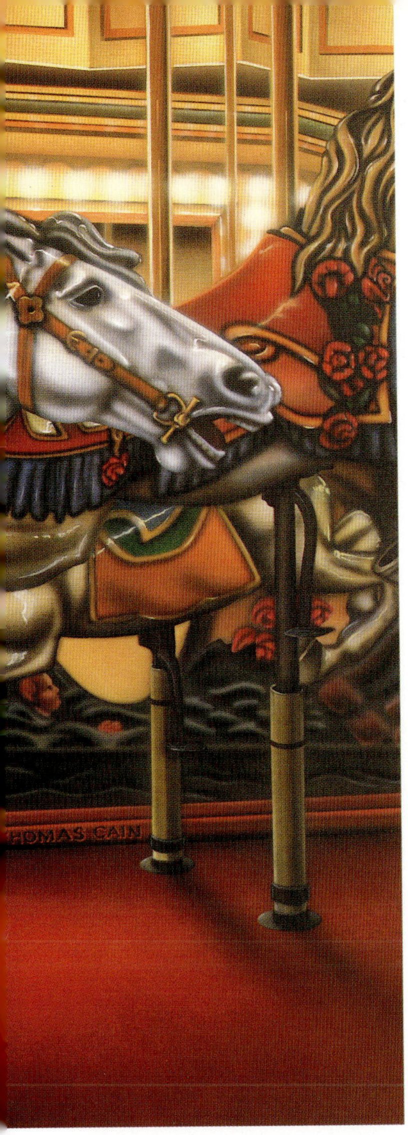

4

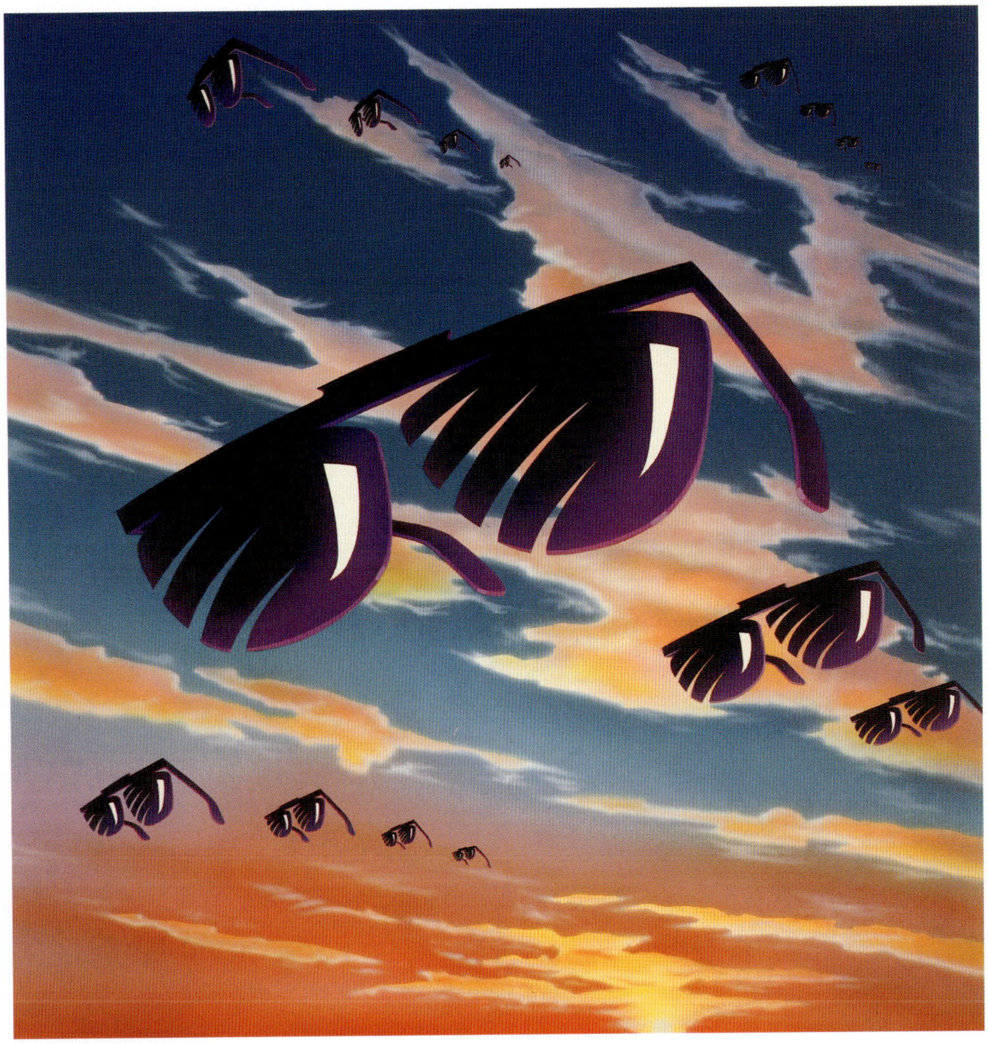

5

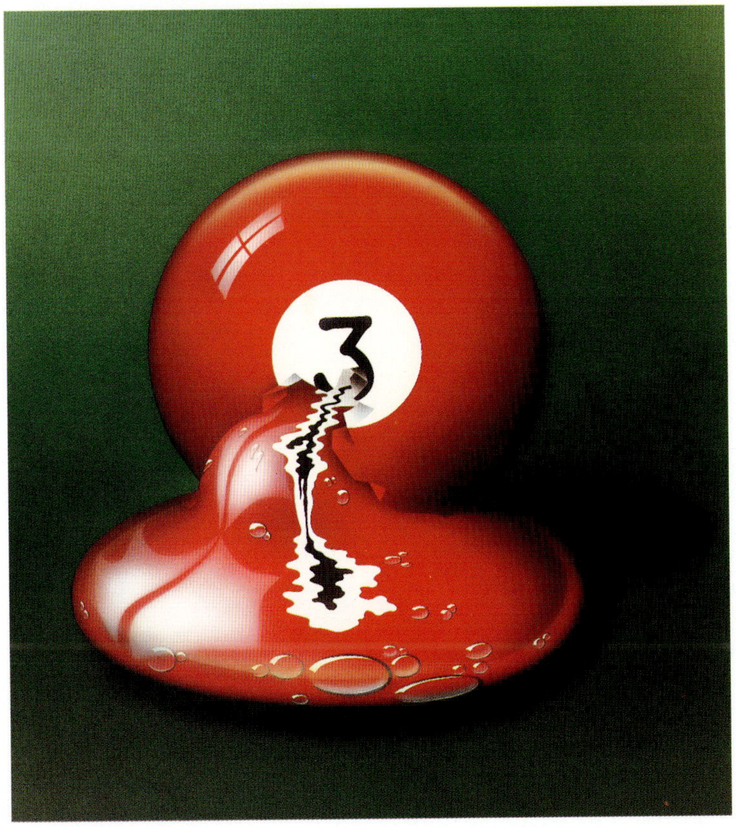

6

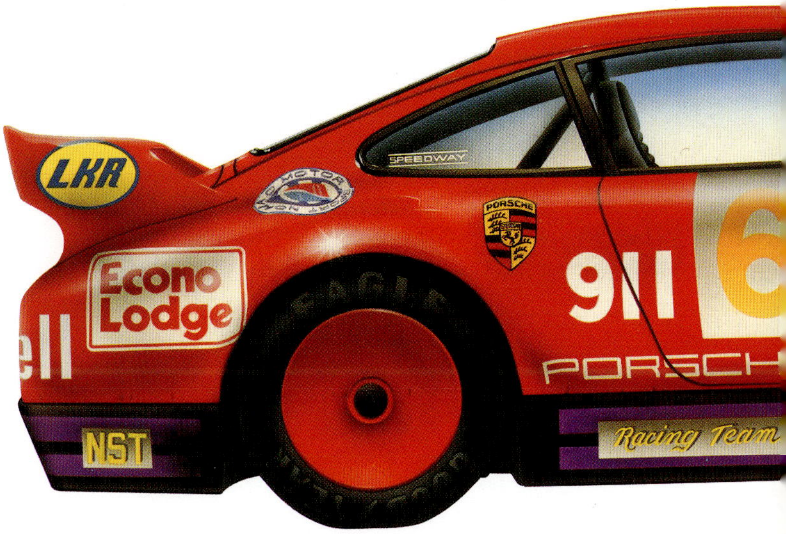

4
Illustrator **THOMAS CAIN**
Client **WFOX-FOX 97 RADIO/ DELTA AIRLINES**
Art Director **STEVE JOHNSON**
Usage **PROMOTIONAL**
Media **ACRYLIC**

5
Illustrator **THOMAS CAIN**
Title **3 BALL**
Usage **SELF PROMOTION**
Media **ACRYLIC**

6
Illustrator **THOMAS CAIN**
Title **STOCK CAR**
Client **ECONO-LODGE**
Art Director **JEFF SCHOTZ**
Usage **ANNUAL REPORT**
Media **ACRYLIC**

1
Illustrator **THOMAS J. HUMPERT**
Title **NEW DIMENSION OF PLAY**
Usage **SELF PROMOTION**
Media **ACRYLIC**

2
Illustrator **THOMAS J. HUMPERT**
Title **HARMONY ROSE**
Usage **SELF PROMOTION**
Media **ACRYLIC**

3
Illustrator **THOMAS J. HUMPERT**
Title **PIECES OF THE PUZZLE**
Usage **SELF PROMOTION**
Media **ACRYLIC**

1

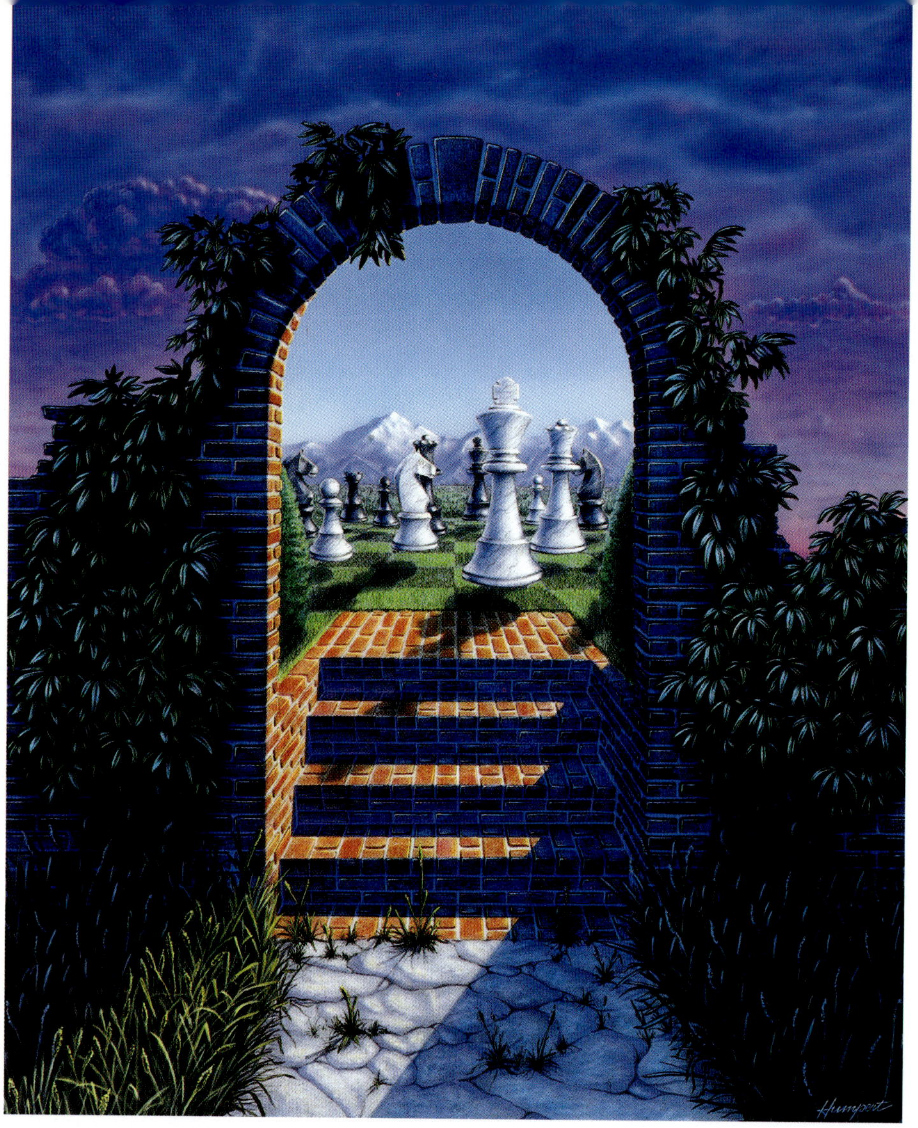

2

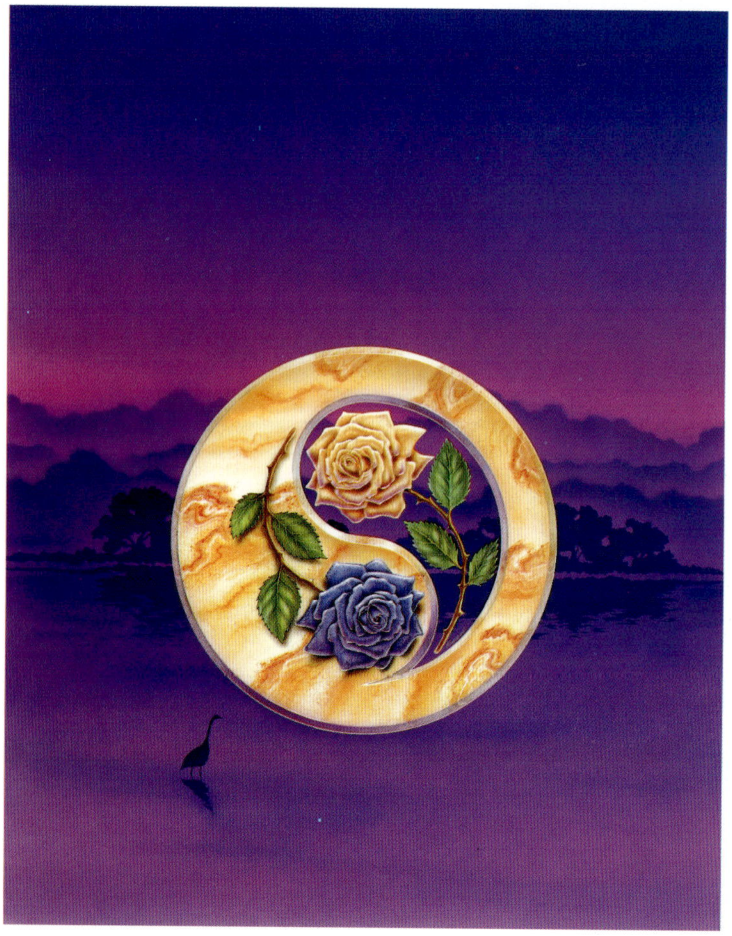

3

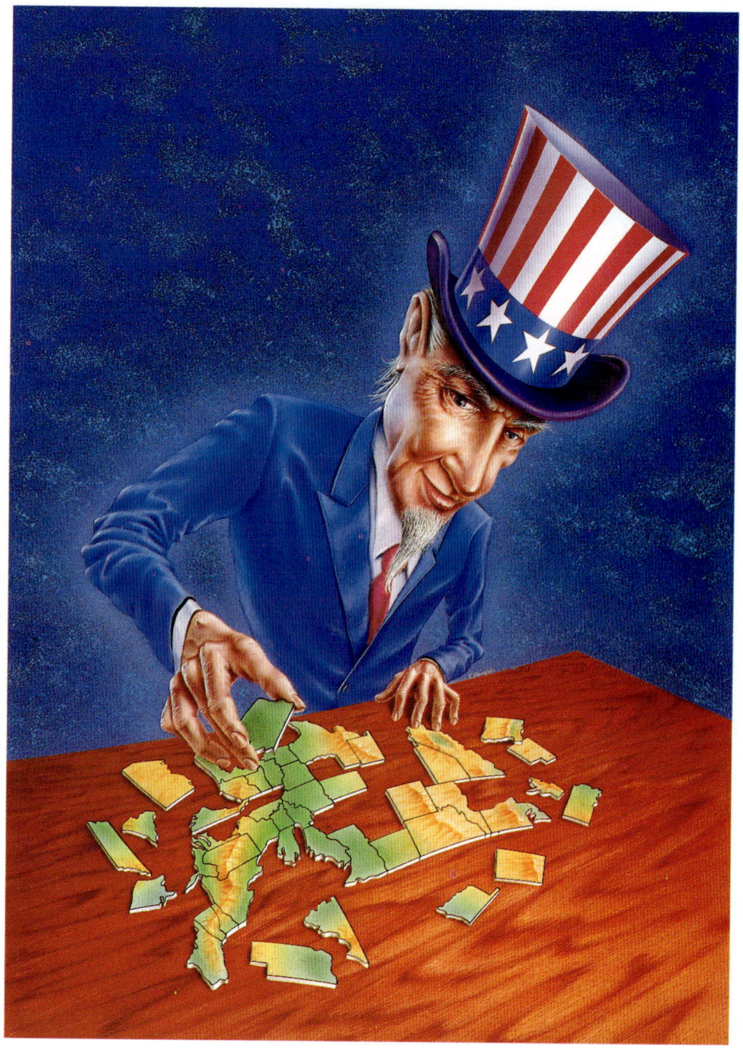

4

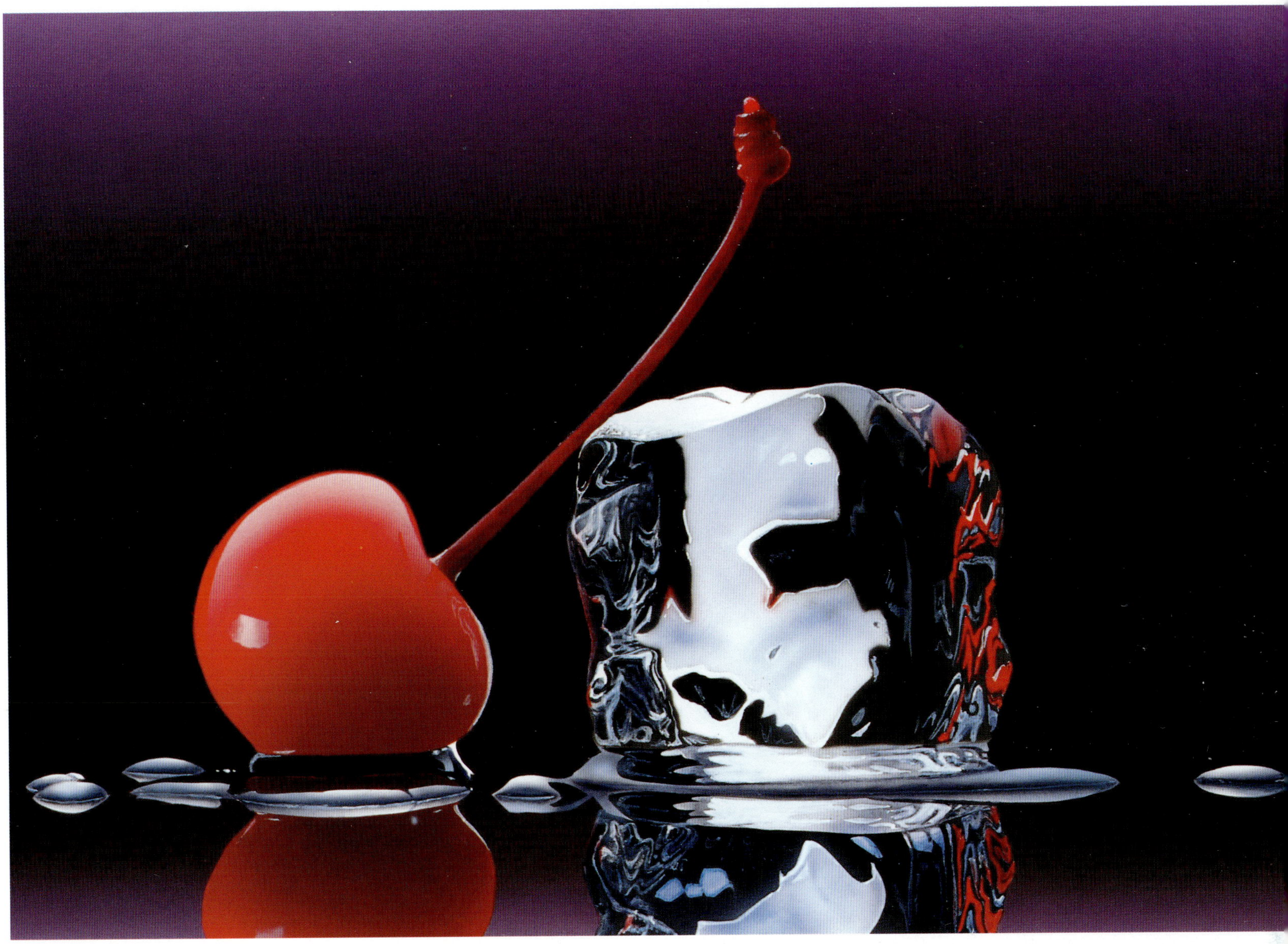

5

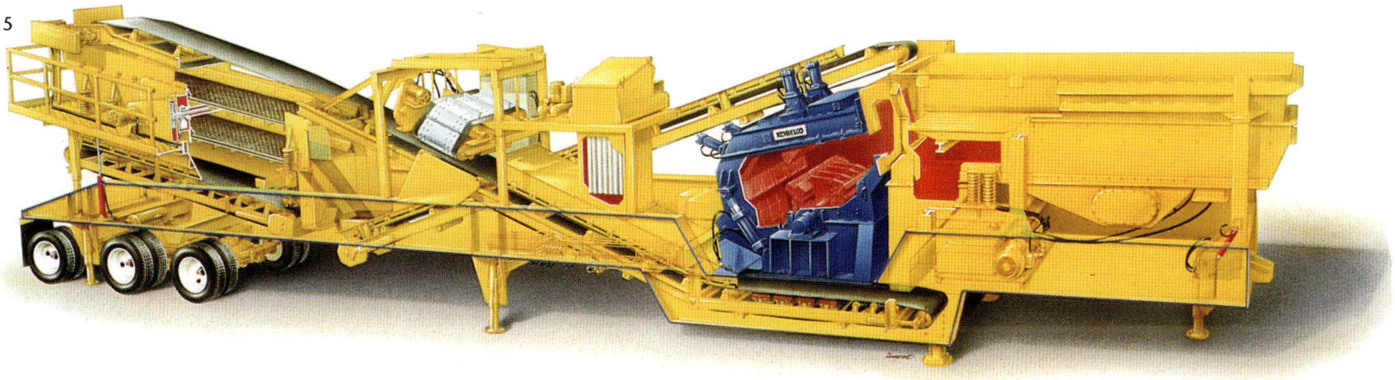

4
Illustrator **THOMAS J. HUMPERT**
Title **ICE CHERRY**
Usage **SELF PROMOTION**
Media **ACRYLIC**

5
Illustrator **THOMAS J. HUMPERT**
Title **PORTABLE CONCRETE RECYCLING PLANT**
Client **THUNDERBIRD INDUSTRIES**
Usage **BROCHURE, TRADE ADVERTISEMENT**
Media **ACRYLIC**

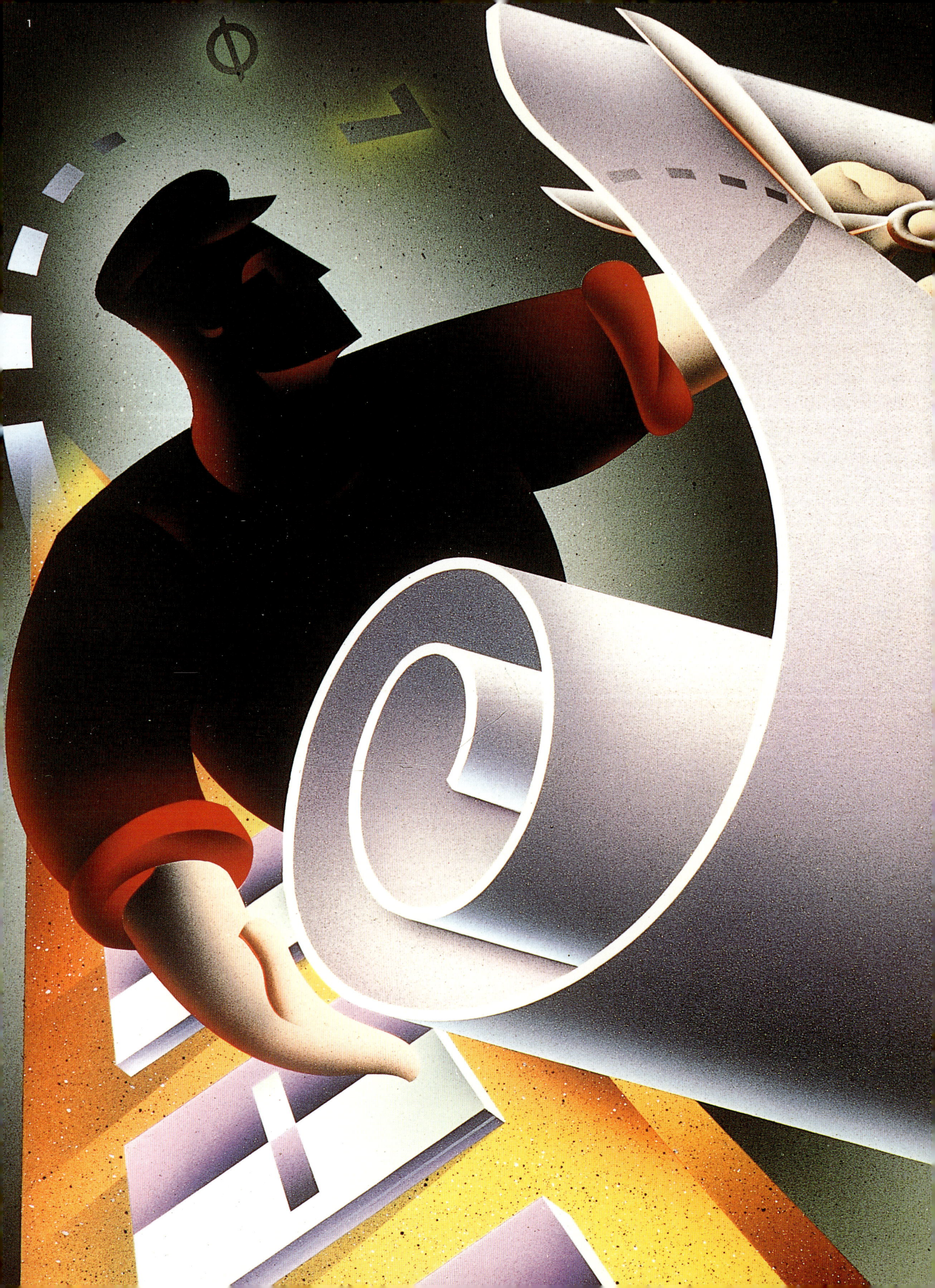

1

1
Illustrator **JEFF KOEGEL**
Client **WORDPERFECT CORP./ WORDPERFECT MAGAZINE**
Art Director **NICKIE EGAN**
Usage **EDITORIAL**
Media **ACRYLIC**

2
Illustrator **JEFF KOEGEL**
Client **INGRAM MICRO**
Art Director **BRIAN BARINGTON**
Usage **EDITORIAL**
Media **ACRYLIC**

3
Illustrator **JEFF KOEGEL**
Usage **SELF PROMOTION**
Media **ACRYLIC**

2

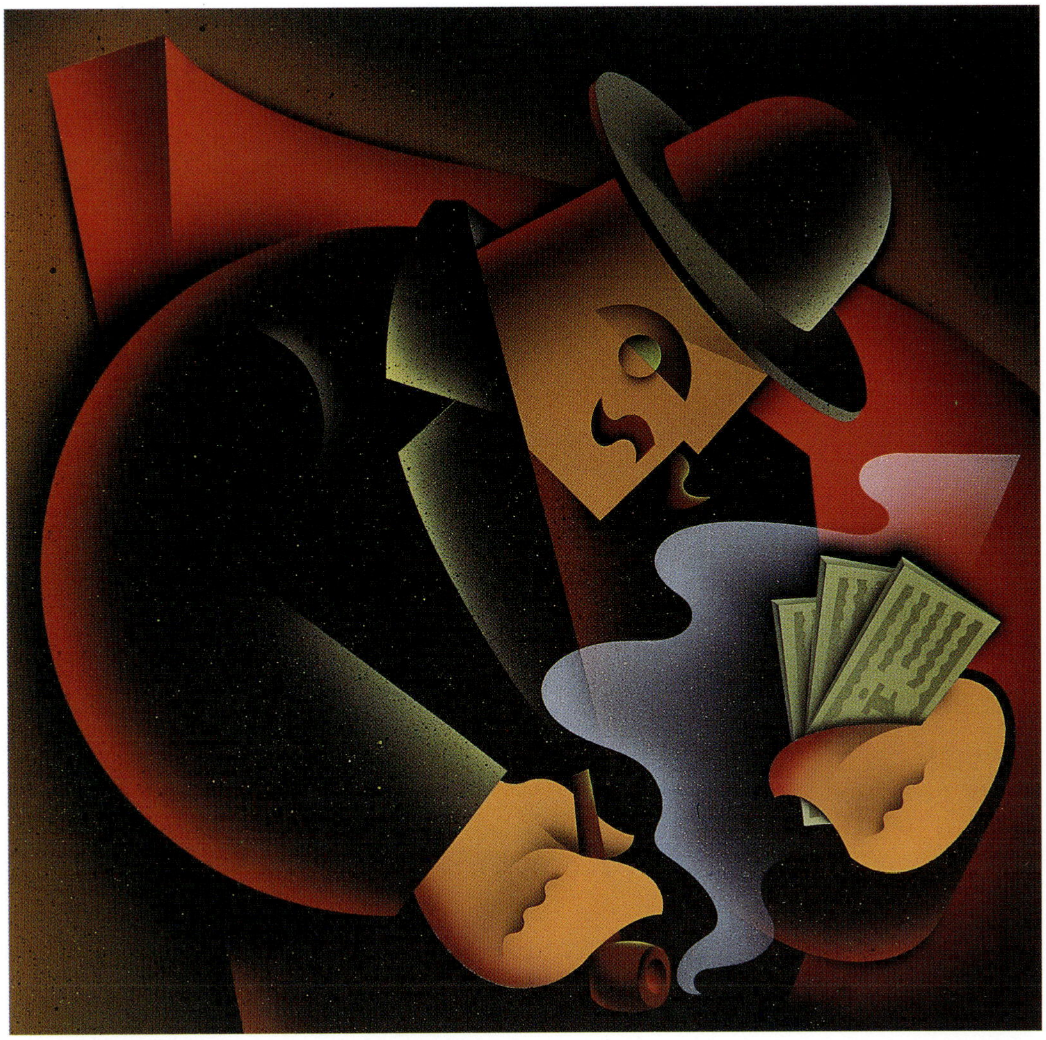

3

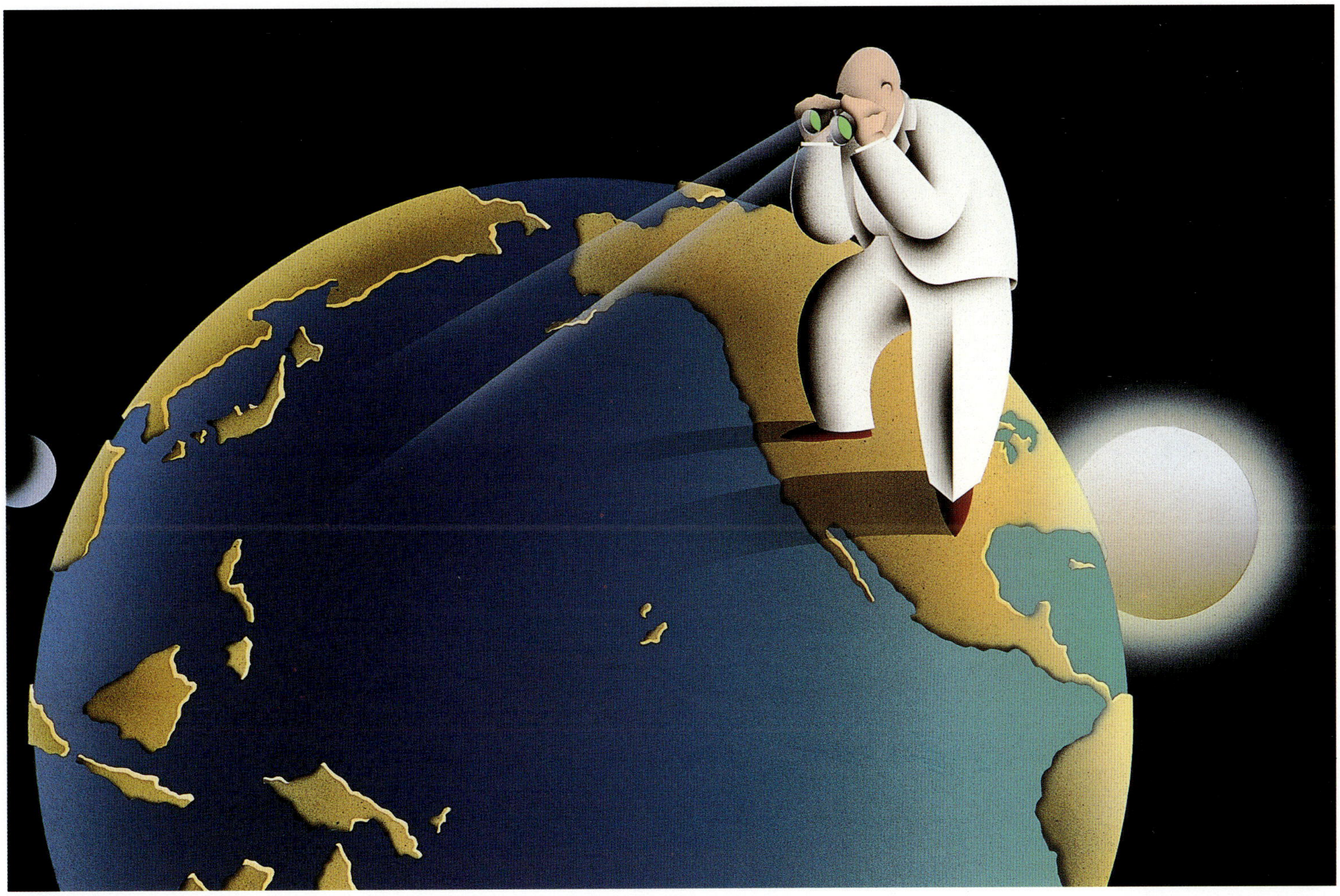

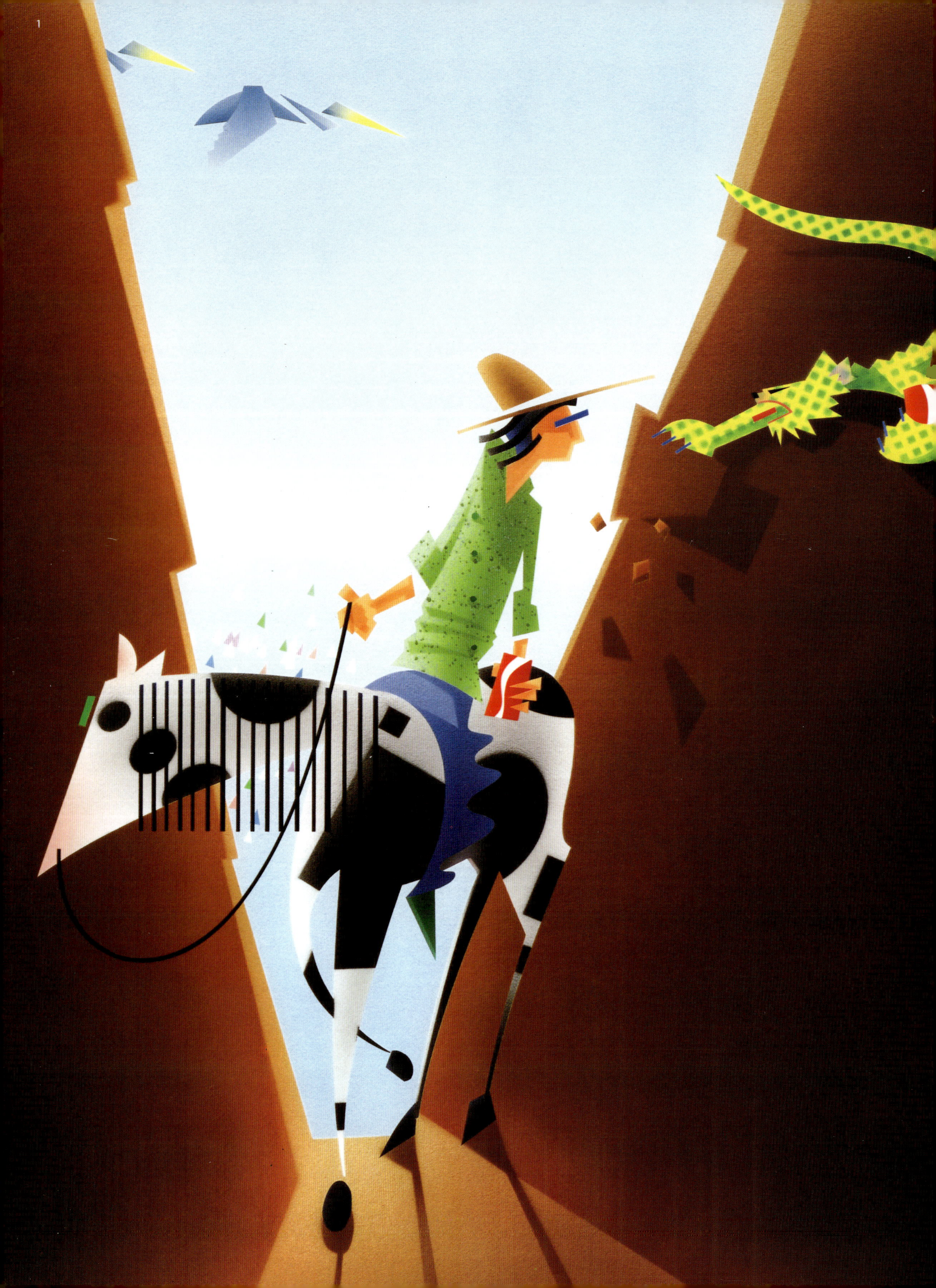

2

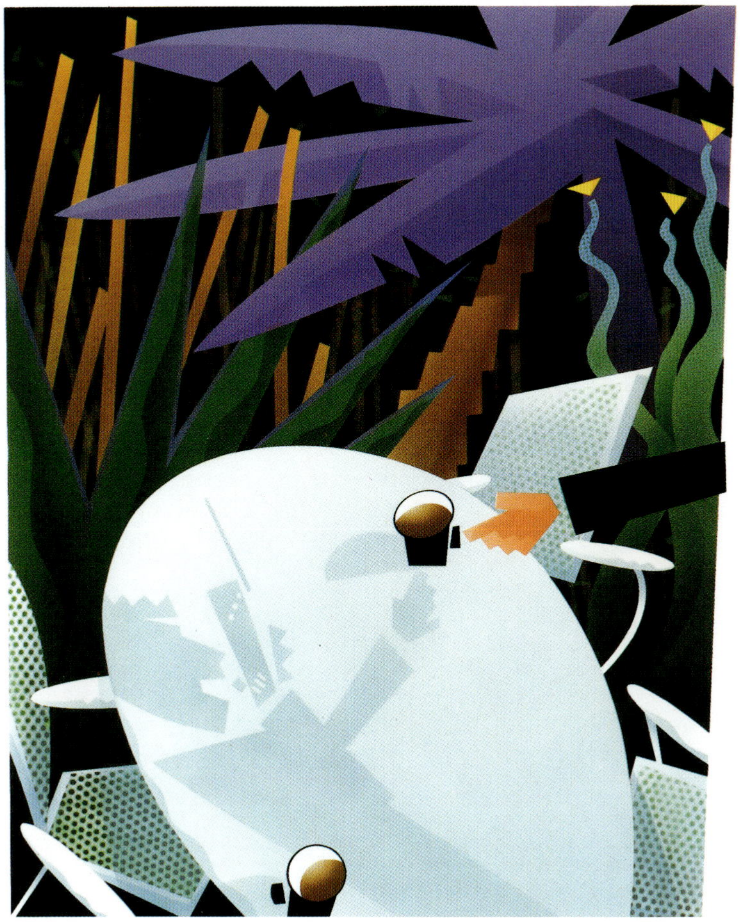

3

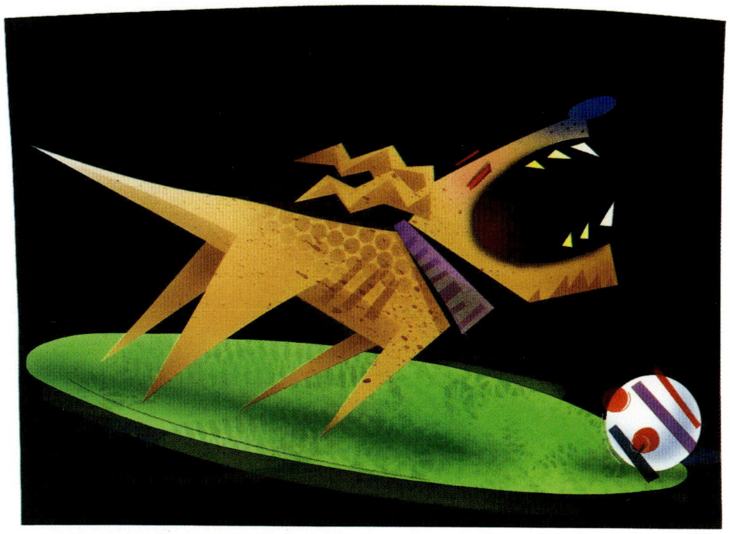

4

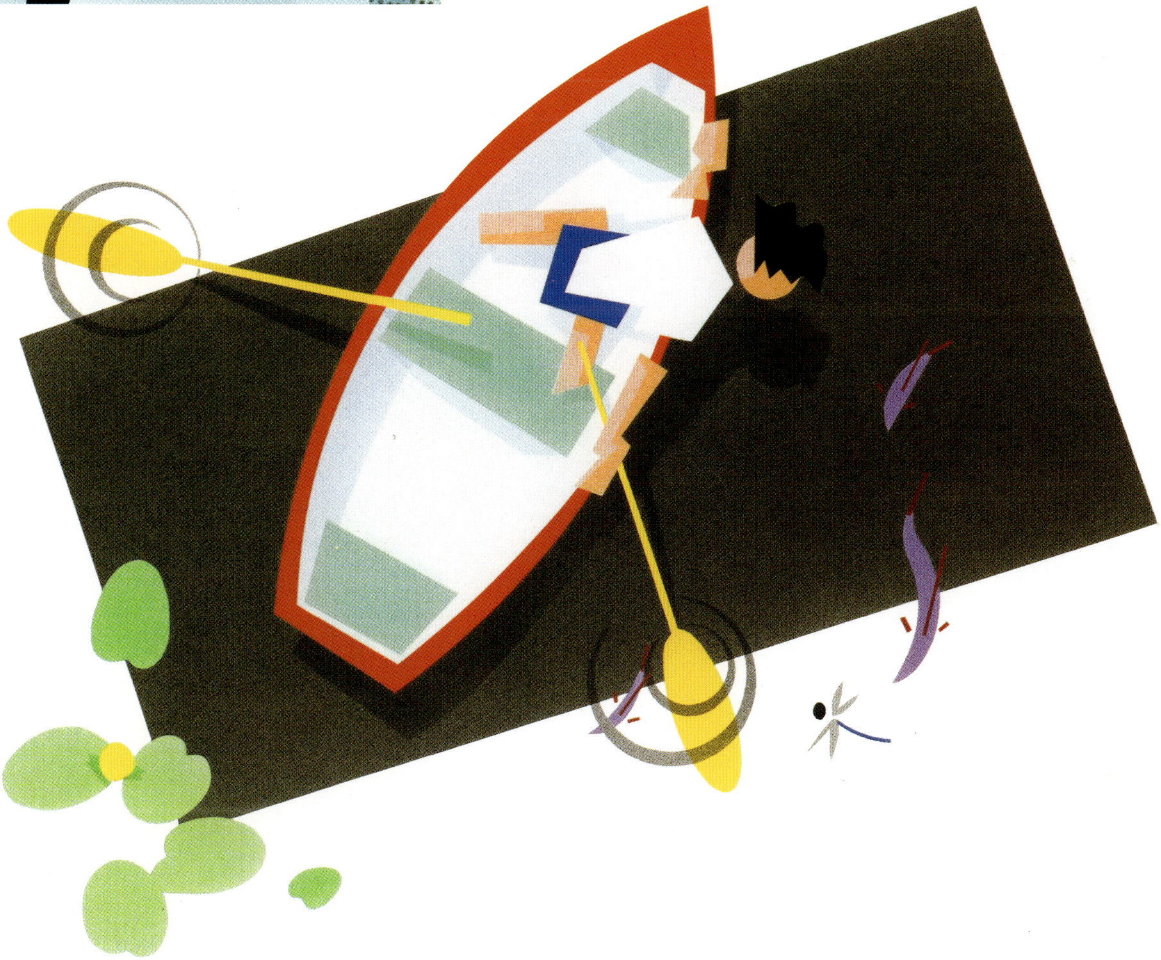

1 - 4
Illustrator **ROGER BOEHM**
Usage **SELF PROMOTION**
Media **GOUACHE**

1 - 3
Illustrator **GARY PENCA**
Usage **SELF PROMOTION**
Media **GOUACHE**

1

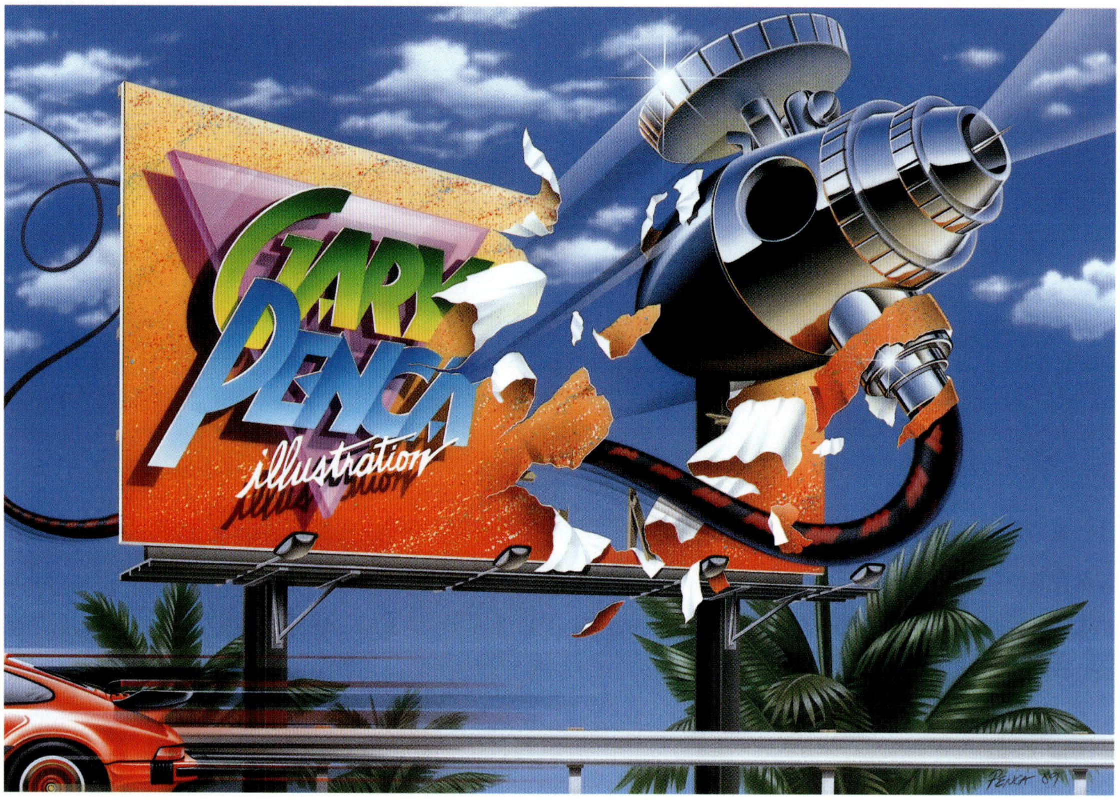

2

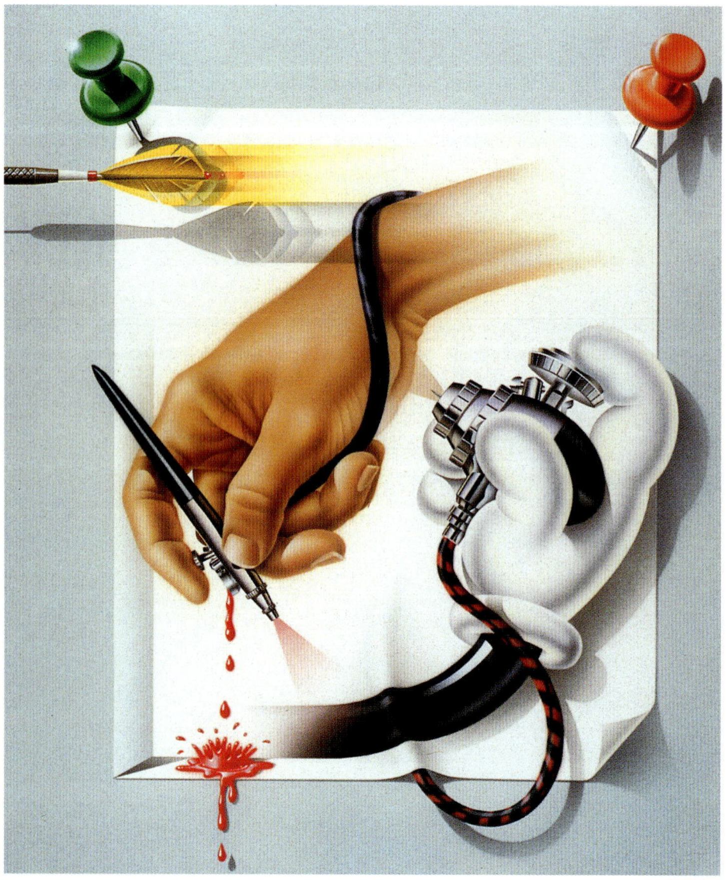

3

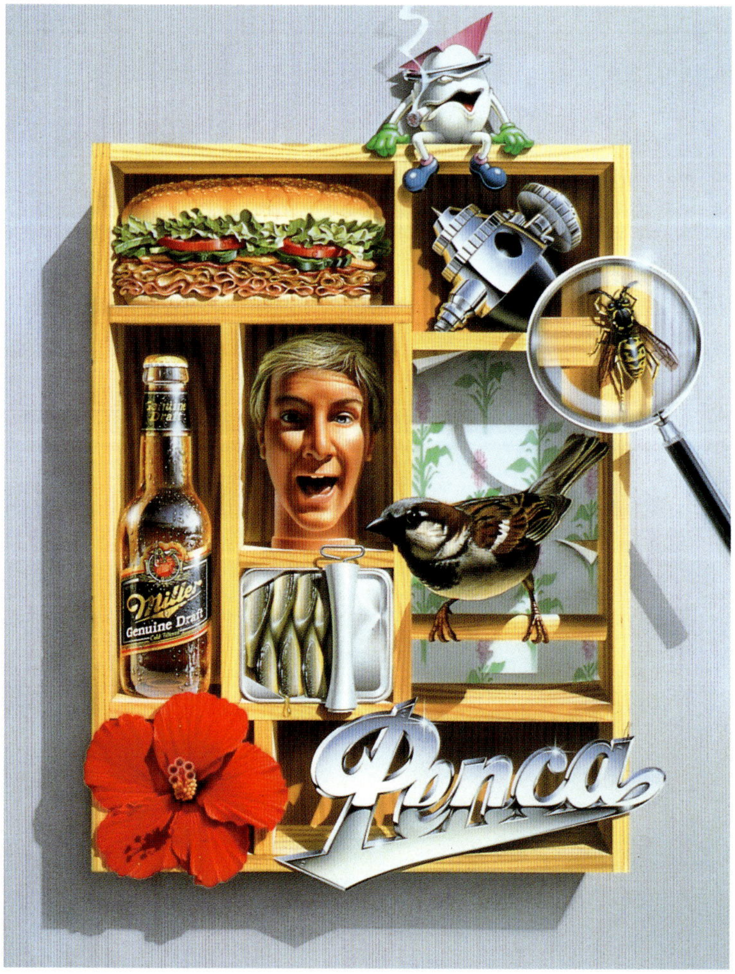

1

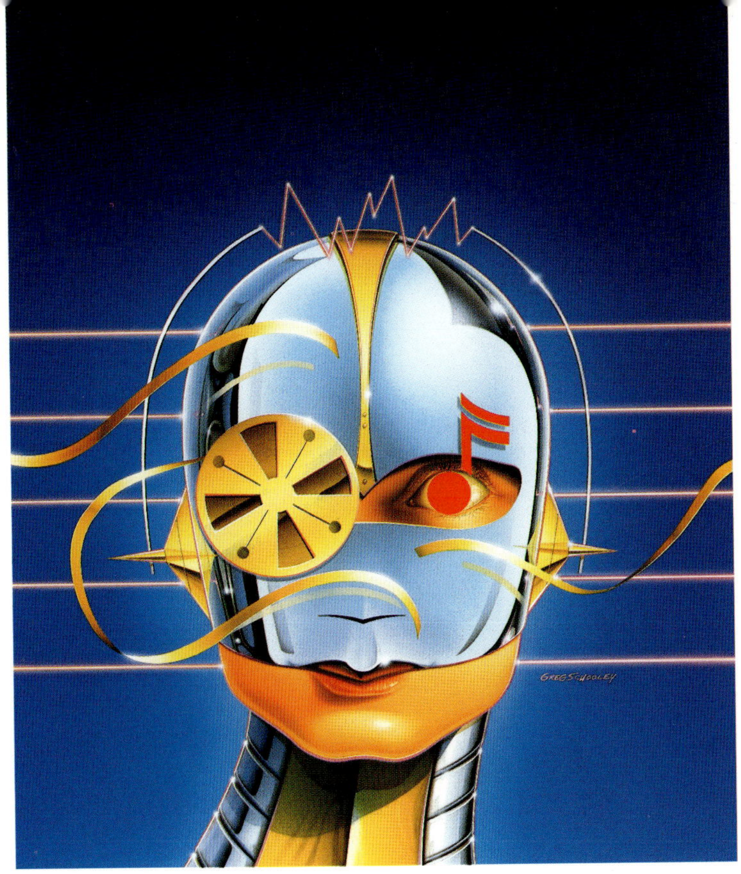

2

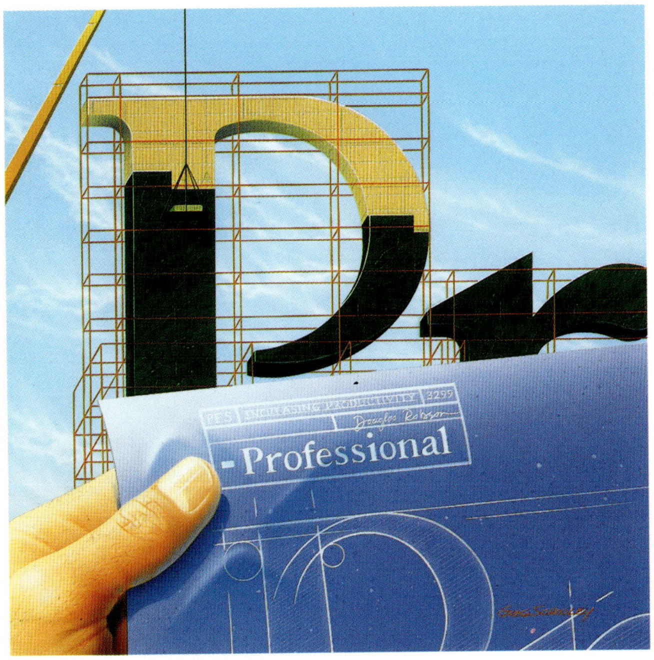

4

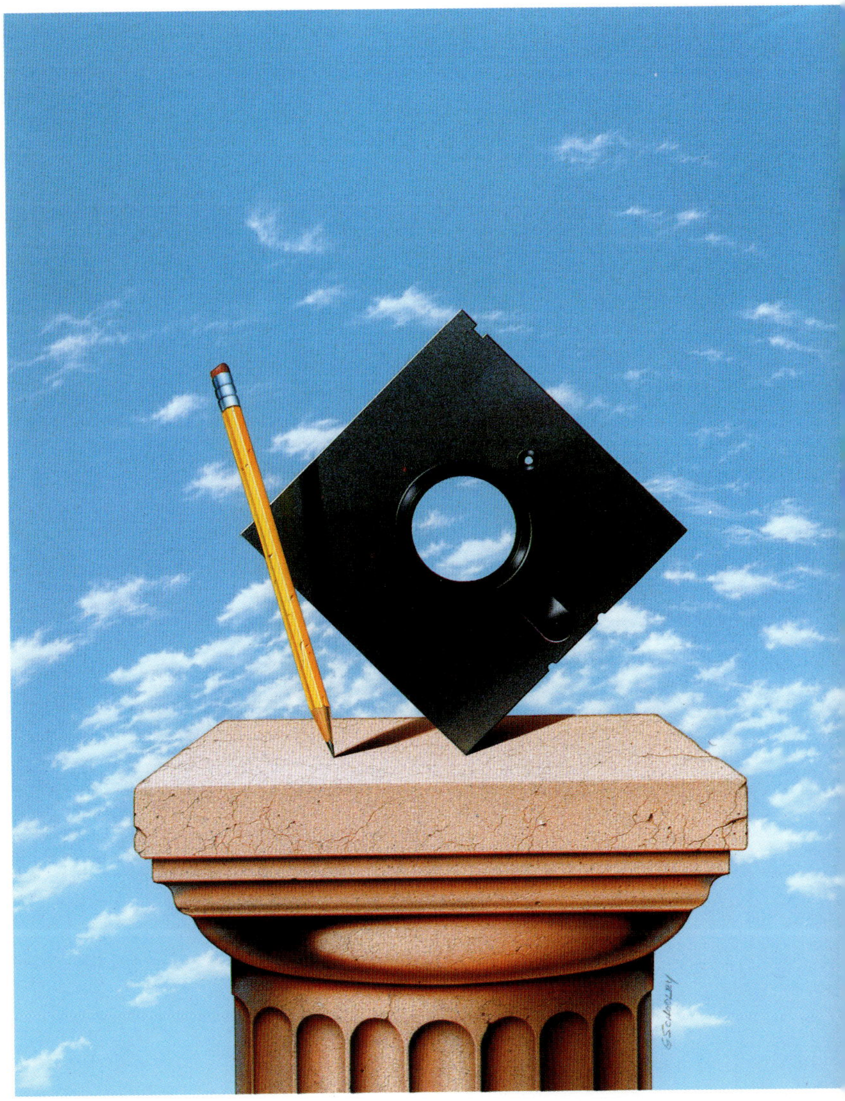

3

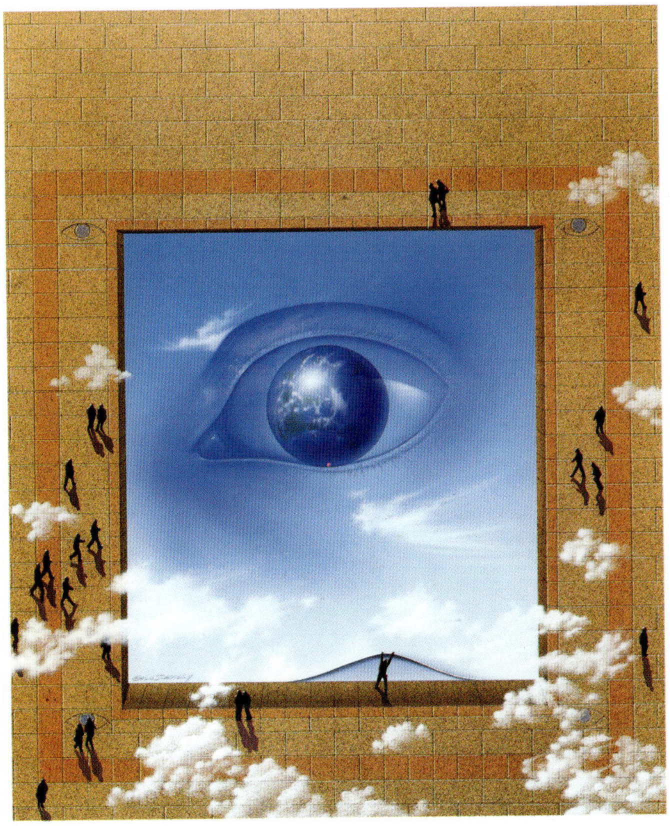

1
Illustrator **GREG SCHOOLEY**
Title **DIGITAL AUDIO TAPE**
Client **TAB/MCGRAW-HILL**
Art Director **LORI SCHLOSSER**
Usage **BOOK AND CATALOG COVER**
Media **GOUACHE, ACRYLIC**

2
Illustrator **GREG SCHOOLEY**
Title **INCREASING PRODUCTIVITY WITH THE PROFESSIONAL SERIES**
Client **TAB/MCGRAW-HILL**
Art Director **JOYCE THOMPSON**
Usage **BOOK COVER**
Media **GOUACHE**

3
Illustrator **GREG SCHOOLEY**
Title **MICROSOFT WORD FOR WINDOWS REVEALED**
Client **TAB/MCGRAW-HILL**
Art Director **LORI SCHLOSSER**
Usage **BOOK COVER**
Media **GOUACHE**

4
Illustrator **GREG SCHOOLEY**
Title **WORDPERFECT POWER: WORD PROCESSING MADE EASY**
Client **TAB/MCGRAW-HILL**
Art Director **LORI SCHLOSSER**
Usage **BOOK COVER**
Media **GOUACHE**

1
Illustrator FARLEY MAGADIA
Client TURNER ENTERTAINMENT CO.
Art Director MICHELLE MAGAT
Usage DIE-CUT COVER TO AN ANIMATION STYLE GUIDE
Media ACRYLIC

2
Illustrator FARLEY MAGADIA
Usage SELF PROMOTION
Media ACRYLIC, COLORED PENCIL

3
Illustrator FARLEY MAGADIA
Usage SELF PROMOTION
Media ACRYLIC

4
Illustrator FARLEY MAGADIA
Client LOS ANGELES SOCIETY OF ILLUSTRATORS/LEARNING TREE UNIVERSITY
Art Director FARLEY MAGADIA, AVALYN LUNDGREN ELLIS
Usage EXHIBITION ANNOUNCEMENTS
Media ACRYLIC, INK, ENAMEL

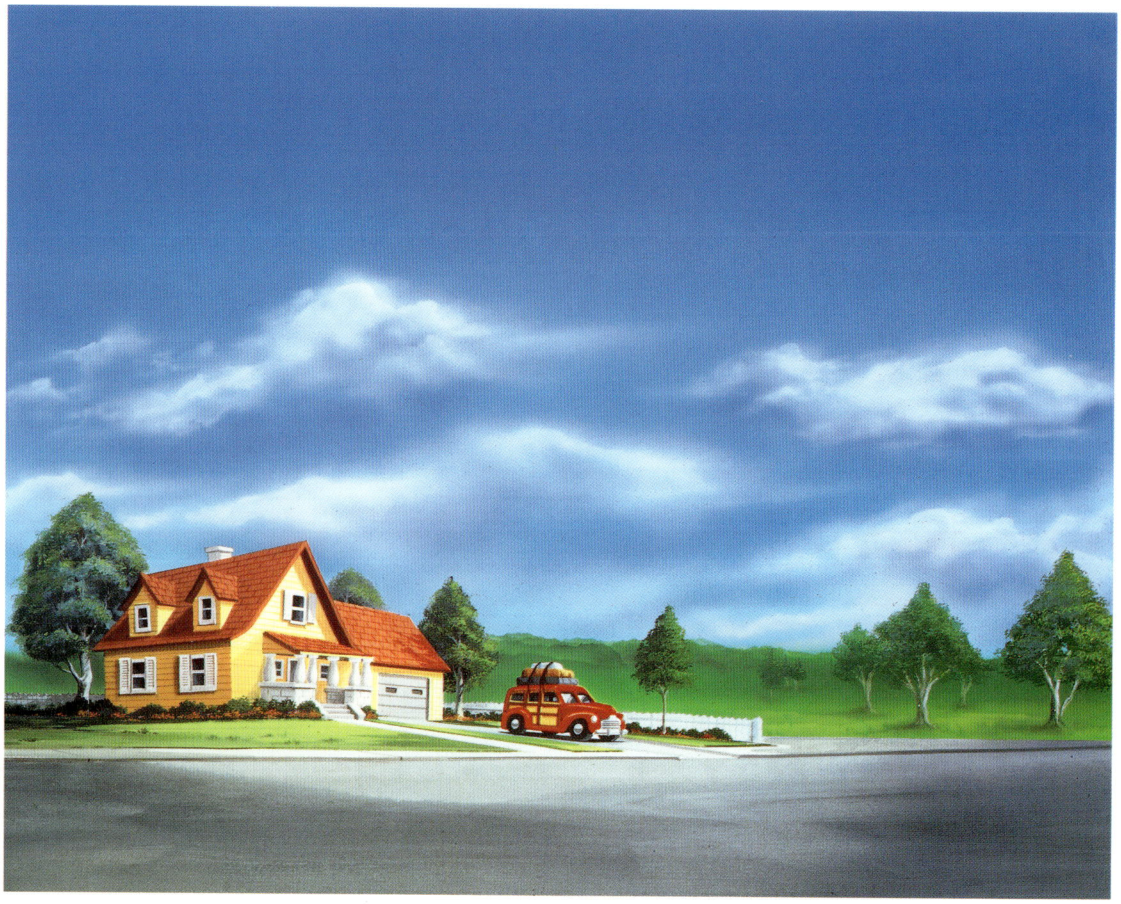

1

2

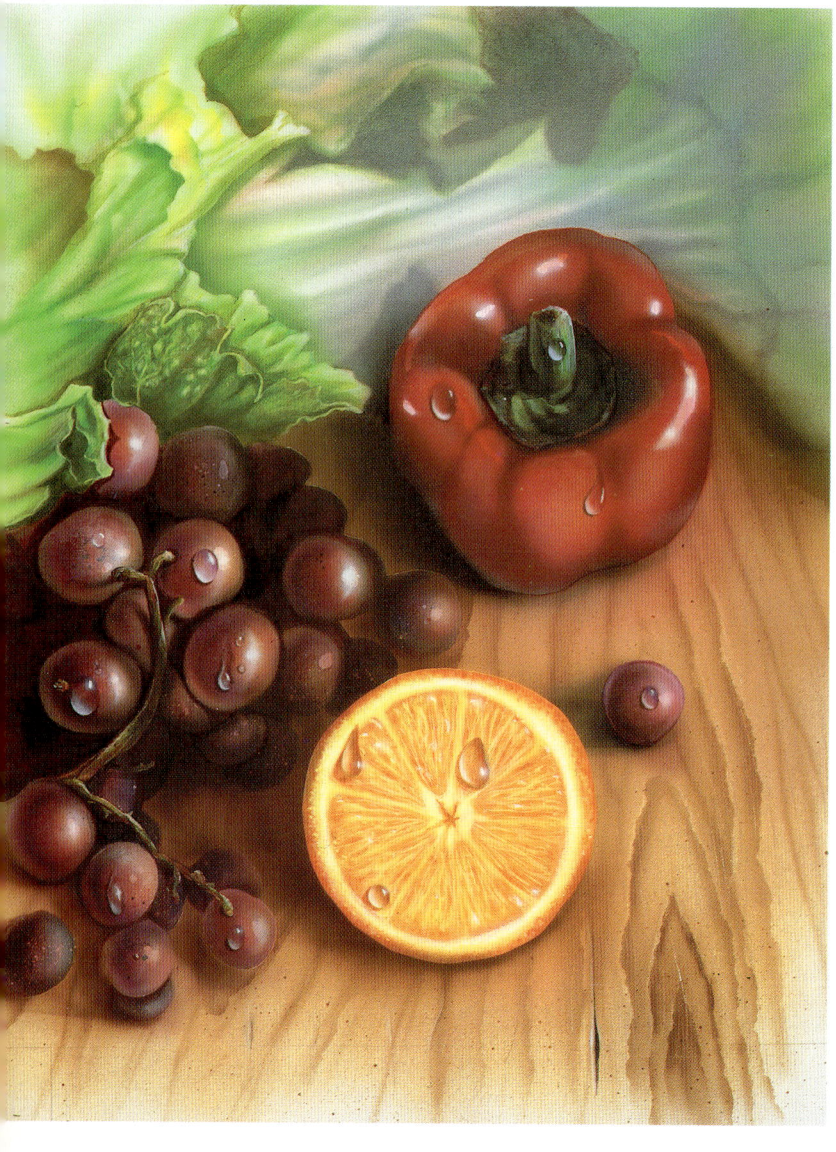

3

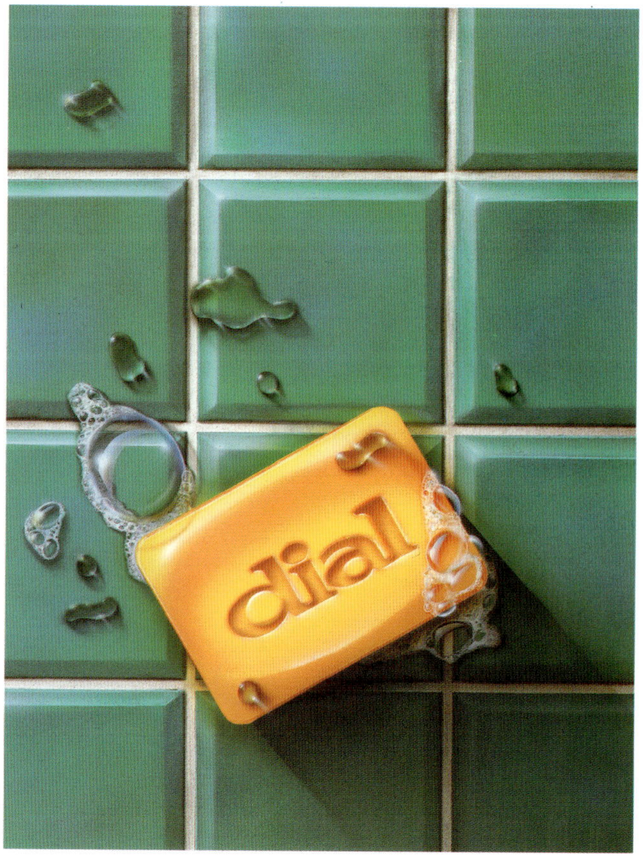

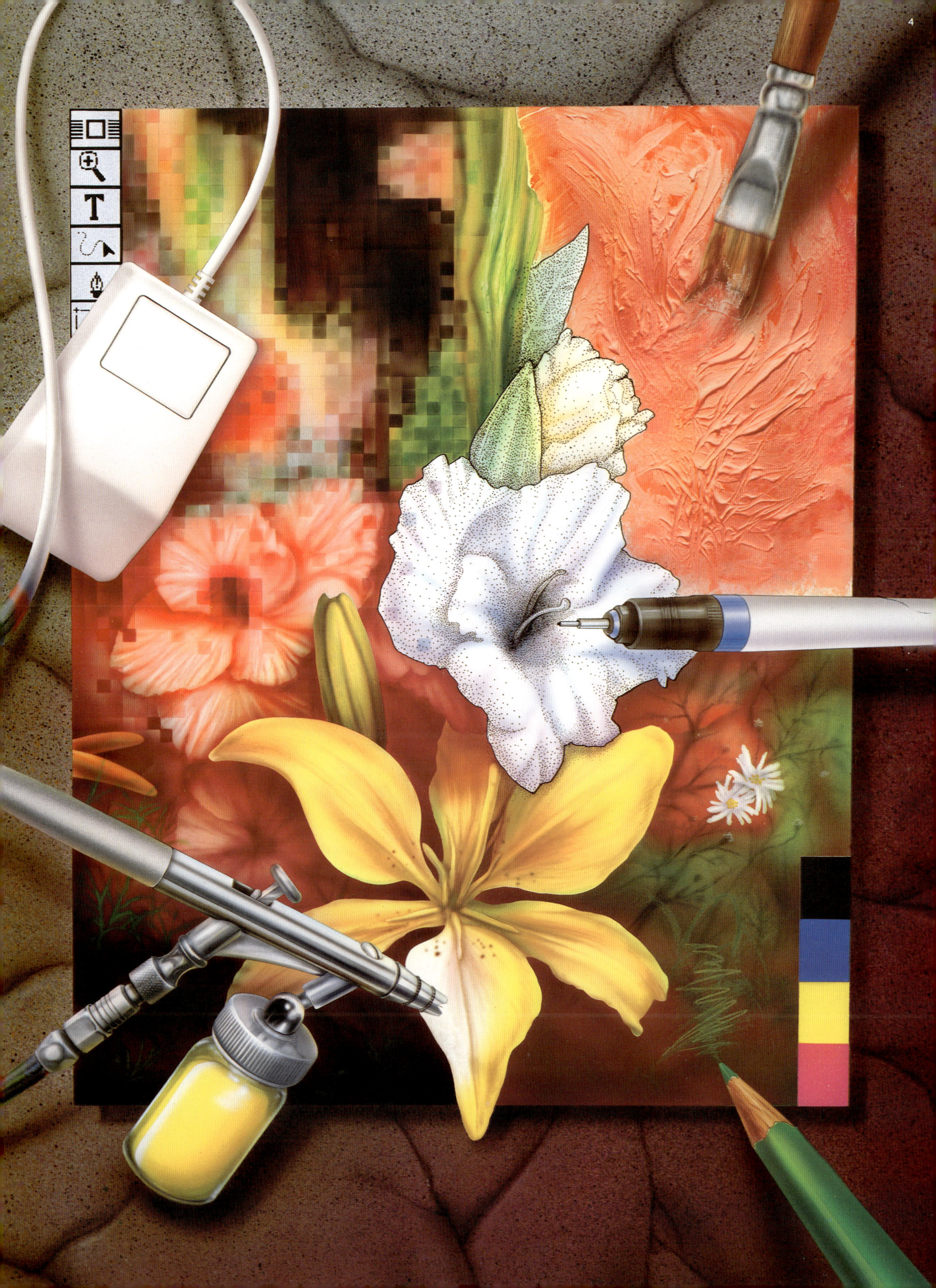

1

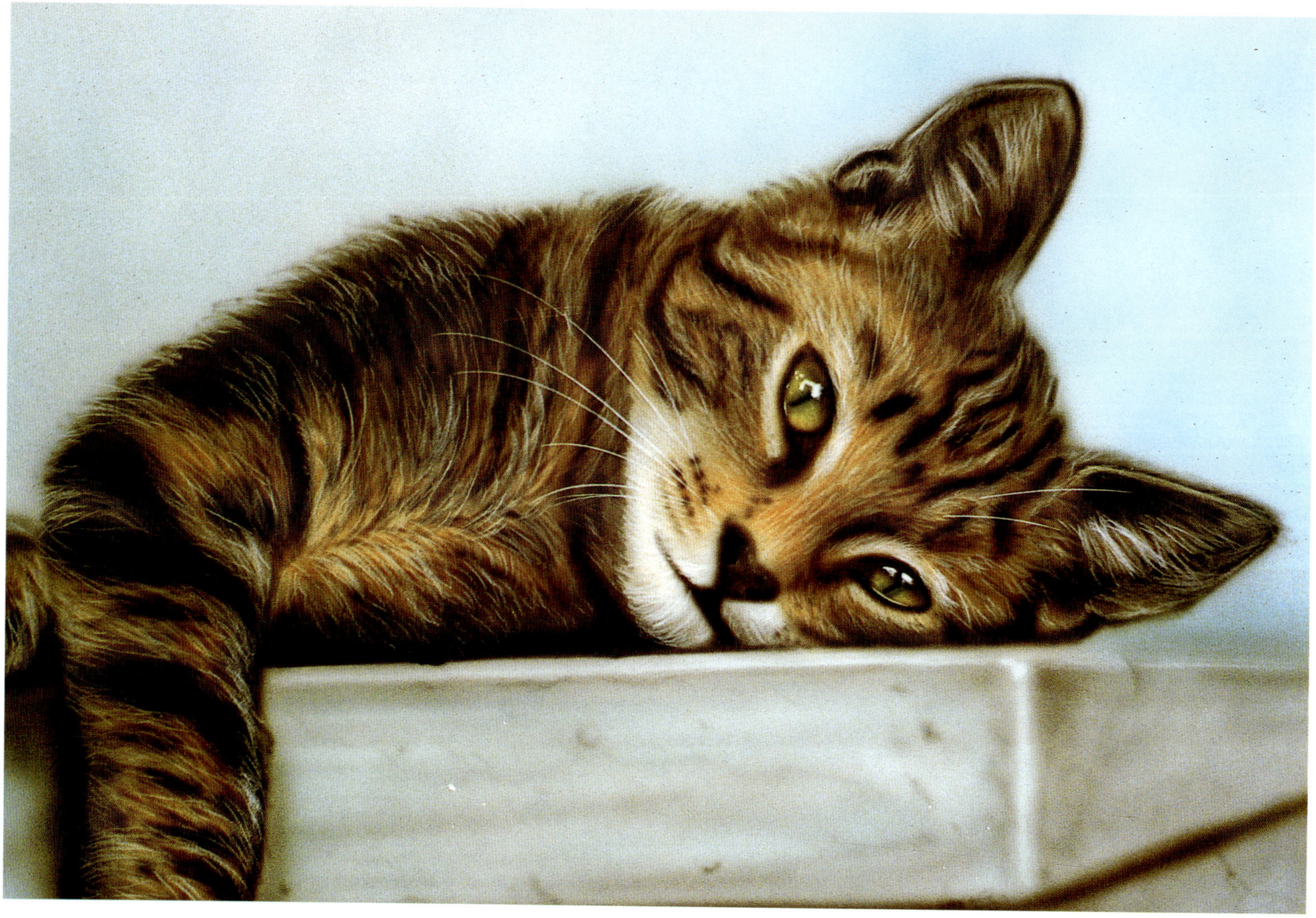

1
Illustrator **GREG HURLEY**
Title **ON THE EDGE**
Usage **SELF PROMOTION**
Media **ACRYLIC**

2
Illustrator **GREG HURLEY**
Title **STARE DOWN**
Usage **SELF PROMOTION**
Media **DYES**

2

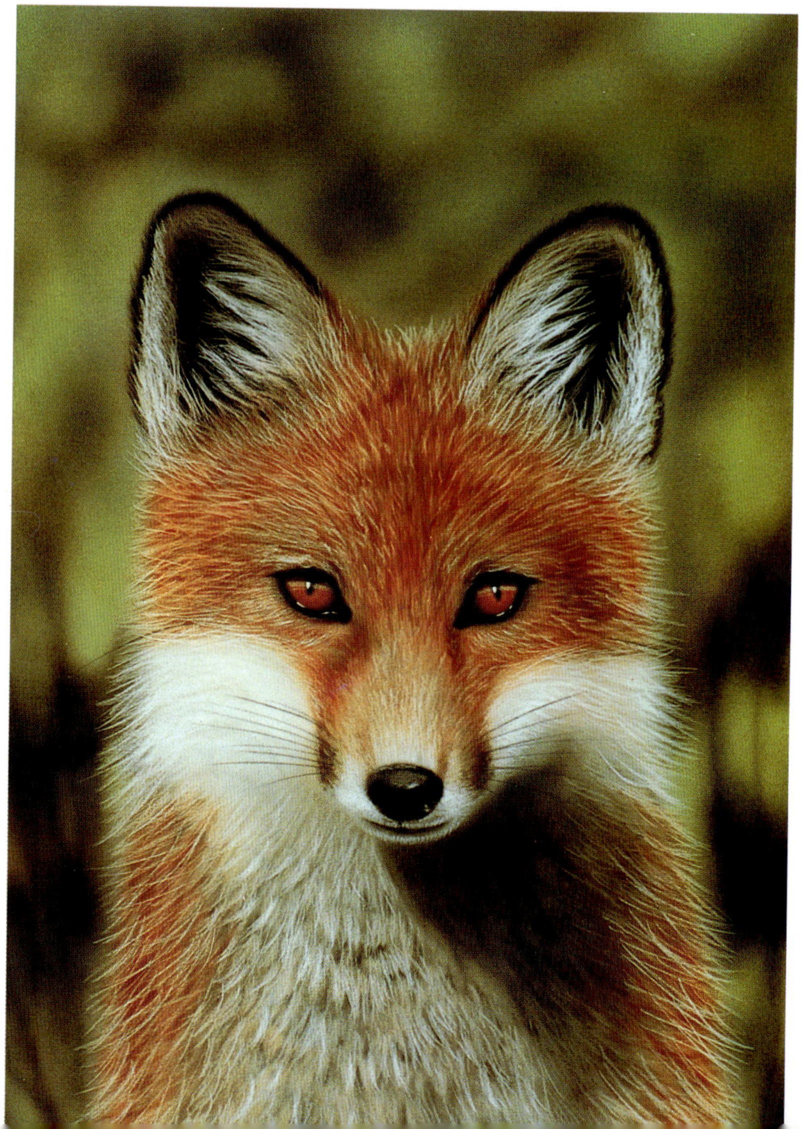

3, 4
Illustrator **GREG HURLEY**
Usage **SELF PROMOTION**
Media **DYES**

3

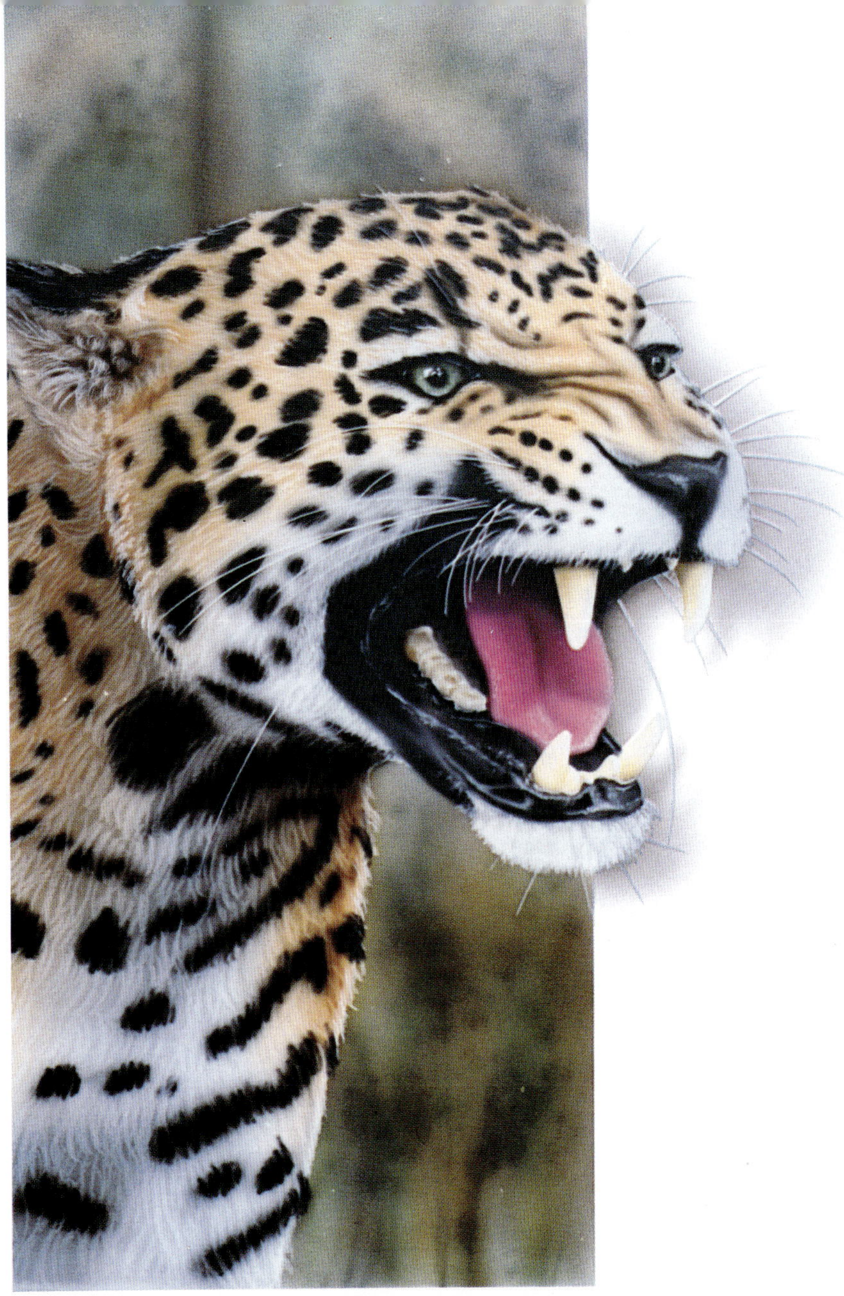

4

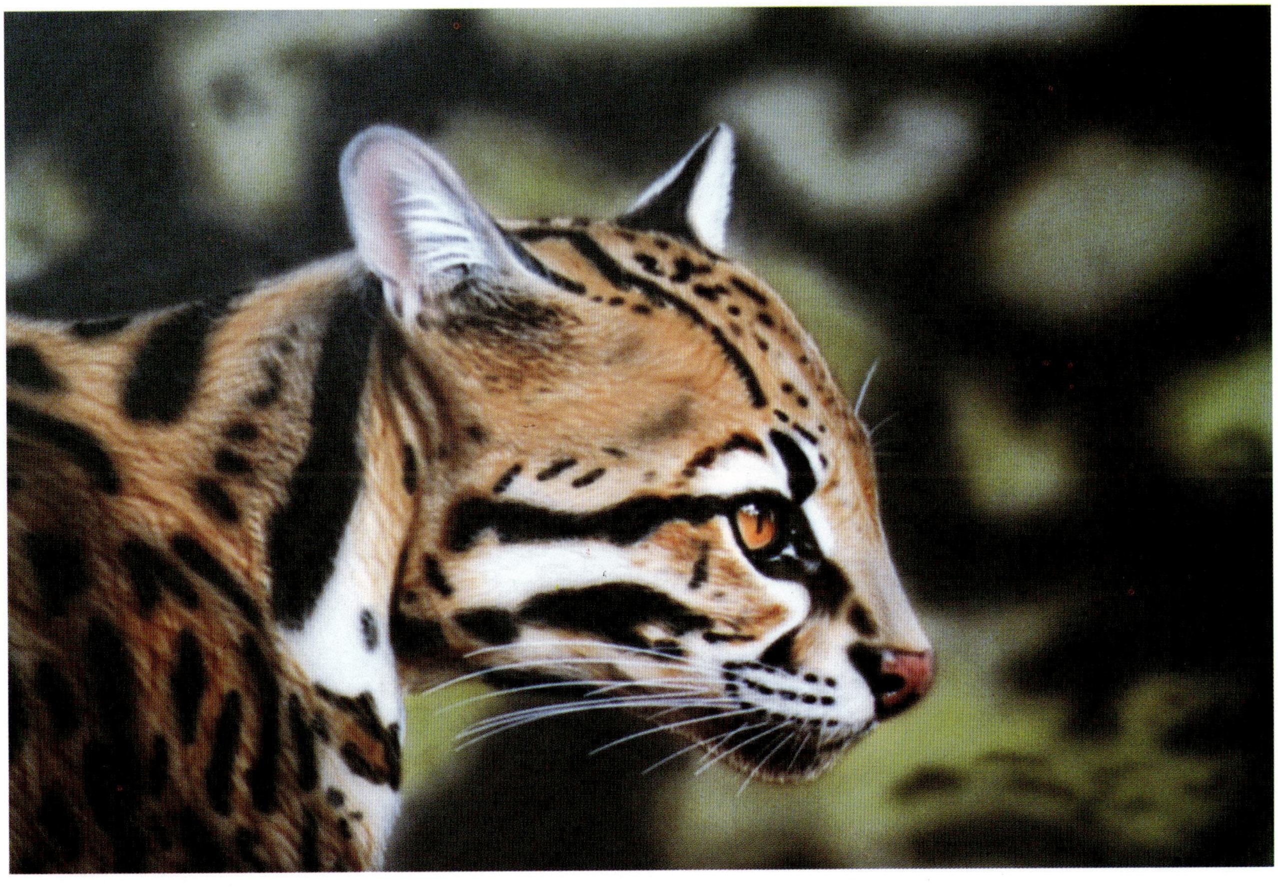

1

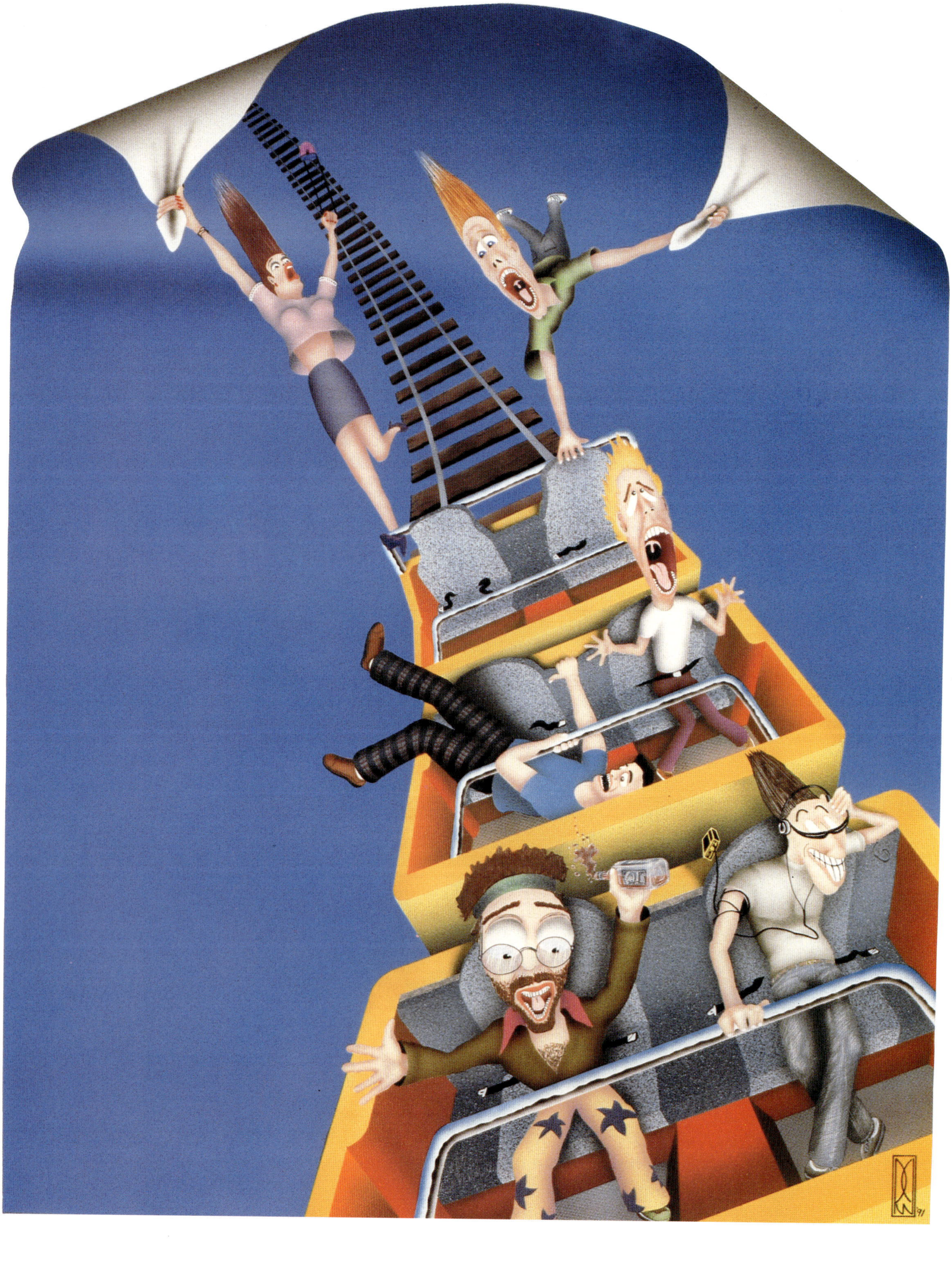

1 - 3
Illustrator **PATRICK WANEBO**
Usage **SELF PROMOTION**
Media **ACRYLIC**

2

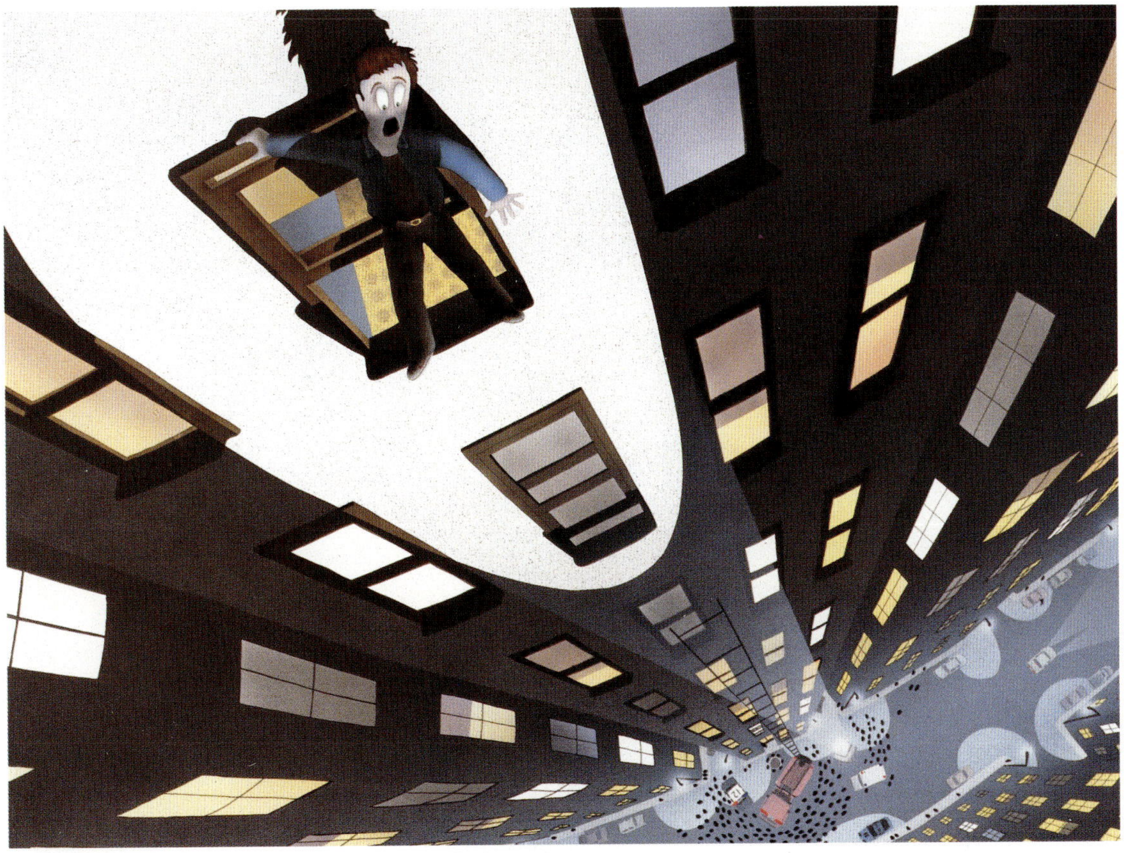

3

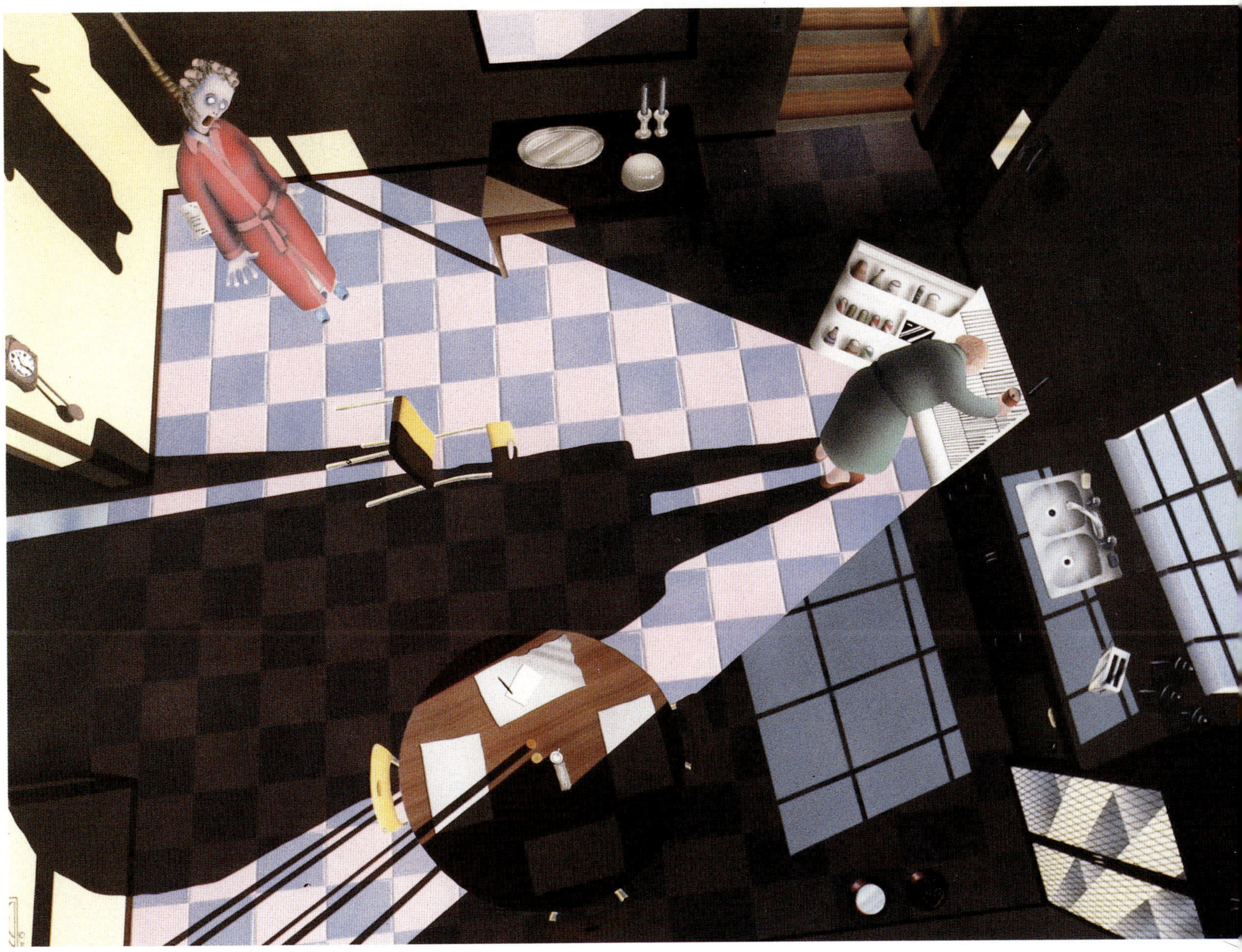

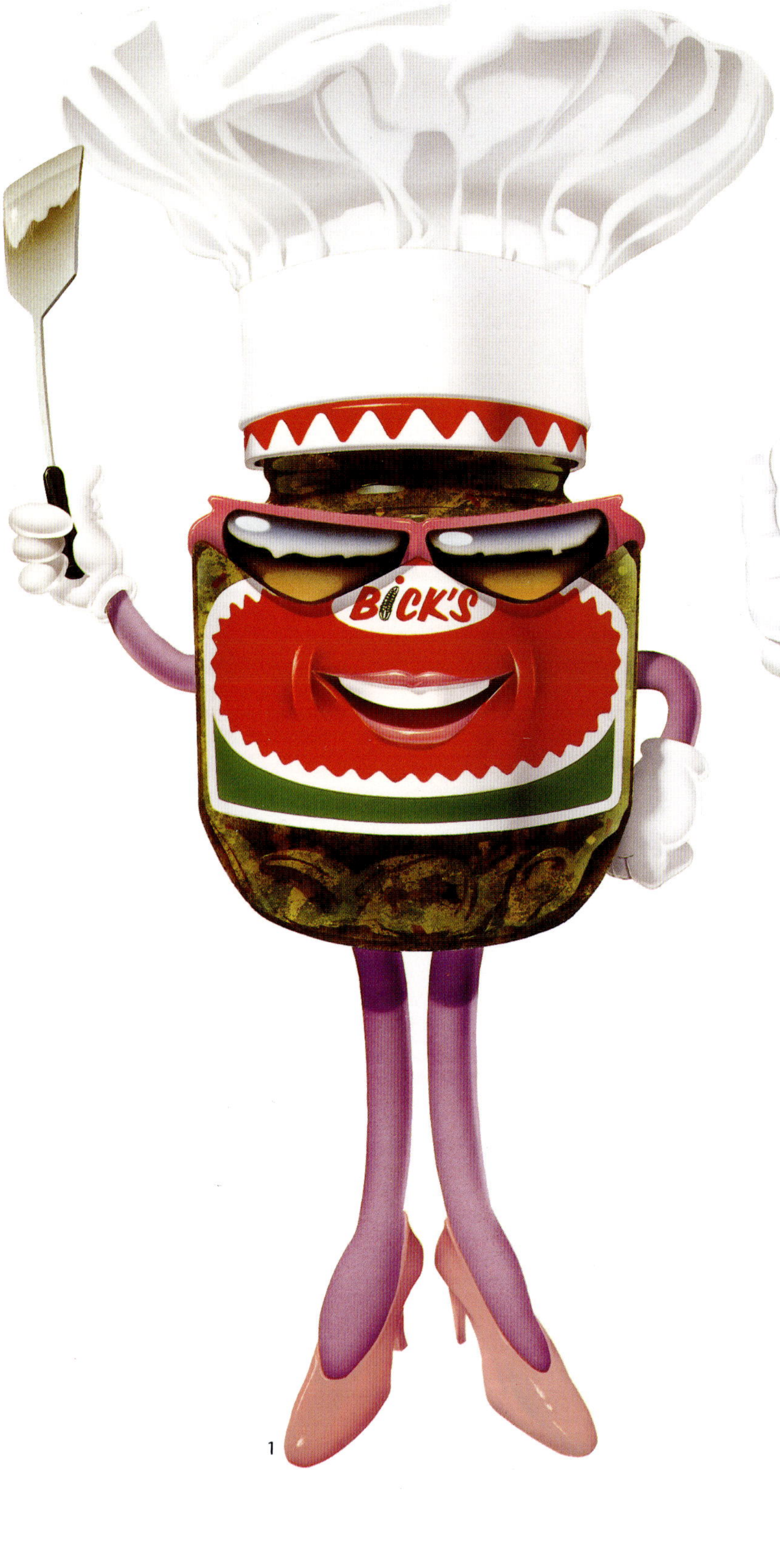

1

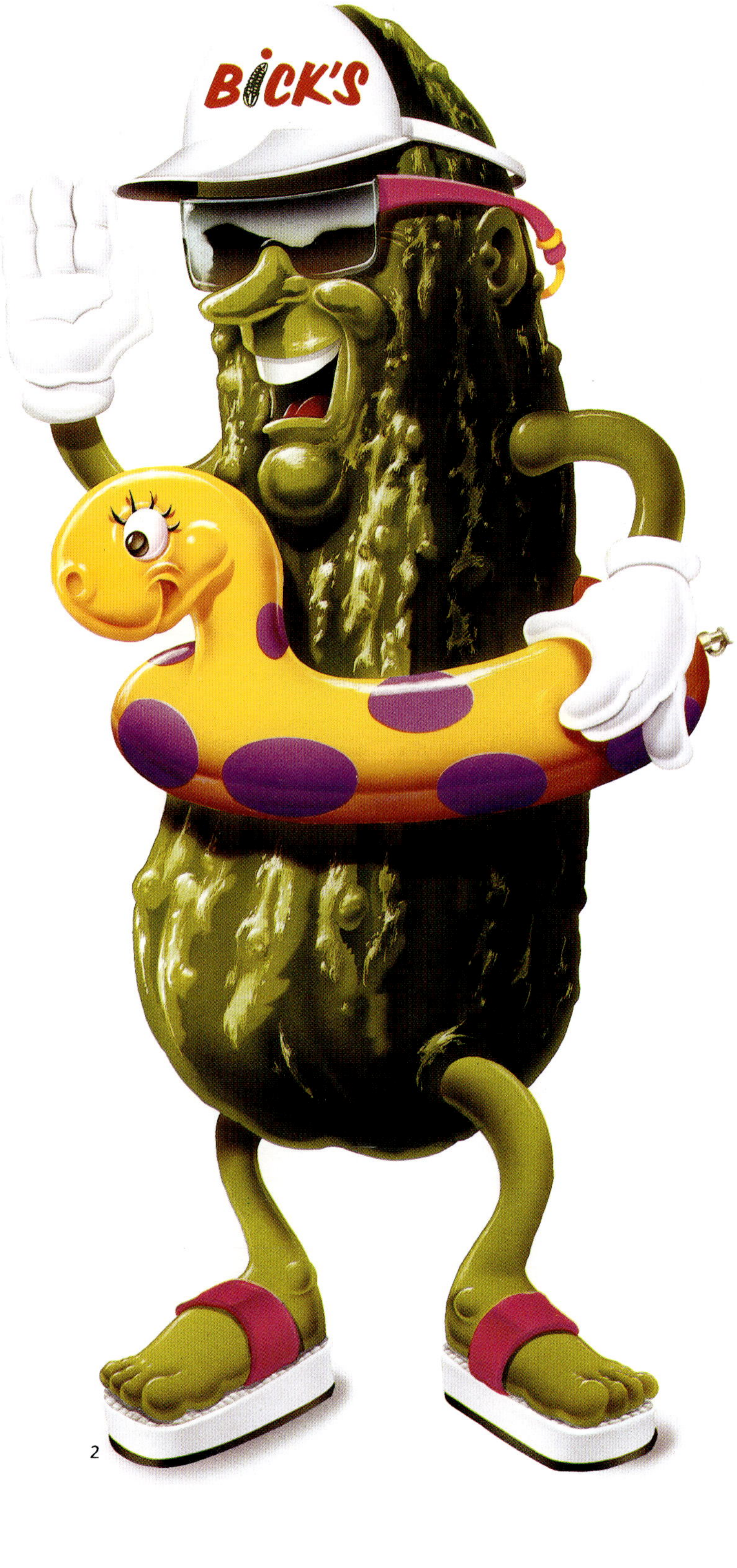

2

1
Illustrator MICK COULAS
Title DOLY BICKLES
Client BICK'S PICKLE COMPANY
Usage DIE-CUT DISPLAY
Media ACRYLIC

2
Illustrator MICK COULAS
Title DON BICKLES
Client BICK'S PICKLES
Usage DIE-CUT DISPLAY
Media ACRYLIC

3
Illustrator MICK COULAS
Title TIME OF YOUR LIFE
Client TIME OF YOUR LIFE GREETING CARDS
Usage LOGO
Media ACRYLIC

4
Illustrator MICK COULAS
Title SOME THINGS IN LIFE ARE IRRITATING
Usage DIRECT-MAIL PIECE
Media ACRYLIC

5
Illustrator MICK COULAS
Title THE HAMBURGLAR
Client MCDONALD'S CANADA
Usage BILLBOARD
Media ACRYLIC

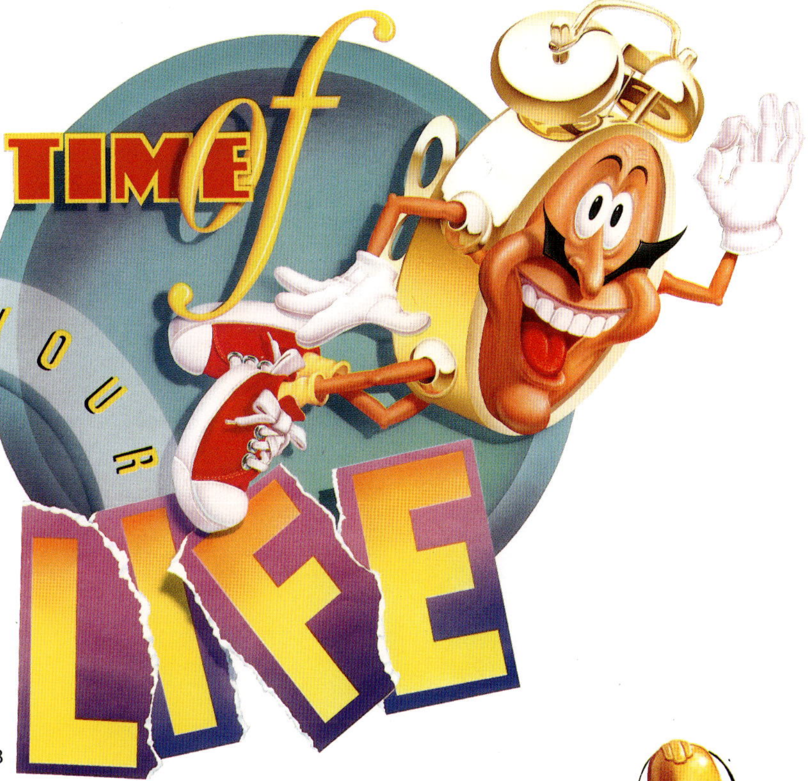

3

4
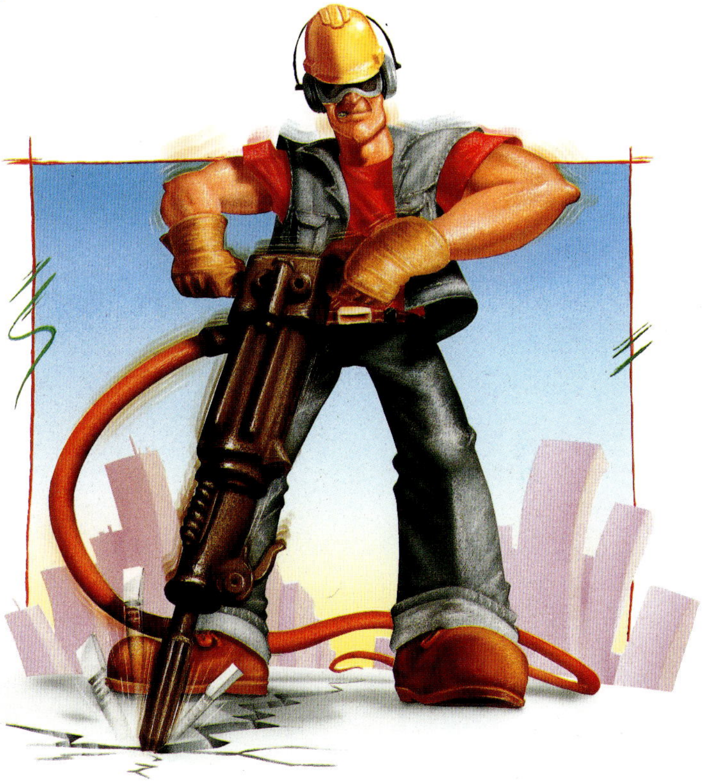

5
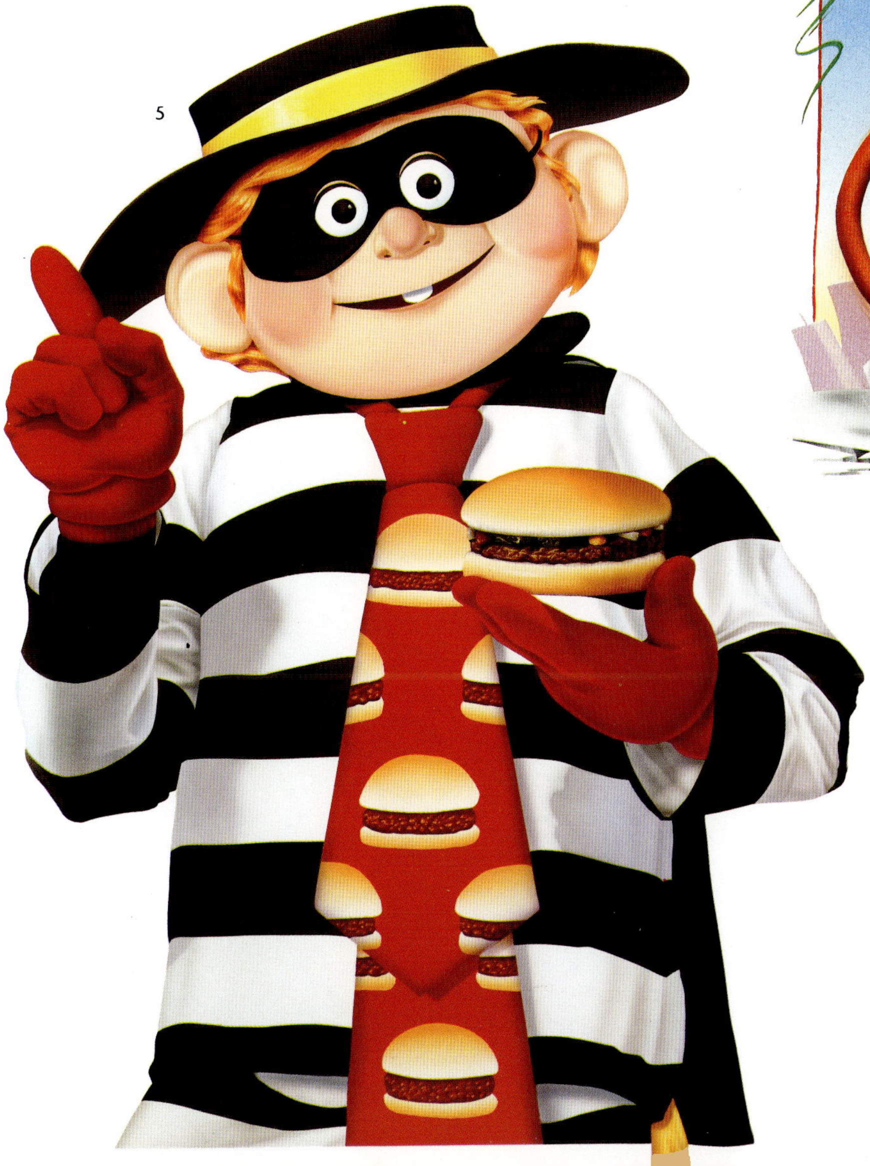

1
Illustrator **JERRY LOFARO**
Title **THERE ARE TIMES WHEN FASTER IS DECIDEDLY BETTER**
Client **MINOLTA**
Media **ACRYLIC**

2
Illustrator **JERRY LOFARO**
Client **ENGLISH MAN'S GUIDE TO SURVIVAL**
Usage **LISTING OF ENGLISH PUBS OUTSIDE OF THE UNITED KINGDOM**
Media **ACRYLIC**

3
Illustrator **JERRY LOFARO**
Title **IDEALLY YOUR EQUIPMENT SHOULD MATCH YOUR NEEDS**
Client **MINOLTA**
Media **ACRYLIC**

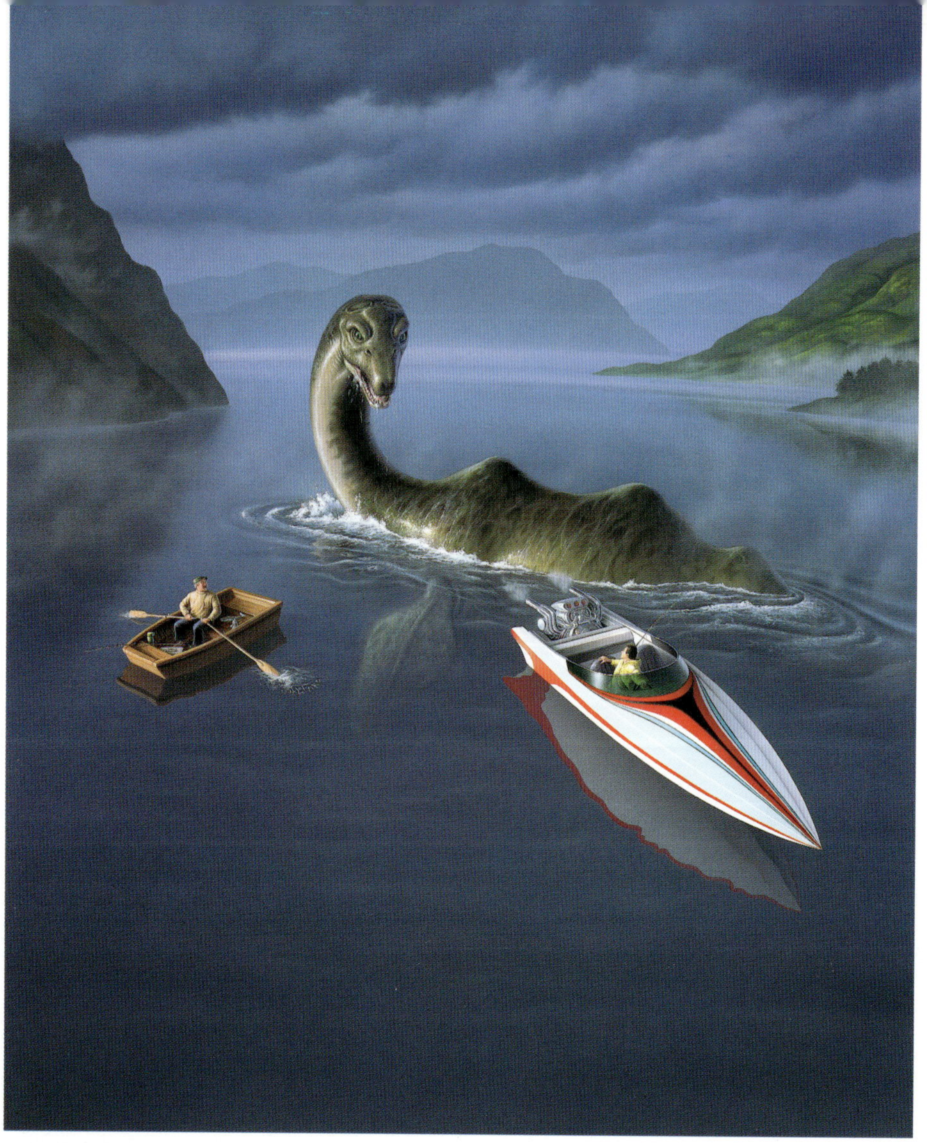

1

2

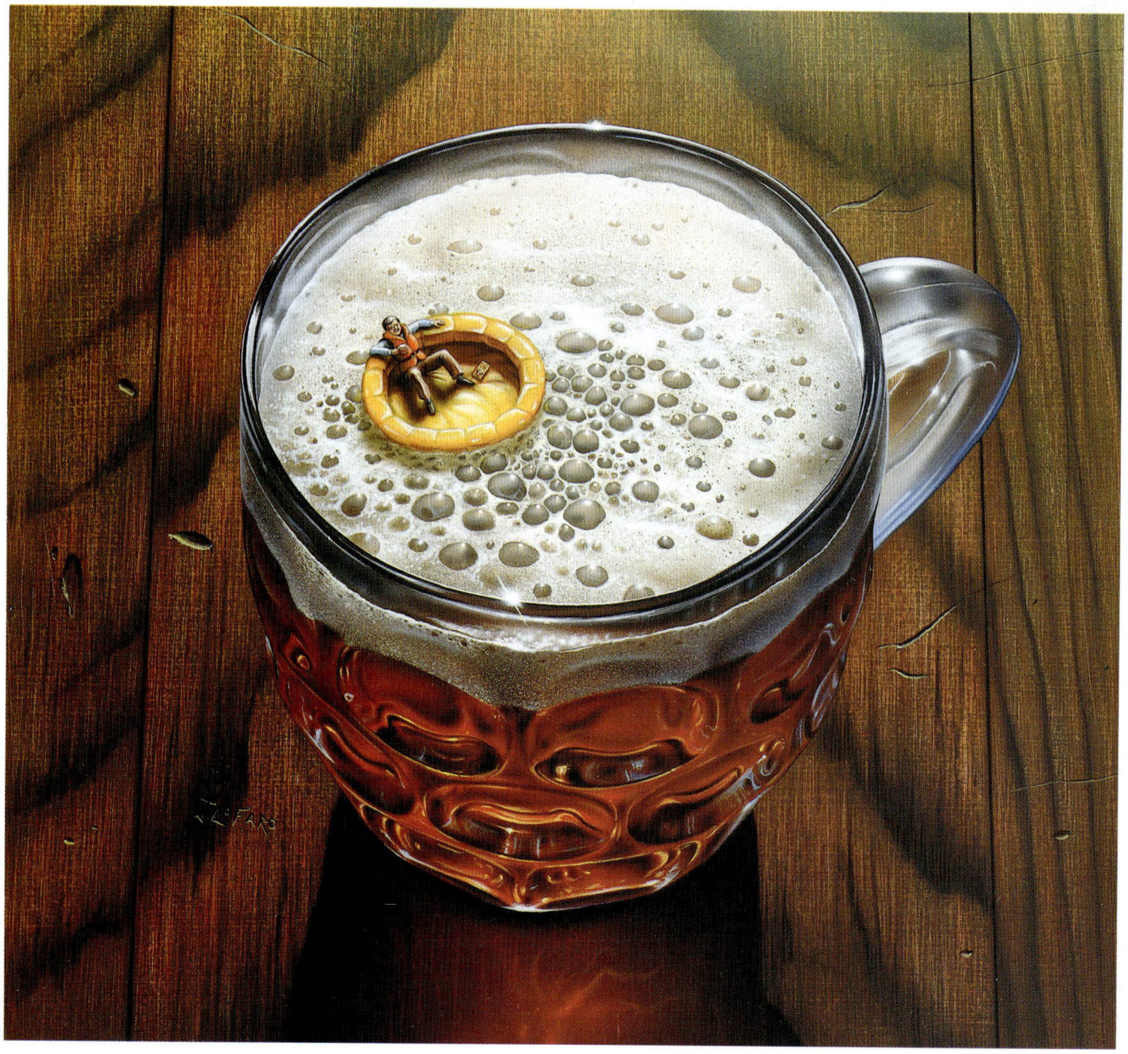

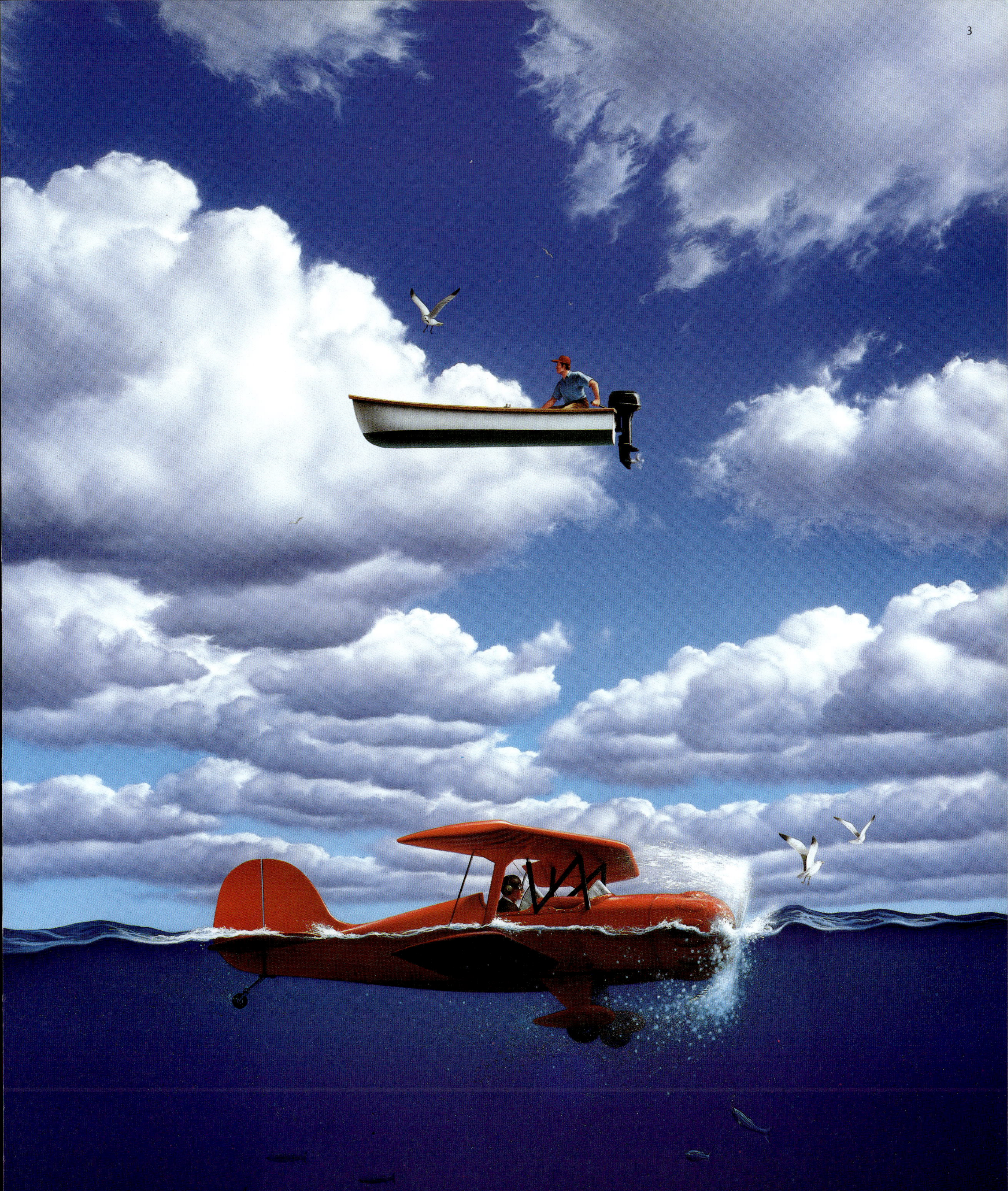

1
Illustrator **CHRIS P. APOSTOLOU**
Title **LIFEBLOOD**
Client **BLIND (BAND)**
Usage **COMMERCIAL ART**
Media Used **BADGER ACRYLICS**

2
Illustrator **CRAIG ATTEBERY**
Title **HRMS ANTENNA SIGNAL PATH**
Client **JET PROPULSION LABORATORY**
Usage **TECHNICAL ILLUSTRATION**
Media Used **GOUACHE**

1

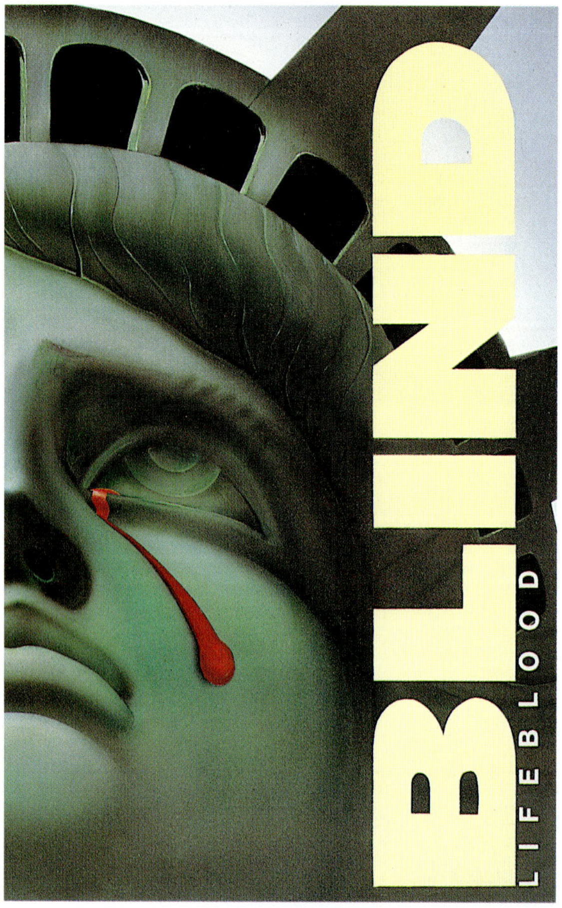

2

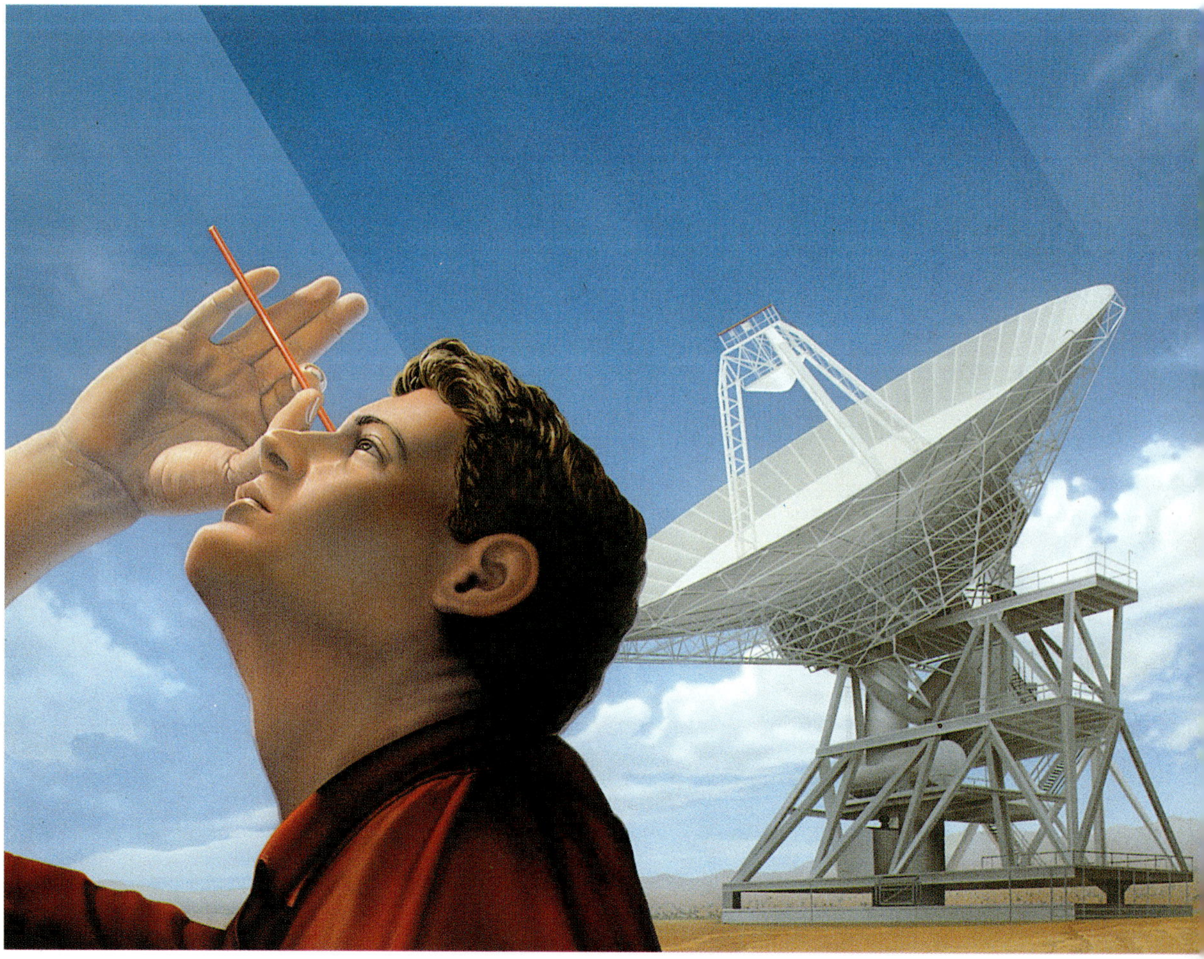

1
Illustrator **PETER BARTCZAK**
Title **BALLERINA**
Client **HI-TECH SOFTWARE**
Media Used **AIRBRUSHED BADGER OPAQUE COLORS**

2
Illustrator **PETER BARTCZAK**
Title **PIG'S SQUEALS & FERRIS WHEELS**
Client **SANTA CRUZ COUNTY FAIR**
Usage **POSTER**
Media Used **GOUACHE**

3
Illustrator **LESLIE BATES**
Title **JOURNEY FROM KRYPTON**
Usage **SELF PROMOTION**
Media Used **ACRYLIC ON GESSOED MASONITE**

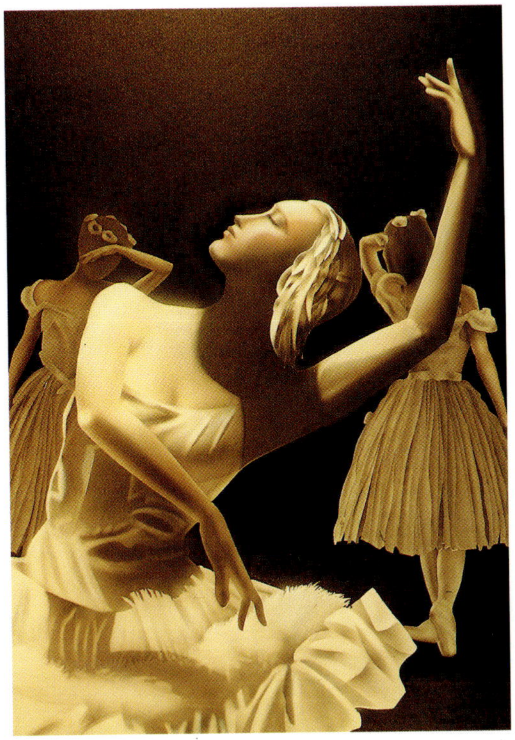

1

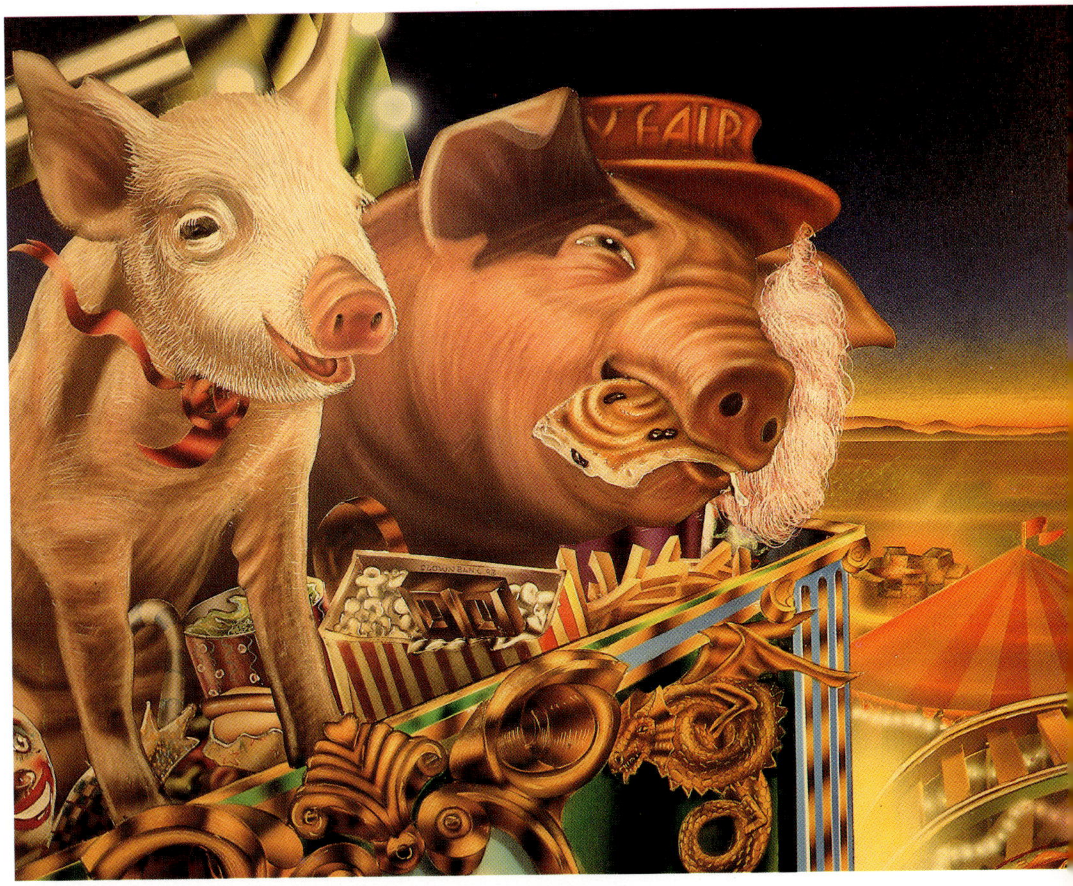

2

3

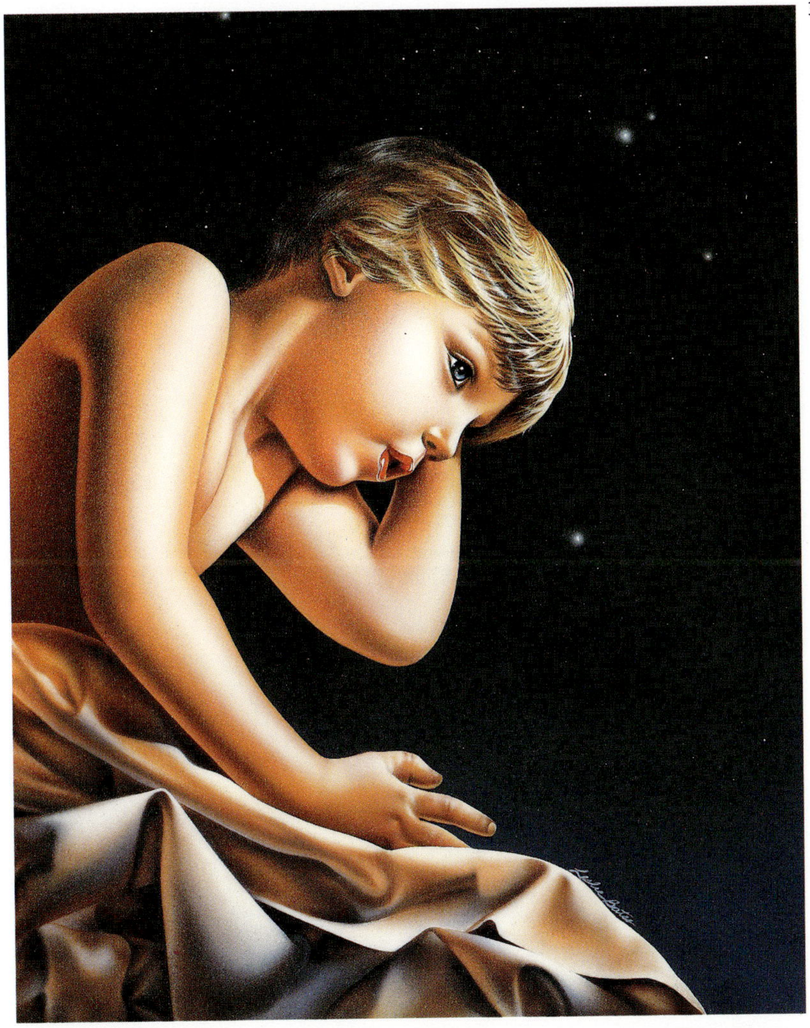

1
Illustrator **SCOTT BECKLEY**
Title **LION HEART**
Usage **FINE ART**
Media Used **ACRYLIC**

2
Illustrator **SCOTT BECKLEY**
Client **TEXAS INSTRUMENTS**
Usage **MAGAZINE ADVERTISEMENT**
Media Used **GOUACHE**

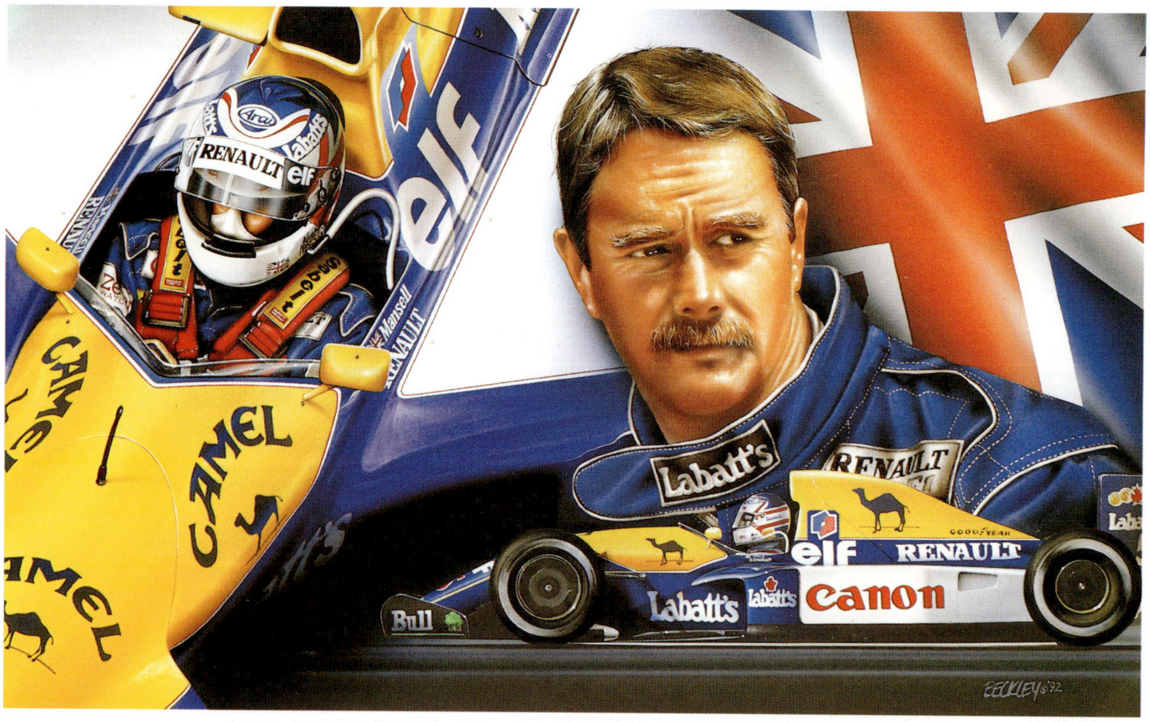

1

2

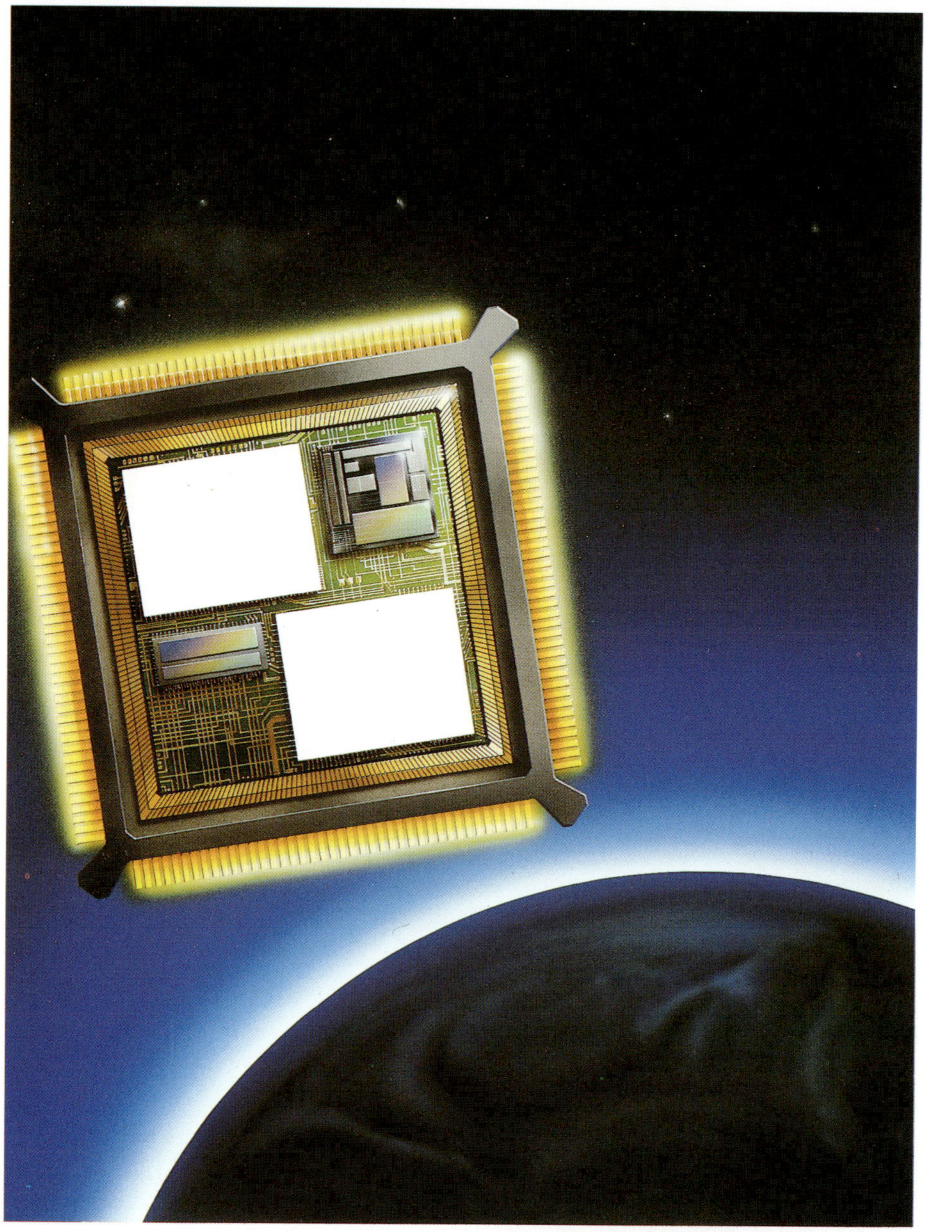

1
Illustrator DORON BEN-AMI
Title LITTLE PEOPLE, BIG PRESSURES
Client SOUTHWEST AIRLINES/SPIRIT MAGAZINE
Media Used ACRYLIC, COLORED PENCIL

2
Illustrator MARK A. BENDER
Client MCDONALDS
Usage CALENDAR FOR MONTH OF FEBRUARY
Media Used GOUACHE

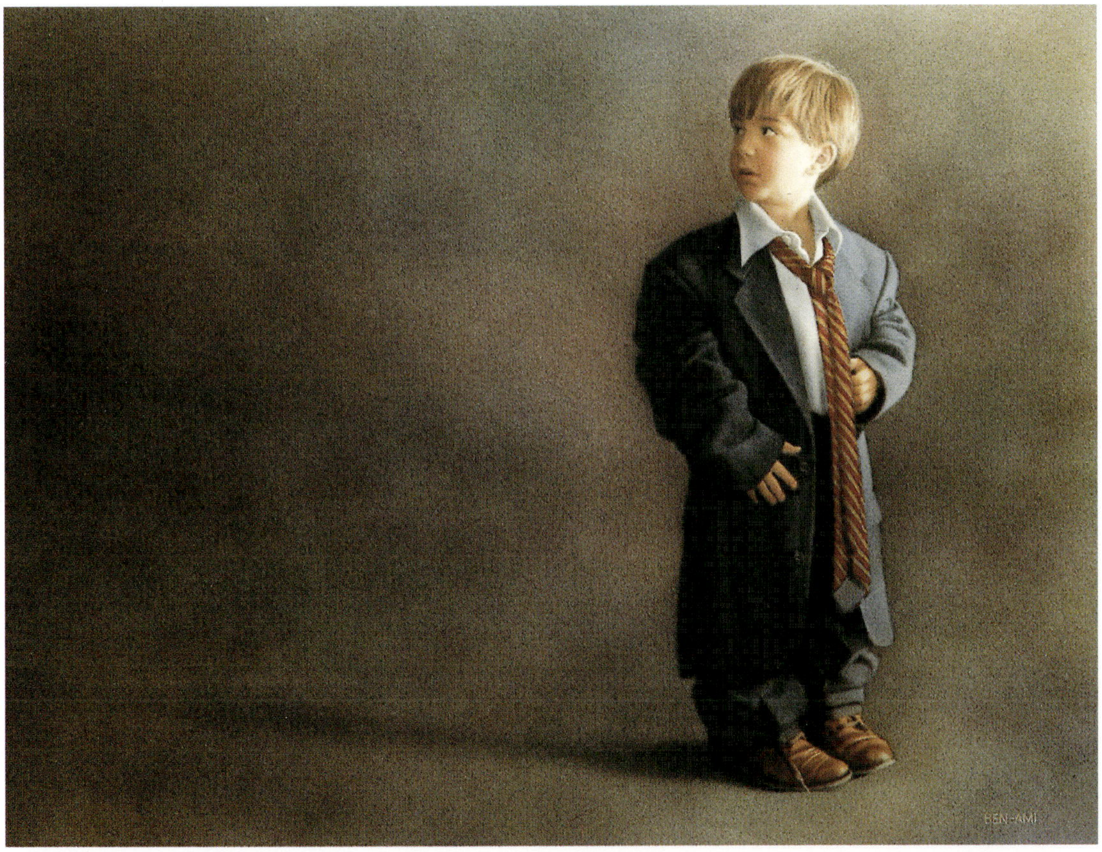

1

2

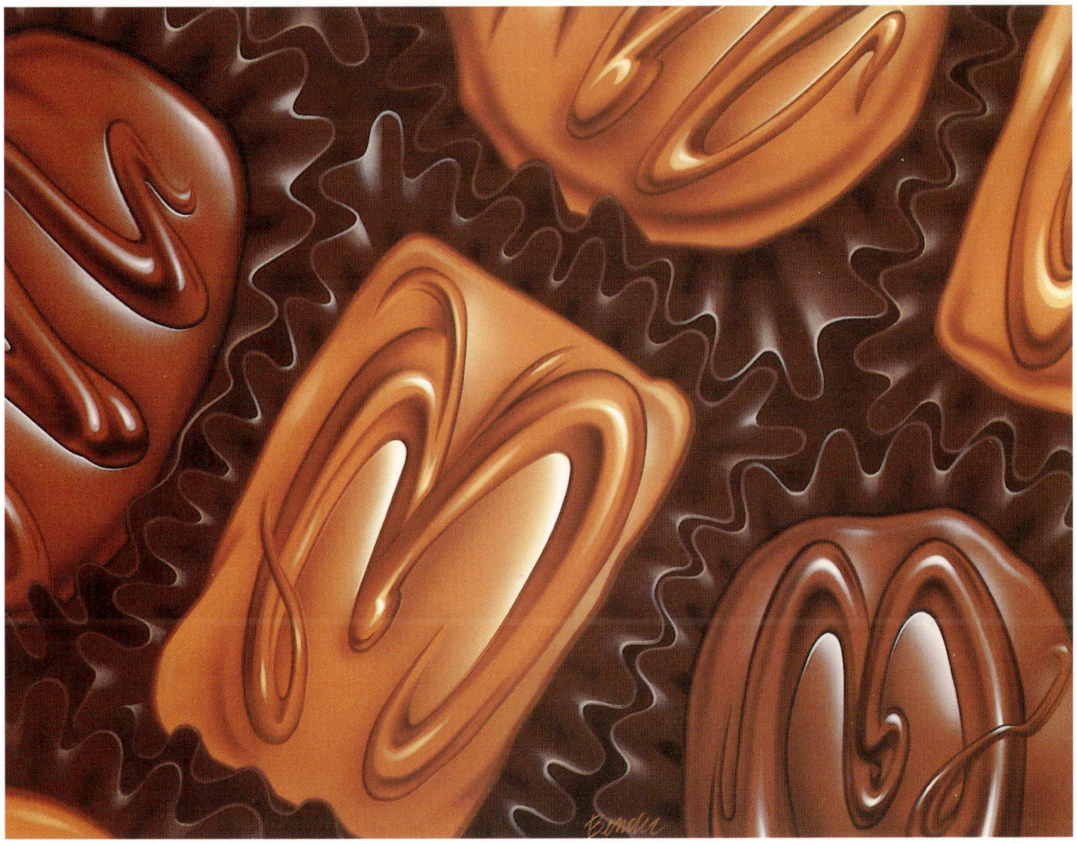

1
Illustrator **ANITA S. BICE**
Title **ON THE DRAWING BOARD**
Art Director **NINA LOWRY**
Usage **EDITORIAL ILLUSTRATION**
Media Used **ACRYLIC**

2
Illustrator **ANITA S. BICE**
Title **WORKING BACK FROM INJURY**
Art Director **NINA LOWRY**
Media Used **ACRYLIC**

3
Illustrator **ANITA S. BICE**
Title **THE QUADRANGLE - HARVARD MEDICAL SCHOOL**
Client **NEW HORIZONS LIMITED**
Usage **FINE ART**
Media Used **MIXED**

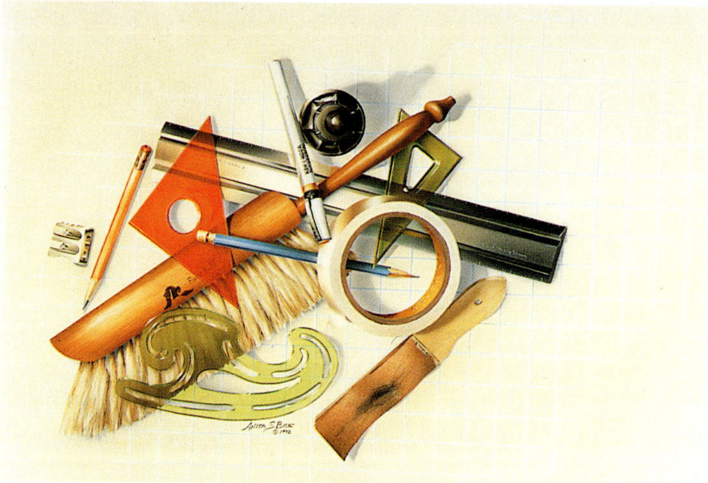

1

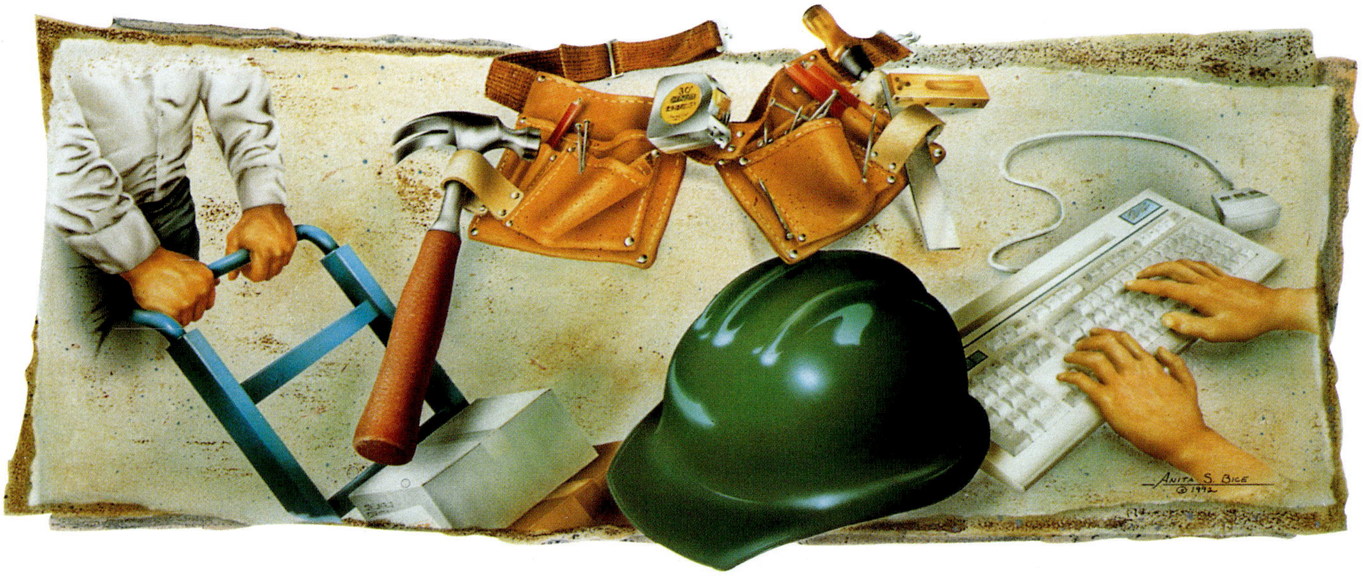

2

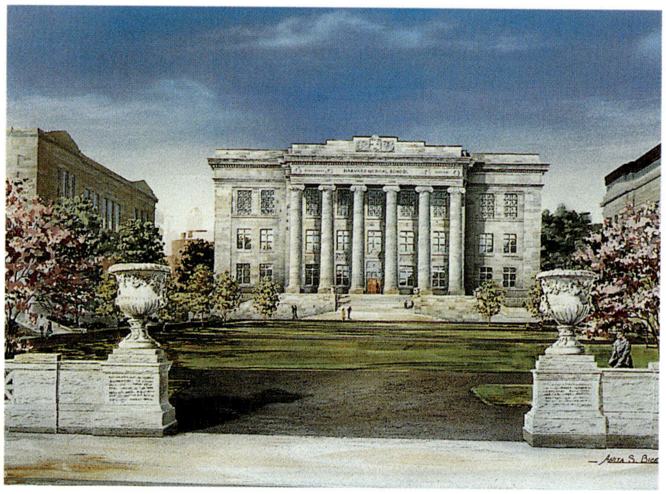

3

1
Illustrator **ANITA S. BICE**
Title **MARSH CHAPEL—BOSTON UNIVERSITY**
Client **NEW HORIZONS LIMITED**
Usage **FINE ART**
Media Used **MIXED**

2
Illustrator **ANITA S. BICE**
Title **ADVANCEMENT WITH NEW LABOR-DELIVERY-RECOVERY SUITES ART**
Art Director **NINA LOWRY**
Usage **EDITORIAL ILLUSTRATION**
Media Used **ACRYLIC**

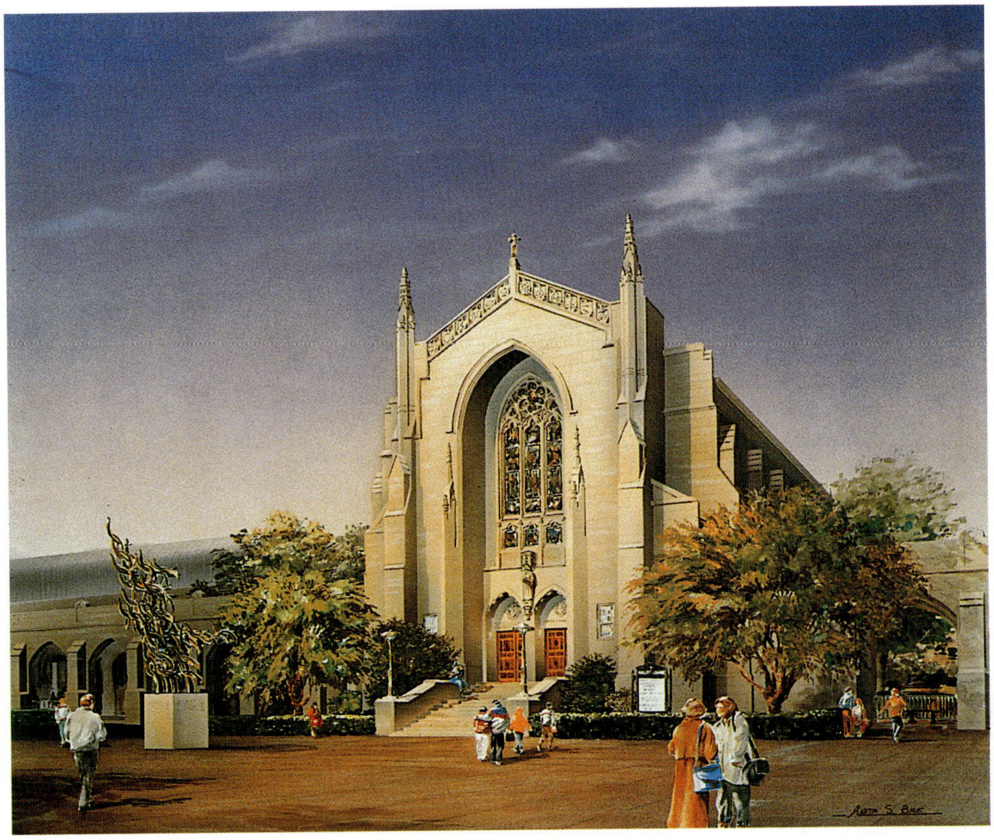

1

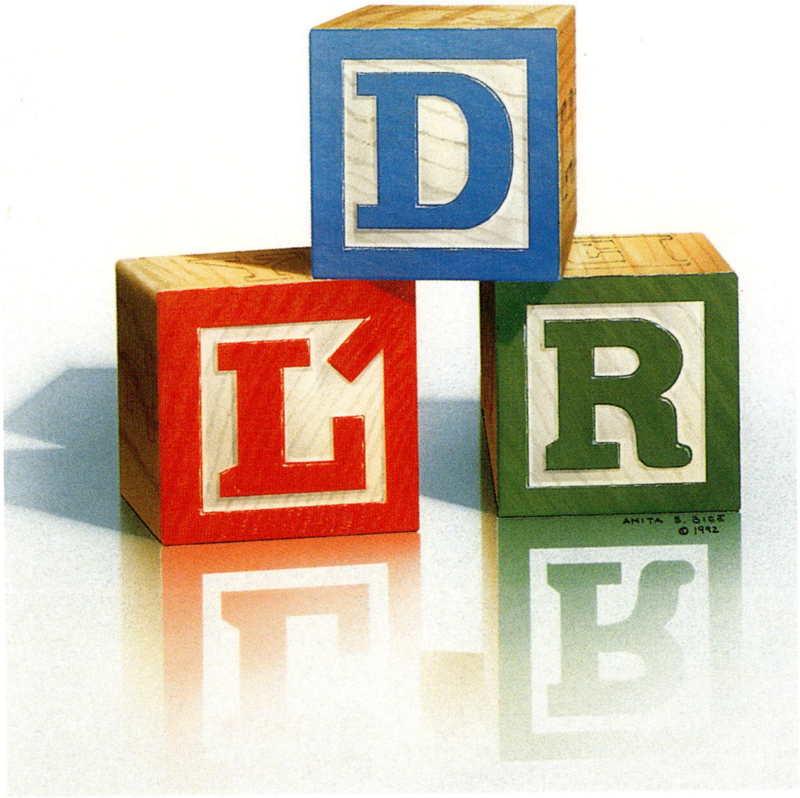

2

1
Illustrator **KURT BITTLE**
Title **OUR VISION**
Client **U.S.D.E.H.A.**
Art Director **NORMAN POSPISIL**
Usage **EDITORIAL ILLUSTRATION**
Media Used **BADGER AIR OPAQUES, BEROL PRISMACOLOR**

2
Illustrator **BRIAN BLAIR**
Title **MA KELLEY**
Client **MA KELLEY (ROCK BAND)**
Usage **COMMERCIAL ART**
Media Used **ACRYLIC**

3
Illustrator **BRIAN BLAIR**
Title **DRUG MONSTER**
Client **"DON'T DO DRUGS" CAMPAIGN**
Usage **POSTER**
Media Used **ACRYLIC**

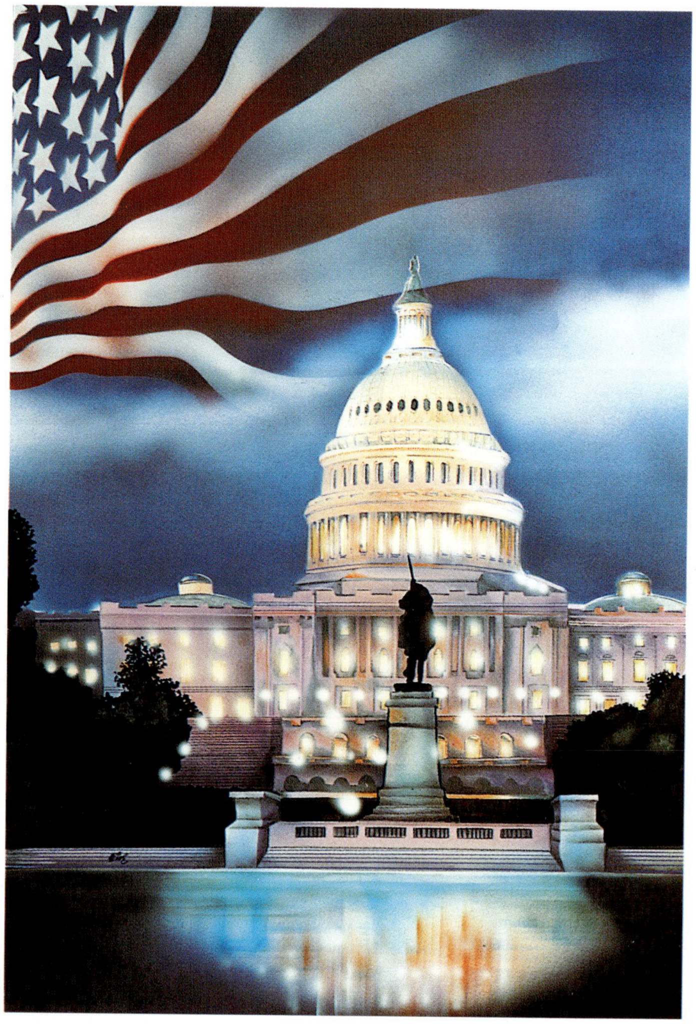

1

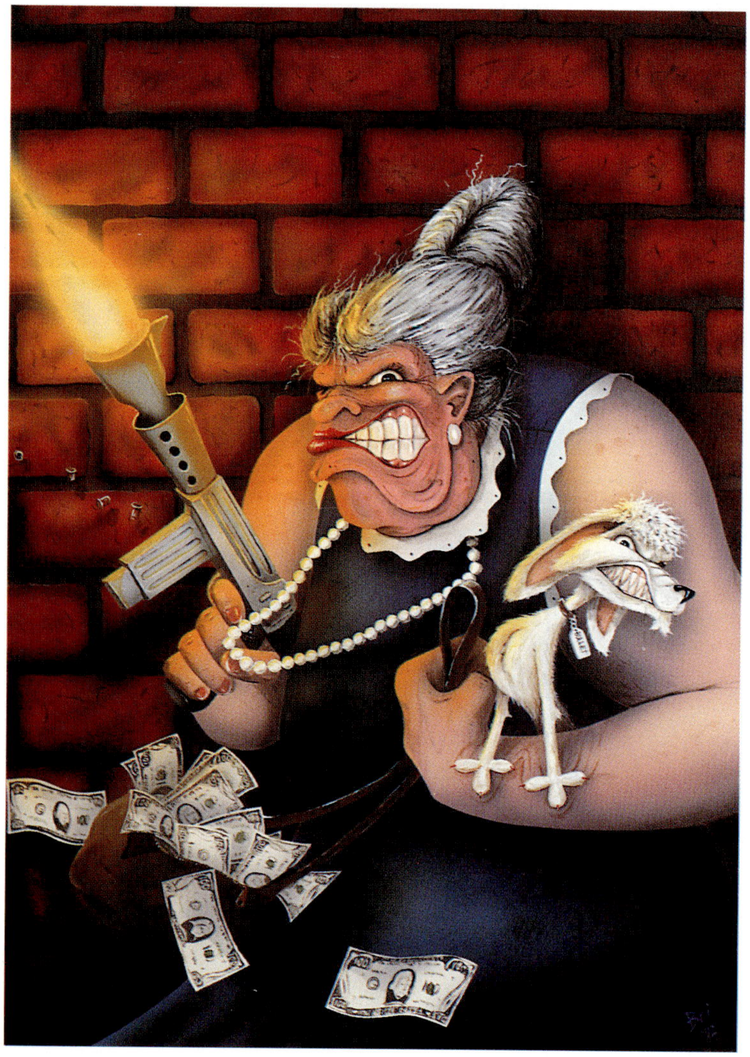

2

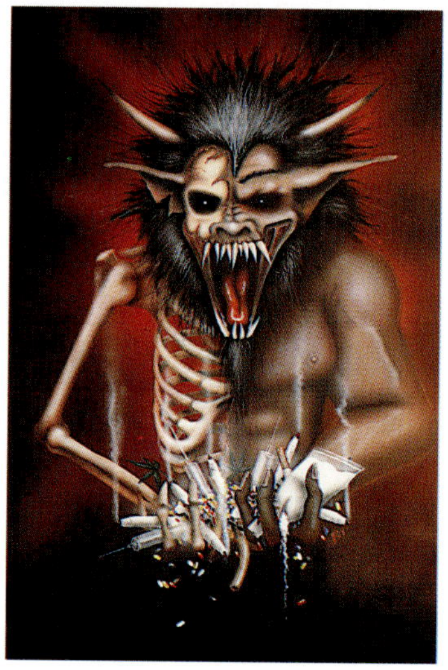

3

1
Illustrator **BRIAN BLAIR**
Title **OPEN SEASON**
Usage **CHILDREN'S BOOK**
Media Used **ACRYLIC**

2
Illustrator **BRIAN BLAIR**
Title **DINO BAIT**
Usage **CHILDREN'S BOOK**
Media Used **ACRYLIC**

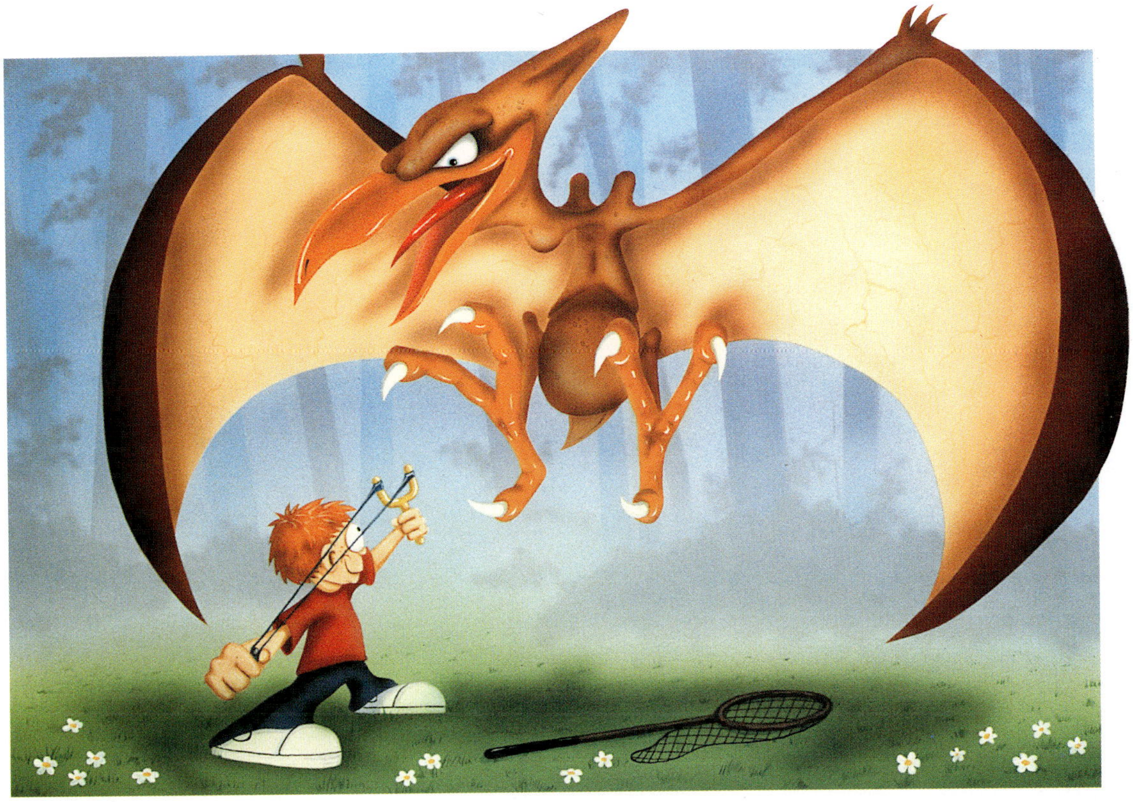

1

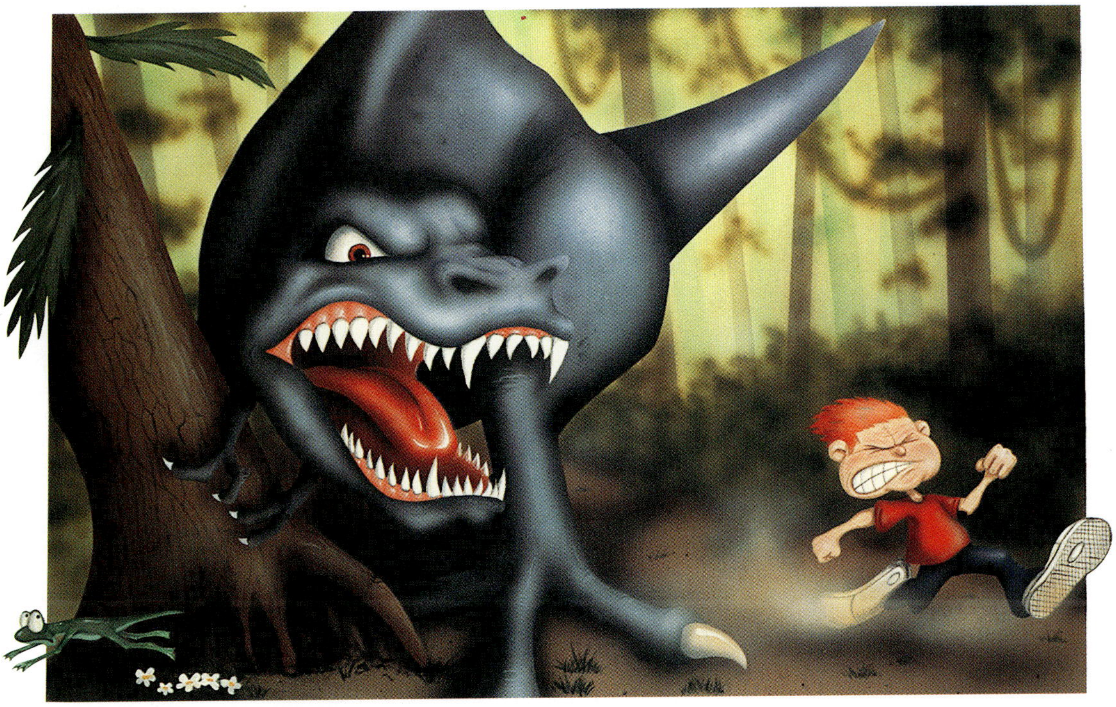

2

1
Illustrator MARTY BRAUN
Title ON THE EDGE OF TECHNOLOGY
Client COMMUNICATIONS WEEK INTERNATIONAL
Art Director ARCH CAREY
Usage MAGAZINE COVER
Media Used ACRYLIC

2
Illustrator MARTY BRAUN
Title BIKING IN VERMONT
Client AMERICAN AIRLINES
Art Director MARILYN CALLEY
Usage IN-FLIGHT MAGAZINE COLUMN
Media Used ACRYLIC

3
Illustrator MARTY BRAUN
Title ONLY TIL DEATH
Client AMERICAN AIRLINES
Art Director ALISANN MARSHALLS
Usage IN-FLIGHT MAGAZINE FICTION
Media Used ACRYLIC

4
Illustrator MARTY BRAUN
Title VALENTINE'S DATE
Client THE WASHINGTON POST
Art Director JOELLEN MURPHY
Usage WEEKEND SECTION COVER
Media Used ACRYLIC

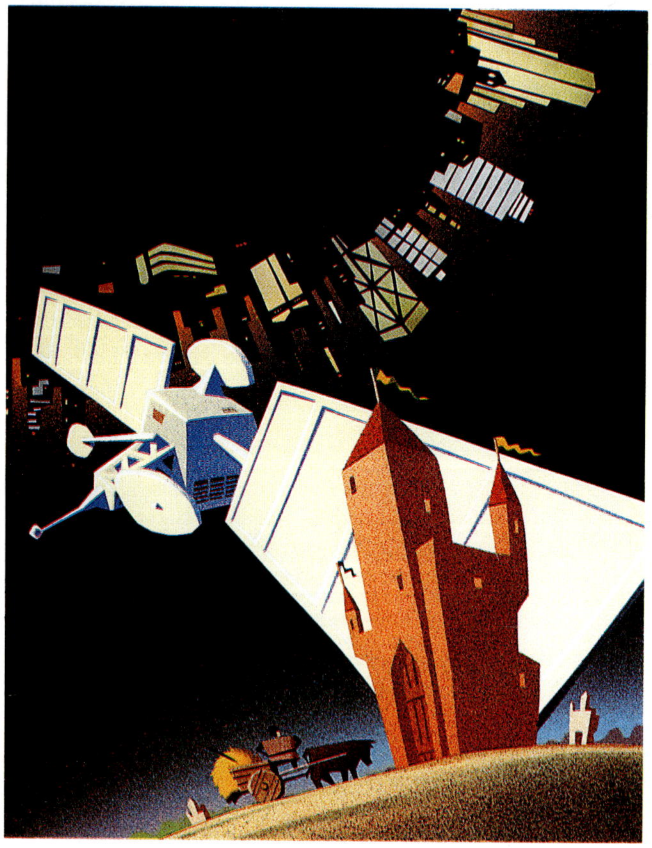
1

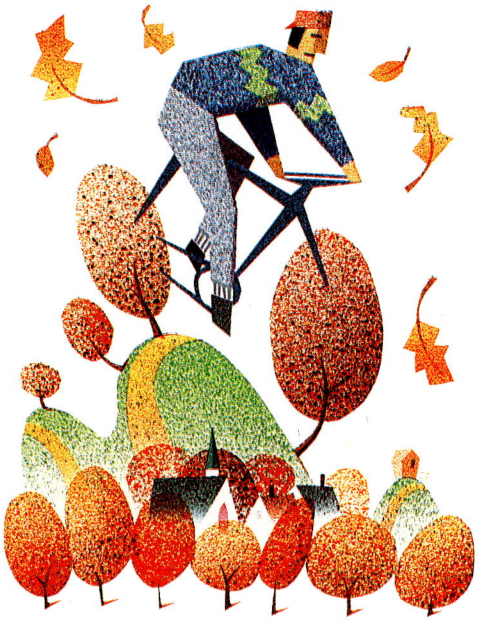
2

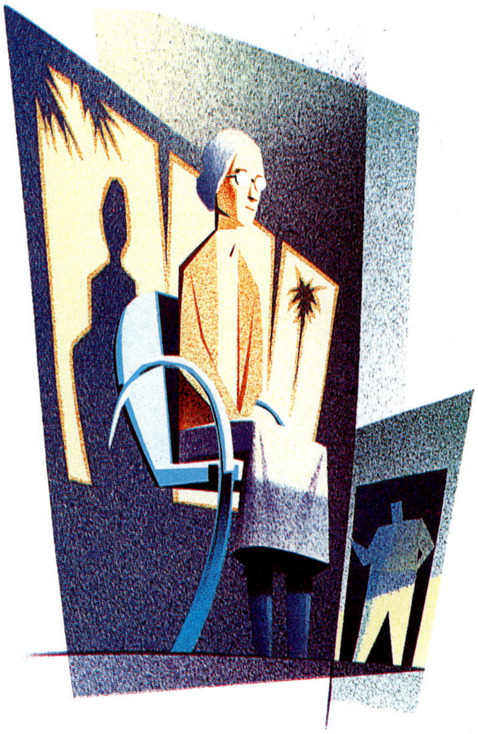
3

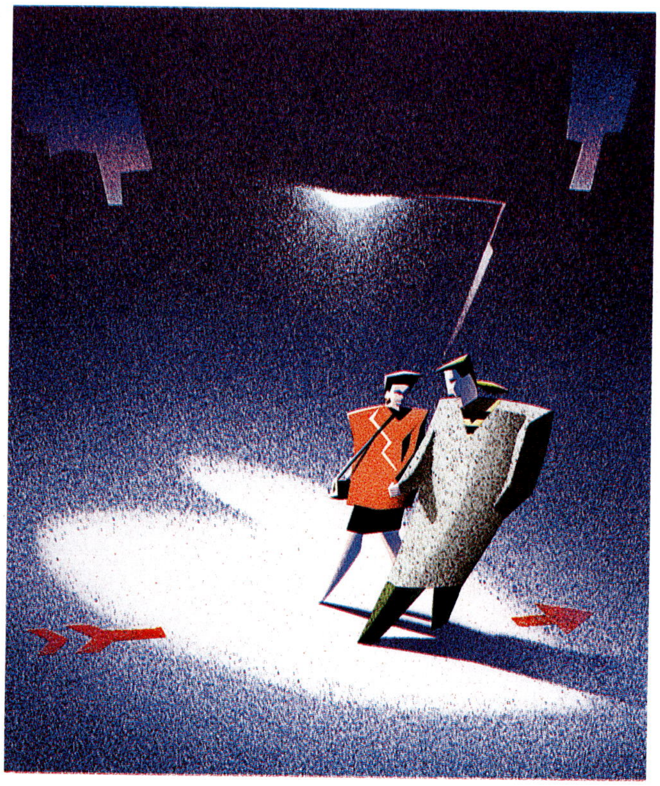
4

1
Illustrator **MARTY BRAUN**
Title **BUDGET CUTS AT DUPONT**
Client **DELAWARE TODAY**
Art Director **INGRID HANSEN LYNCH**
Usage **MAGAZINE COVER**
Media Used **ACRYLIC**

2
Illustrator **MARTY BRAUN**
Title **THE BLUE BIKES OF AMSTERDAM**
Client **EUROPEAN TRAVEL AND LIFE**
Art Director **ANDREA KARMAN**
Usage **EDITORIAL**
Media Used **ACRYLIC**

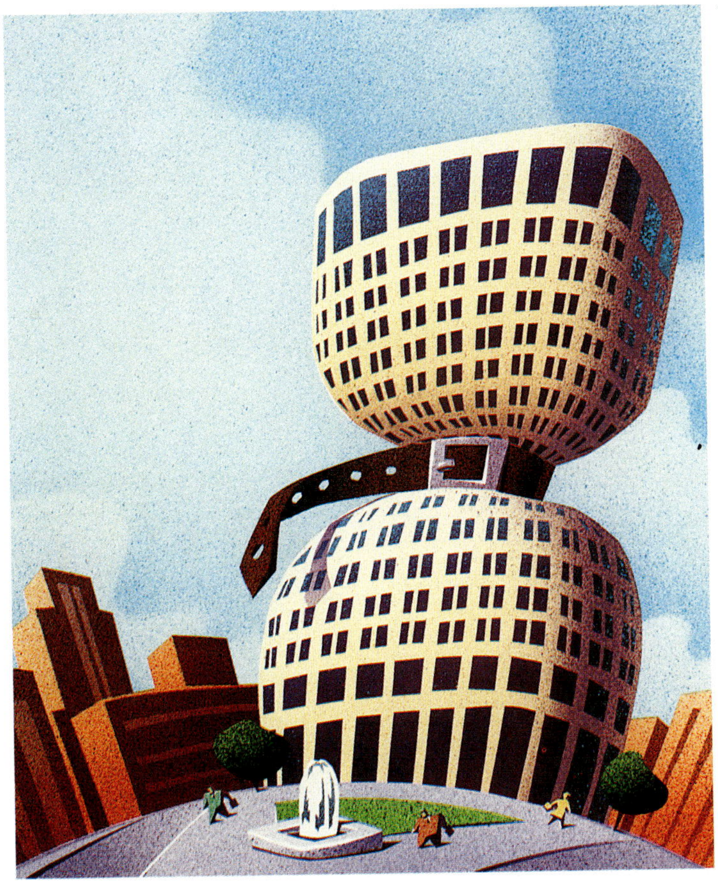

1

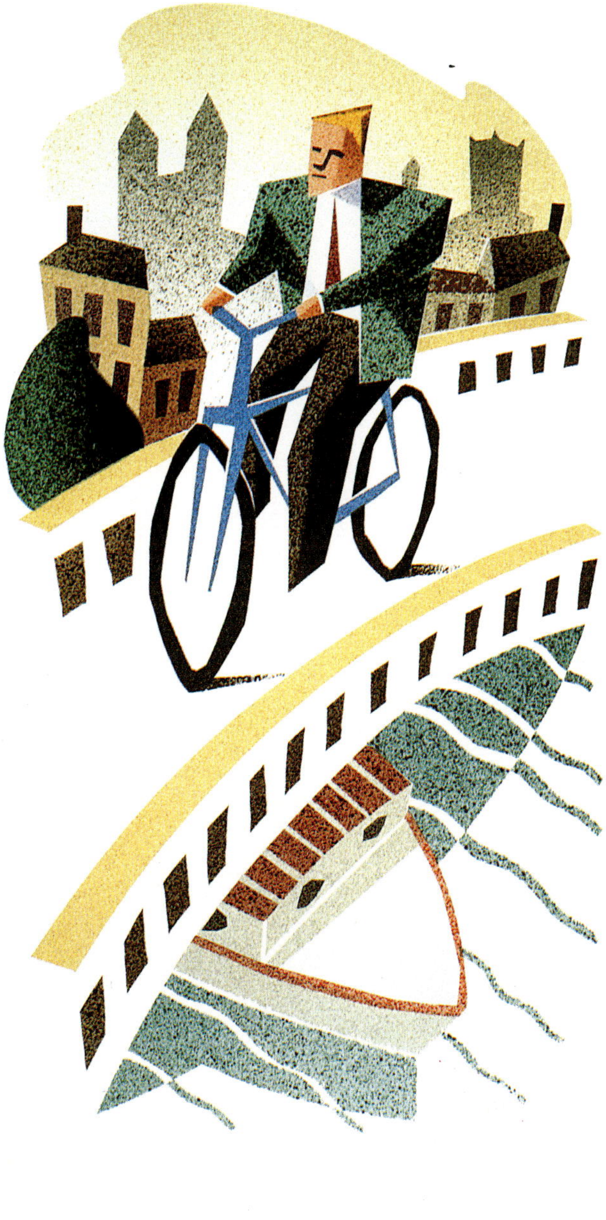

2

1
Illustrator HANK BUFFINGTON
Usage STUDENT ART
Media Used ROTRING ARTIST COLOR

2
Illustrator LONNIE BUSCH
Title WHITE MOUNTAIN COOLER
Media Used ACRYLIC

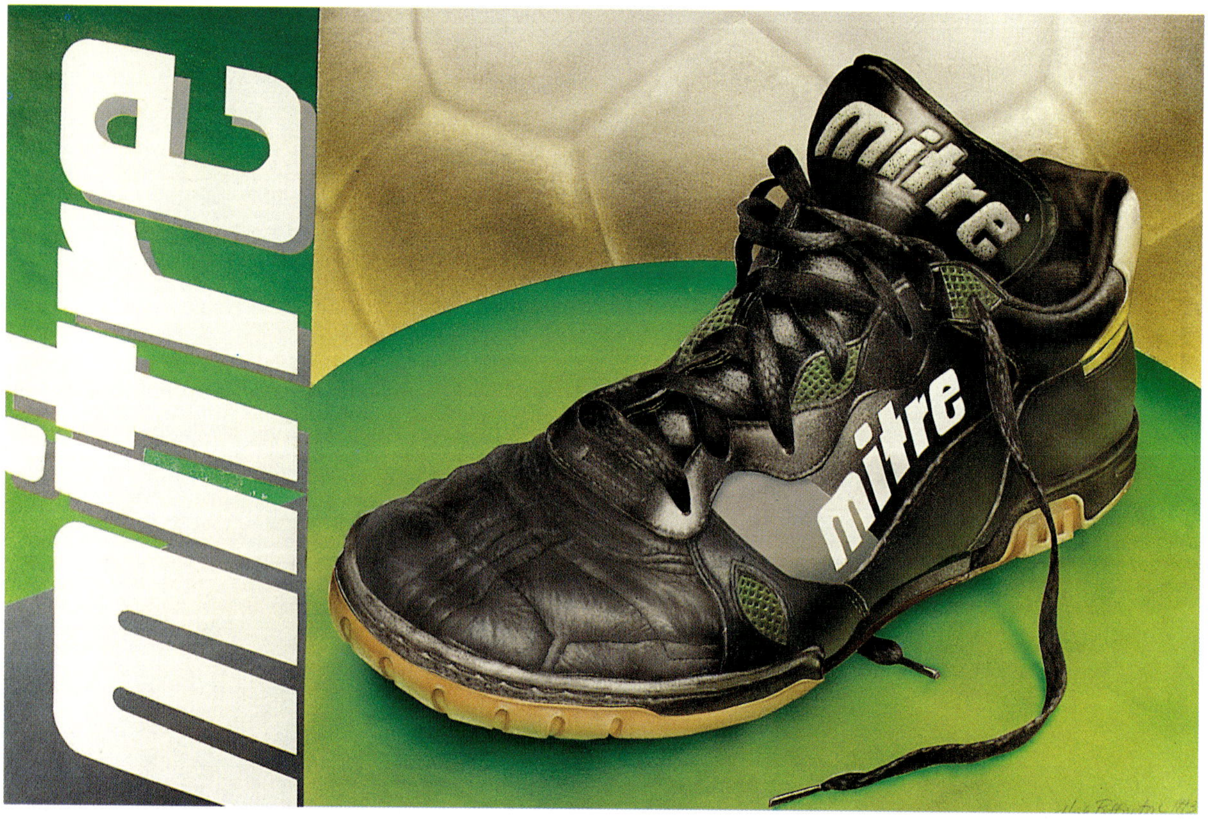

1

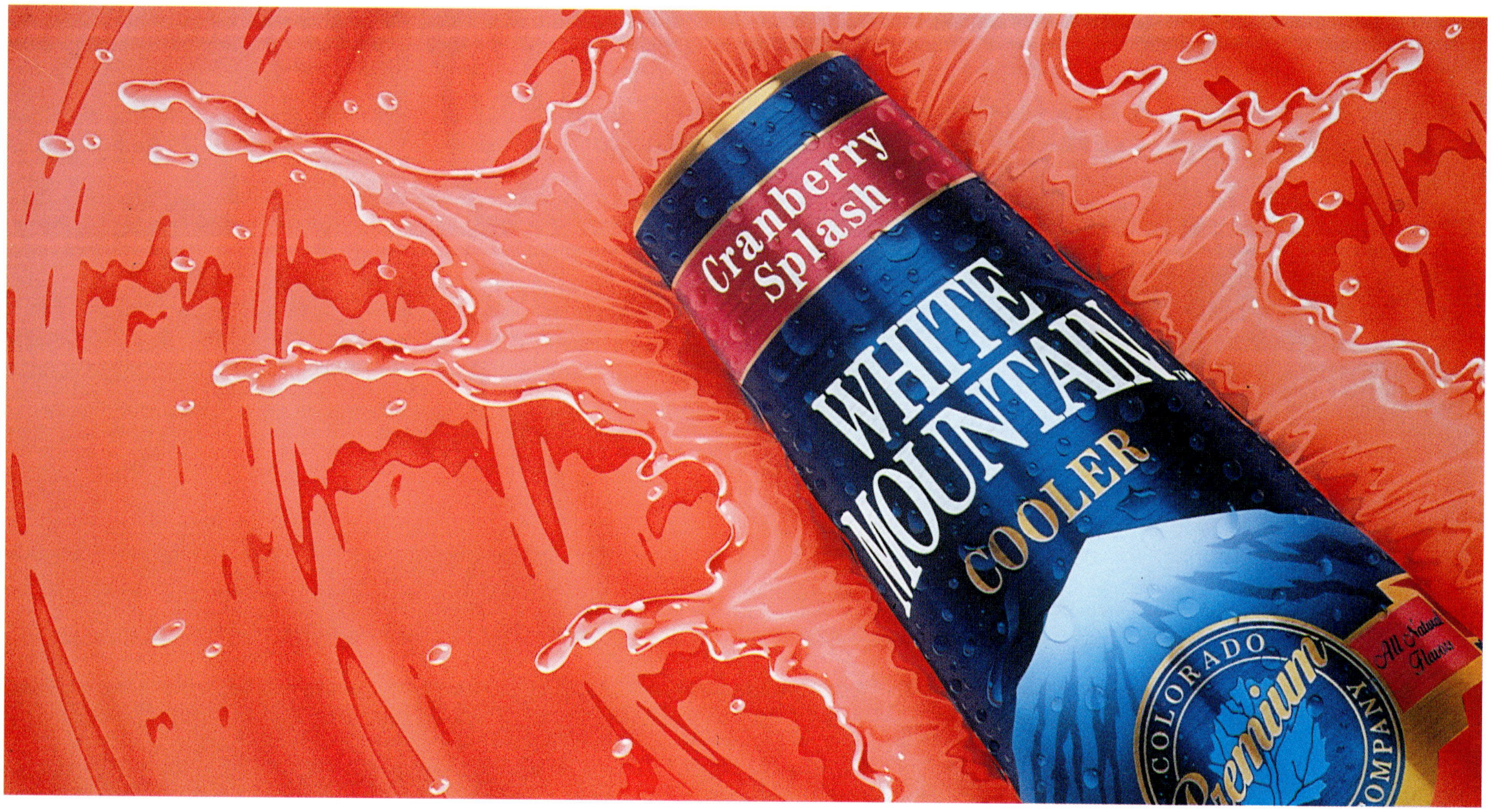

2

1
Illustrator **LONNIE BUSCH**
Title **MASTERCARD DISHES**
Media Used **ACRYLIC**

2
Illustrator **LONNIE BUSCH**
Title **BUD SURFERS**
Media Used **ACRYLIC**

3
Illustrator **LONNIE BUSCH**
Title **7.UP FOUNTAIN**
Media Used **ACRYLIC**

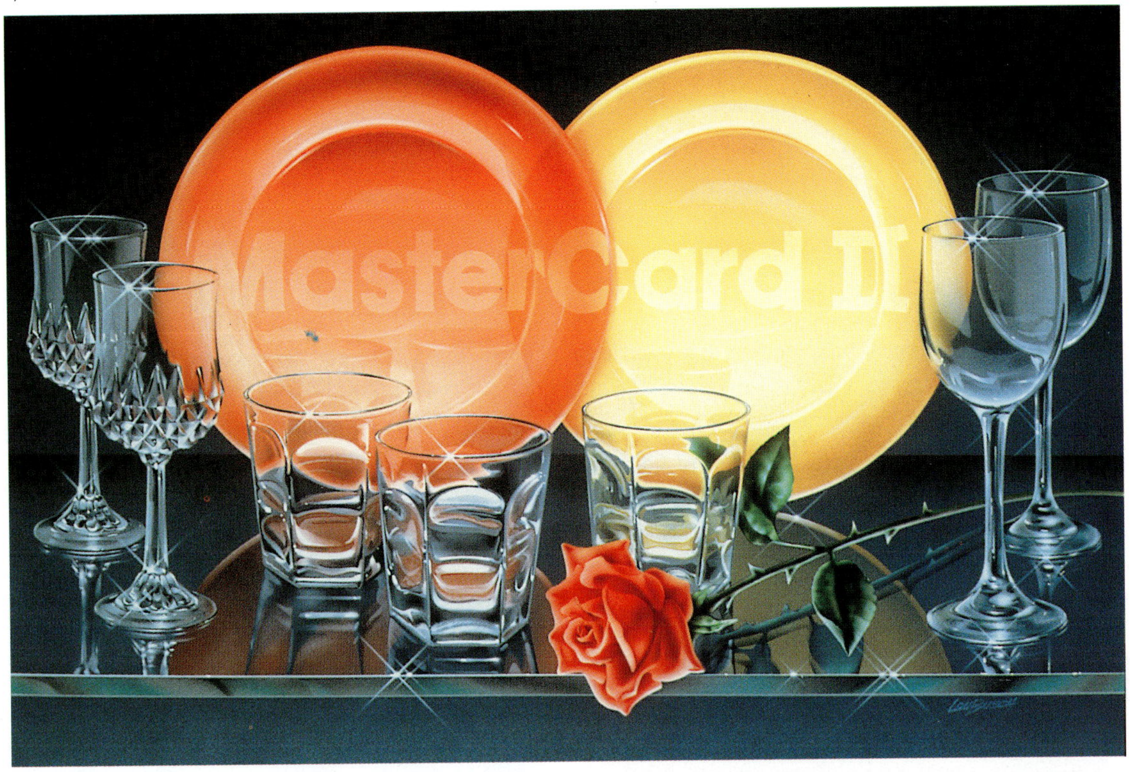

1

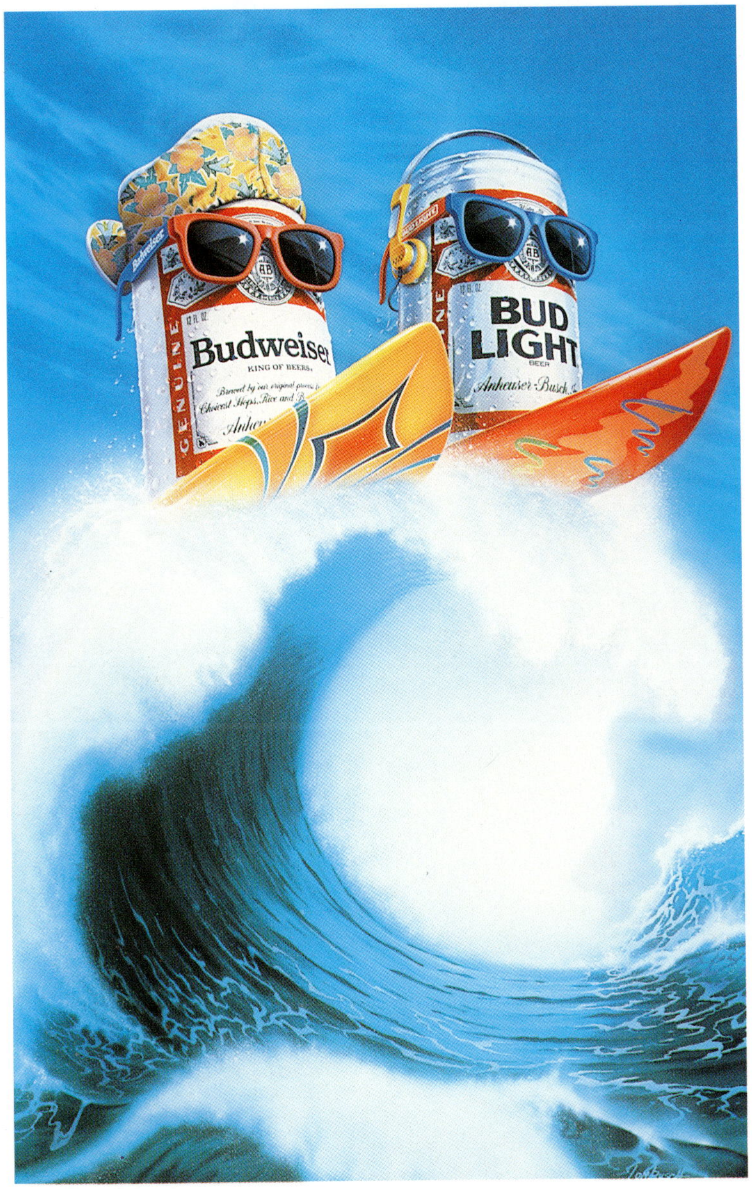

2

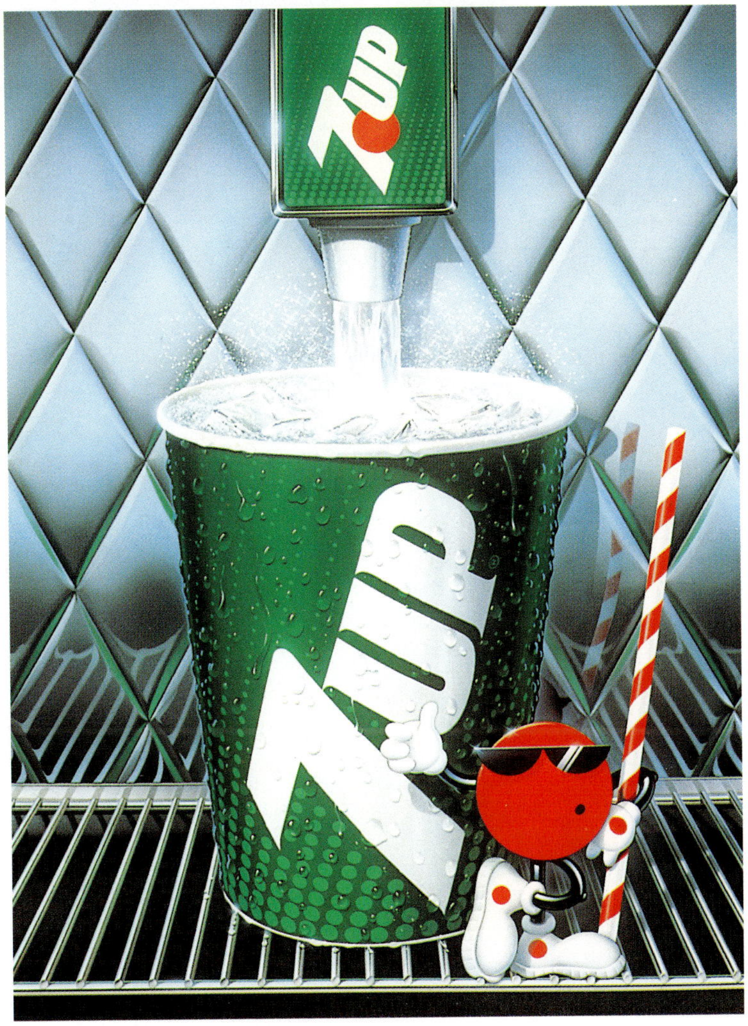

3

1
Illustrator **LONNIE BUSCH**
Title **ELEPHANT MALT LIQUOR**
Media Used **ACRYLIC**

2
Illustrator **LONNIE BUSCH**
Title **7.UP SKIER**
Media Used **ACRYLIC**

1 2

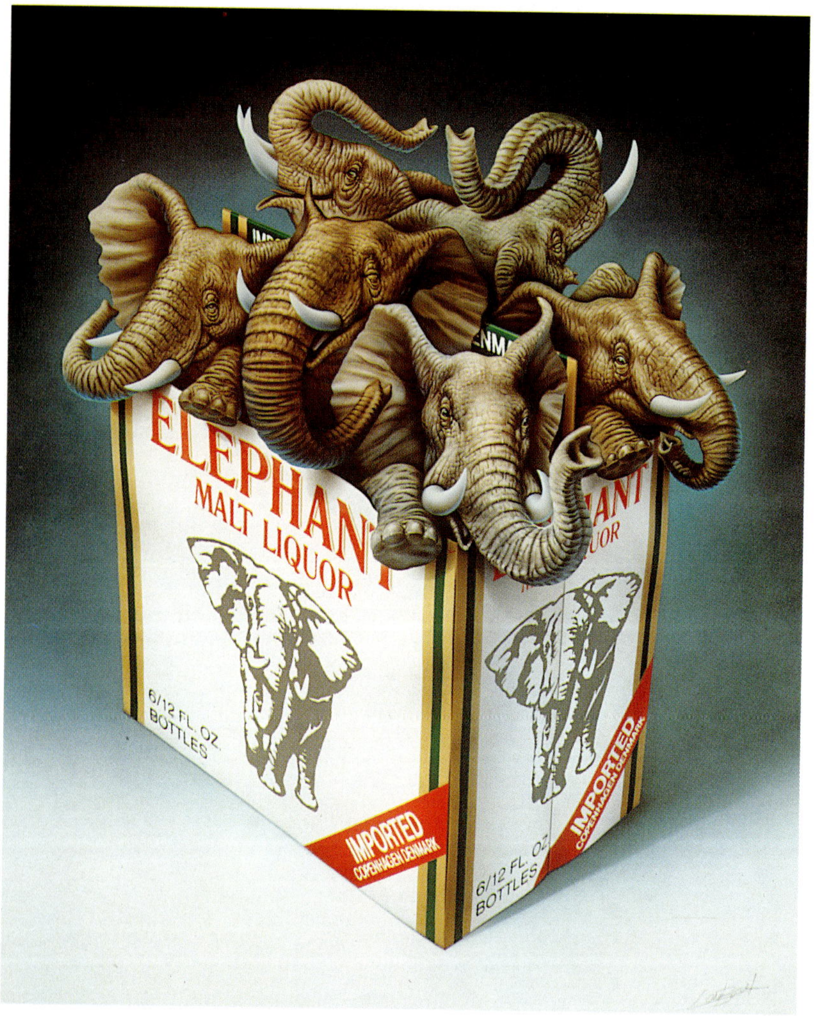

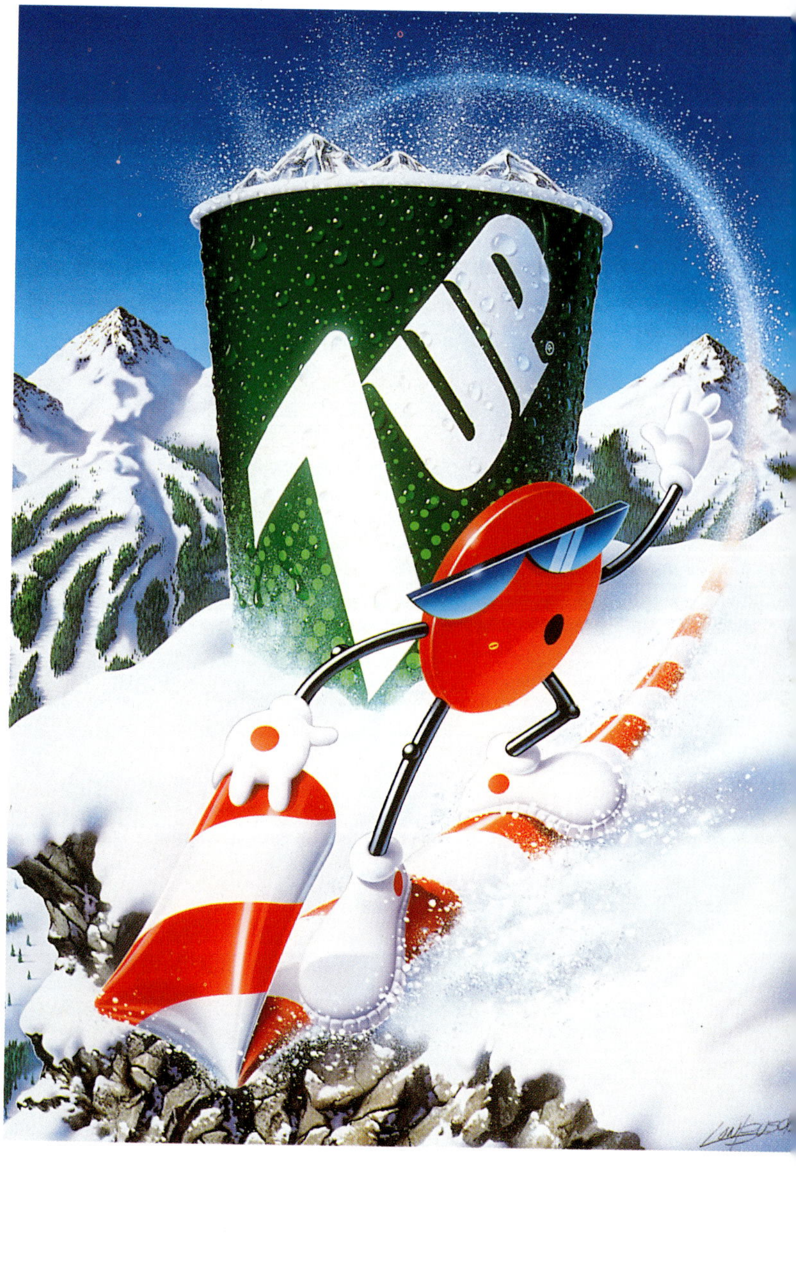

1
Illustrator **LONNIE BUSCH**
Title **PINNOCHIO**
Media Used **ACRYLIC**

2
Illustrator **LONNIE BUSCH**
Title **MILLER GENUINE DRAFT**
Media Used **ACRYLIC**

3
Illustrator **LONNIE BUSCH**
Title **TACO SALAD**
Media Used **ACRYLIC**

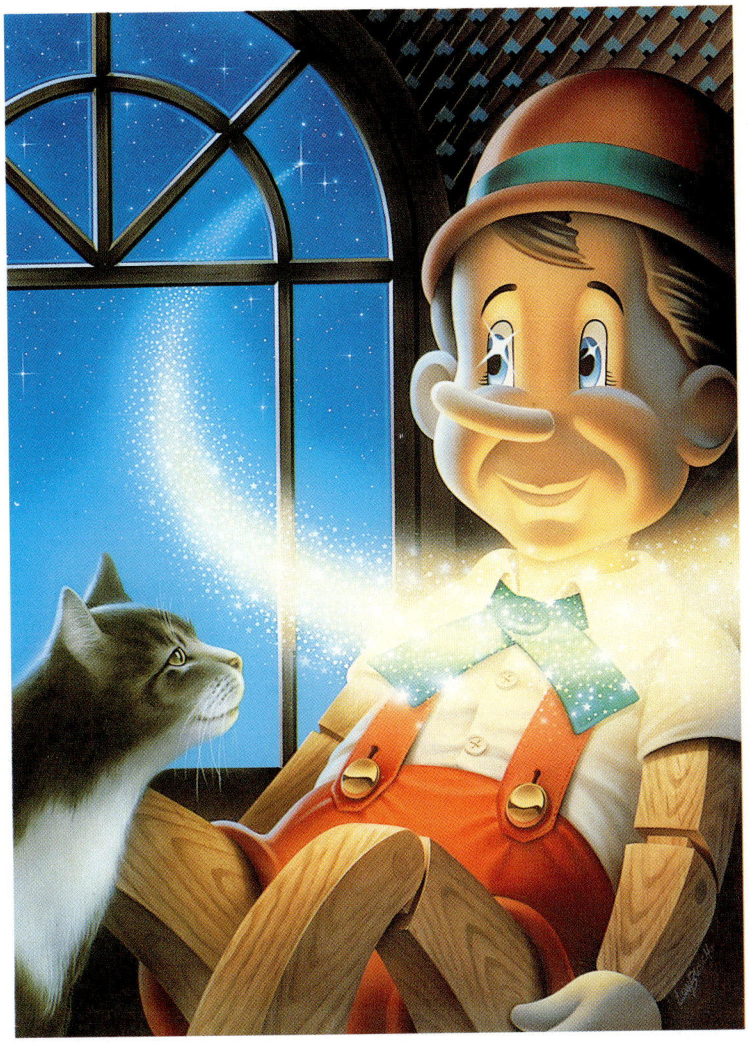

1

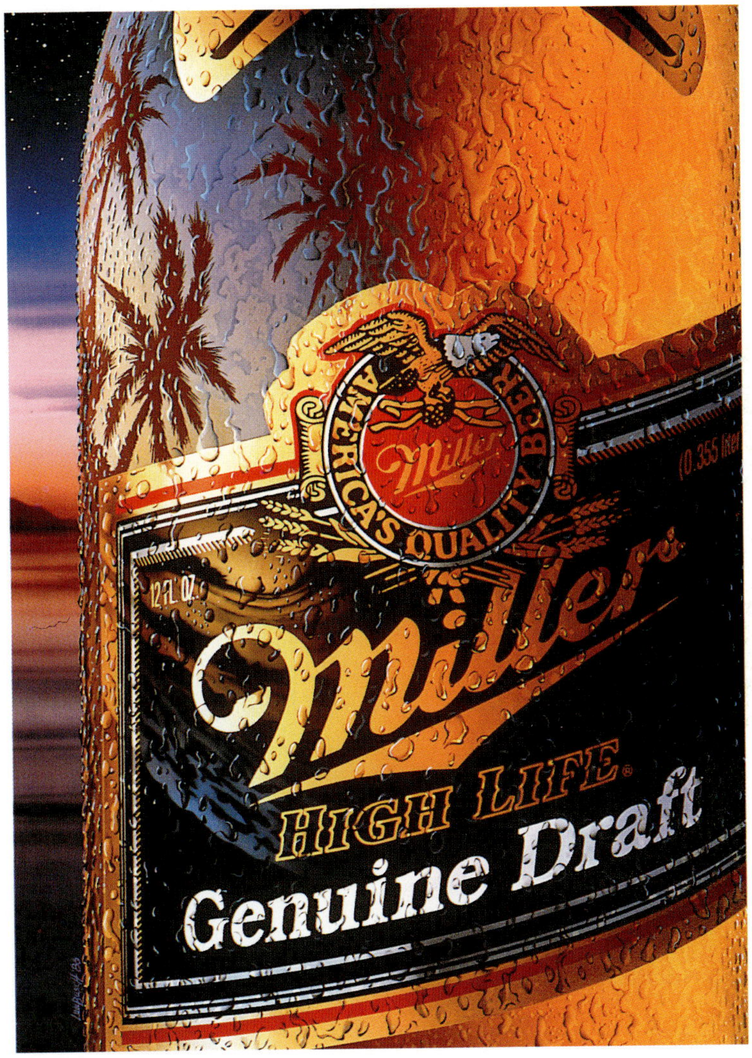

2

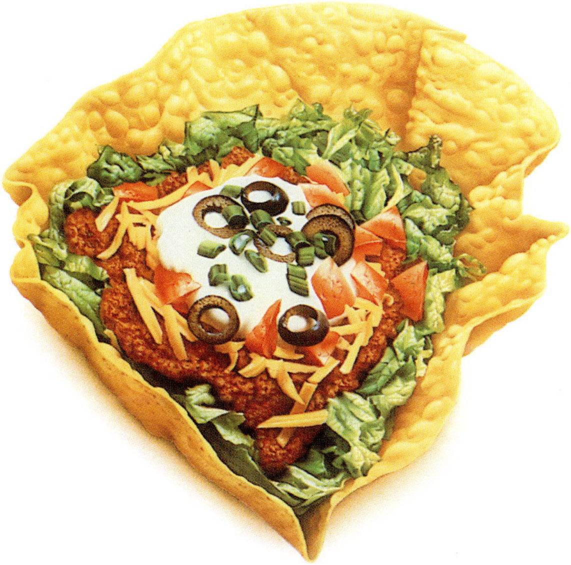

3

1
Illustrator **GARY GLOVER**
Title **EASTER ISLAND**
Usage **SELF PROMOTION**
Media Used **ACRYLIC**

2
Illustrator **GARY GLOVER**
Title **WORF**
Client **UNIVERSAL PICTURES/STATIX**
Usage **ADVERTISEMENT**
Media Used **ACRYLIC**

3
Illustrator **STUART HALL**
Title **ZAGRA THE FORBIDDEN**
Usage **EDITORIAL**
Media Used **WATERCOLOR**

4
Illustrator **ANDY HICKES**
Title **INTERIOR IRS NATIONAL HEADQUARTERS LOBBY**
Client **IRS**
Architect **CARLOS ZAPATA FOR THE HILLER GROUP**
Usage **ARCHITECTURAL RENDERING**
Media Used **MIXED**

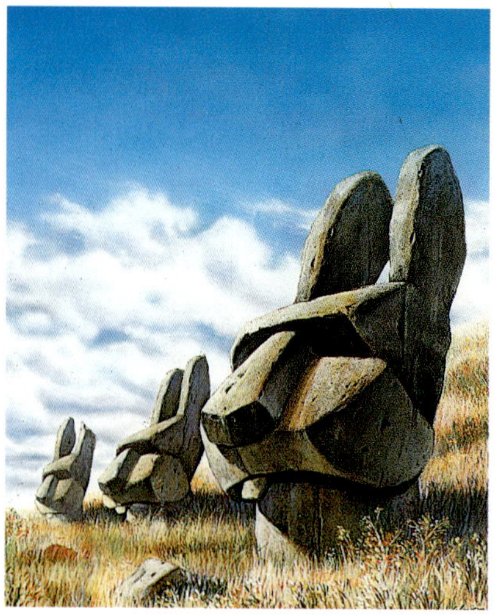

1

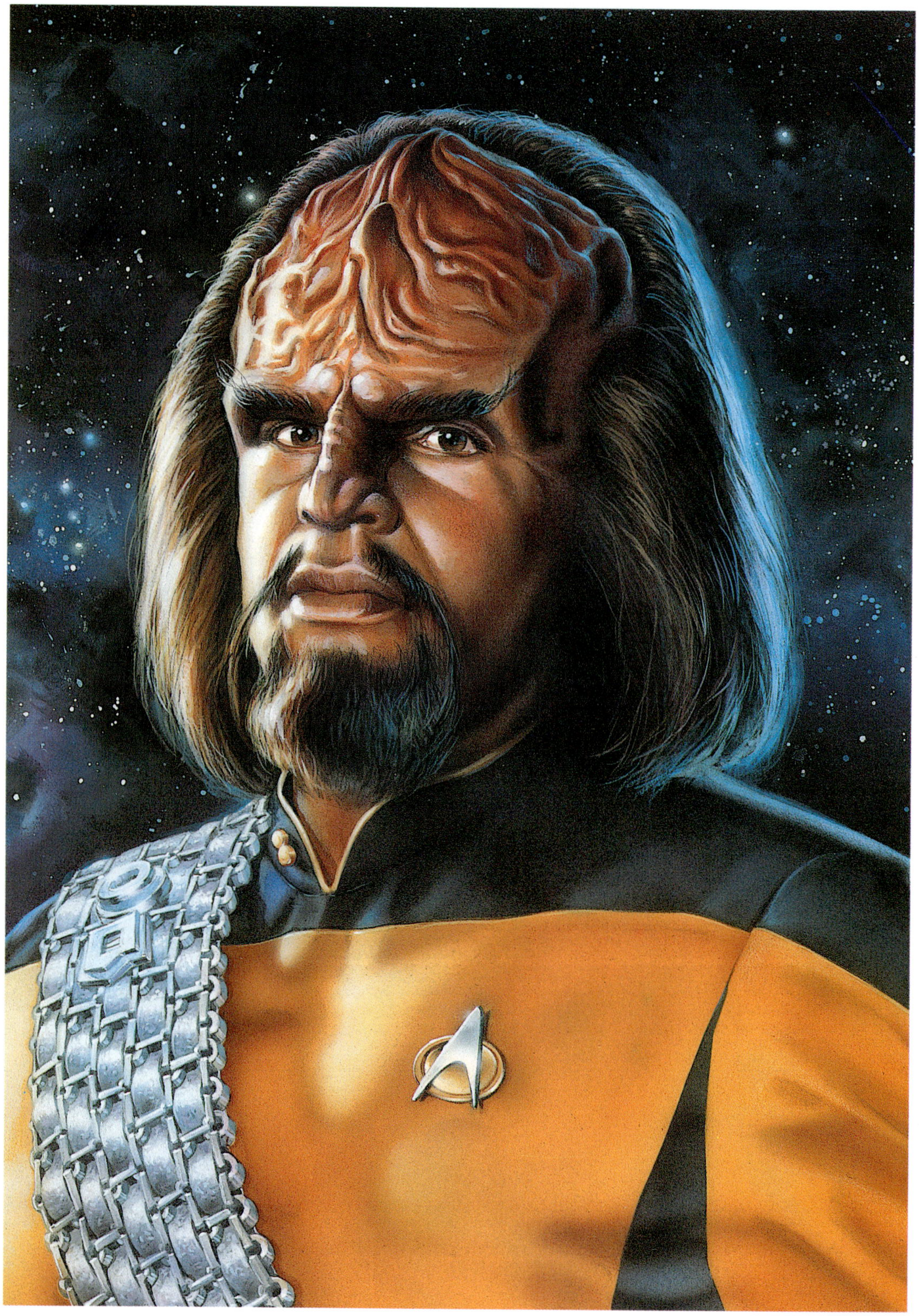

2

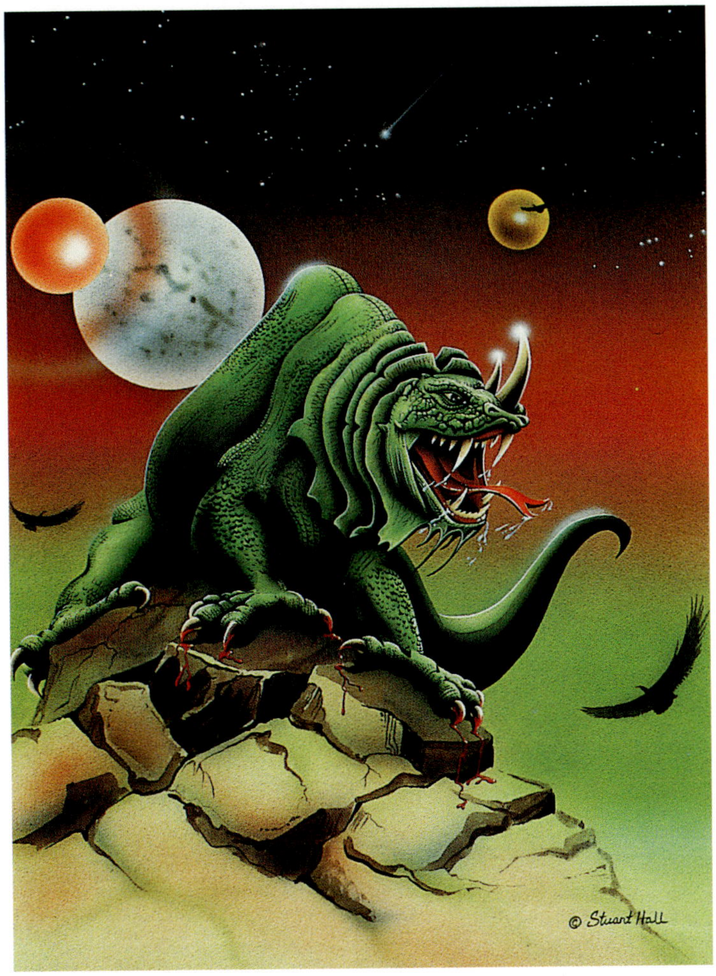

3

4

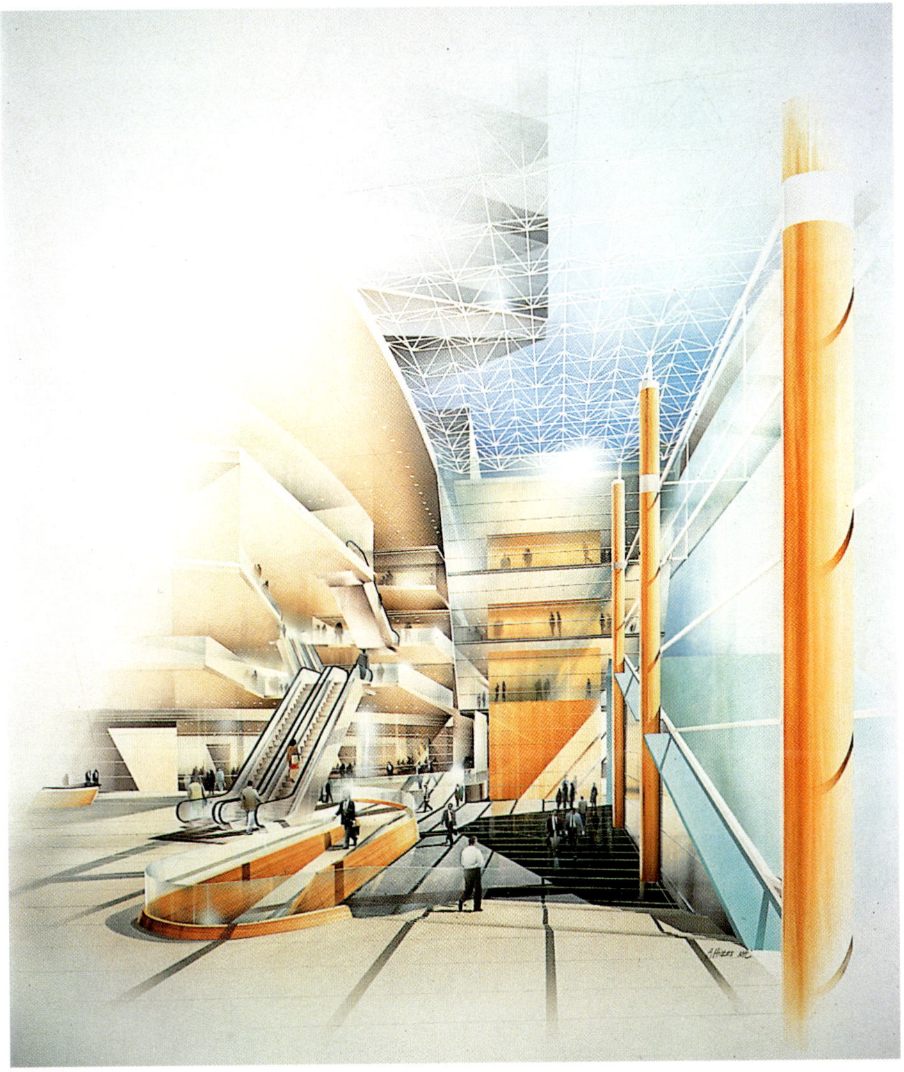

1
Illustrator TOM HOOVER
Title FRANK RAINES
Client PRIVATE COMMISSION
Media Used ACRYLIC

2
Illustrator TOM HOOVER
Title NIGERIAN NIGHTMARE
Client SELF PROMOTION
Media Used ACRYLIC

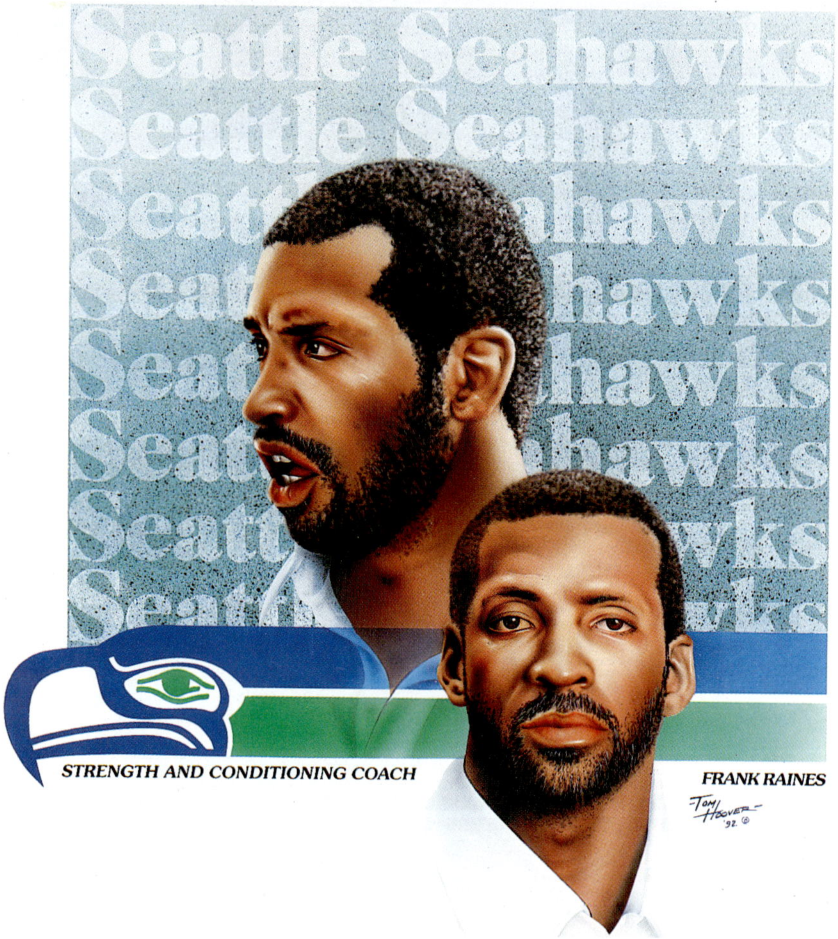

1

2

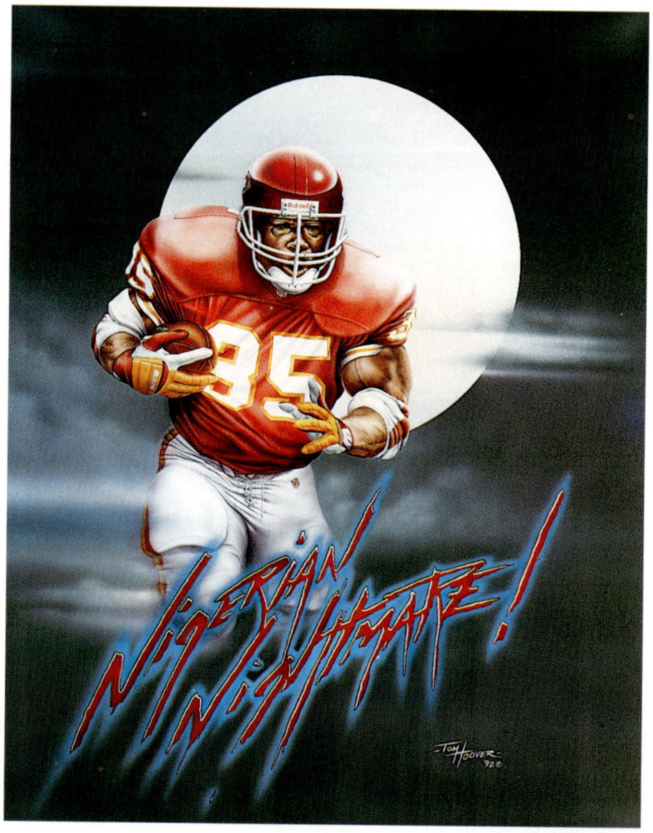

1
Illustrator **ROBERT L. HORWATH**
Title **AT&T SEABED TRACTOR**
Art Director **FRANK MESSINA**
Usage **TECHNICAL ILLUSTRATION**
Media Used **COMART, ACRYLIC**

2
Illustrator **RON HOUGHTON, JR.**
Title **ENDANGERED SPECIES**
Art Director **RON HOUGHTON, JR.**
Usage **COMMERCIAL ART**

3
Illustrator **THOMAS J. HUMPERT**
Title **NOTHING BUT BERRIES**
Usage **SELF PROMOTION**
Media Used **ACRYLIC COMART COLORS**

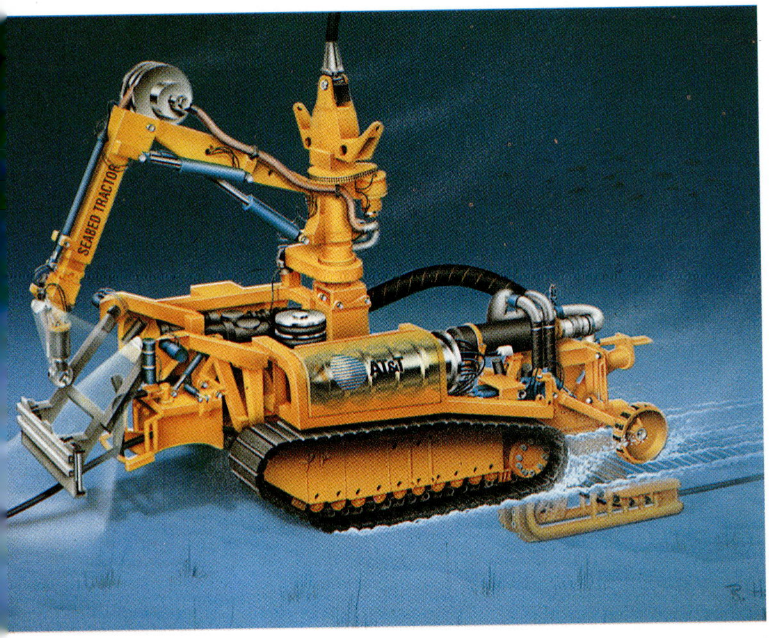

1

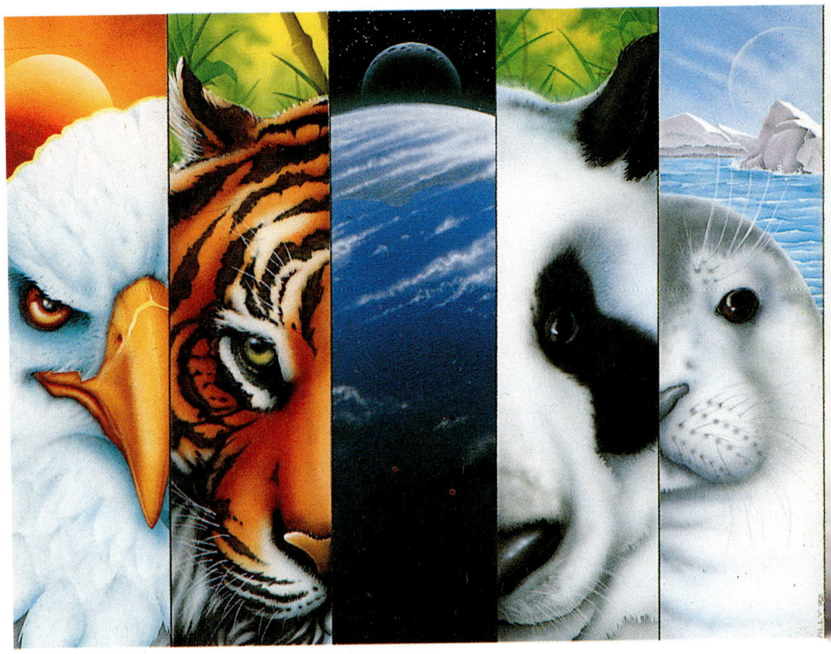

2

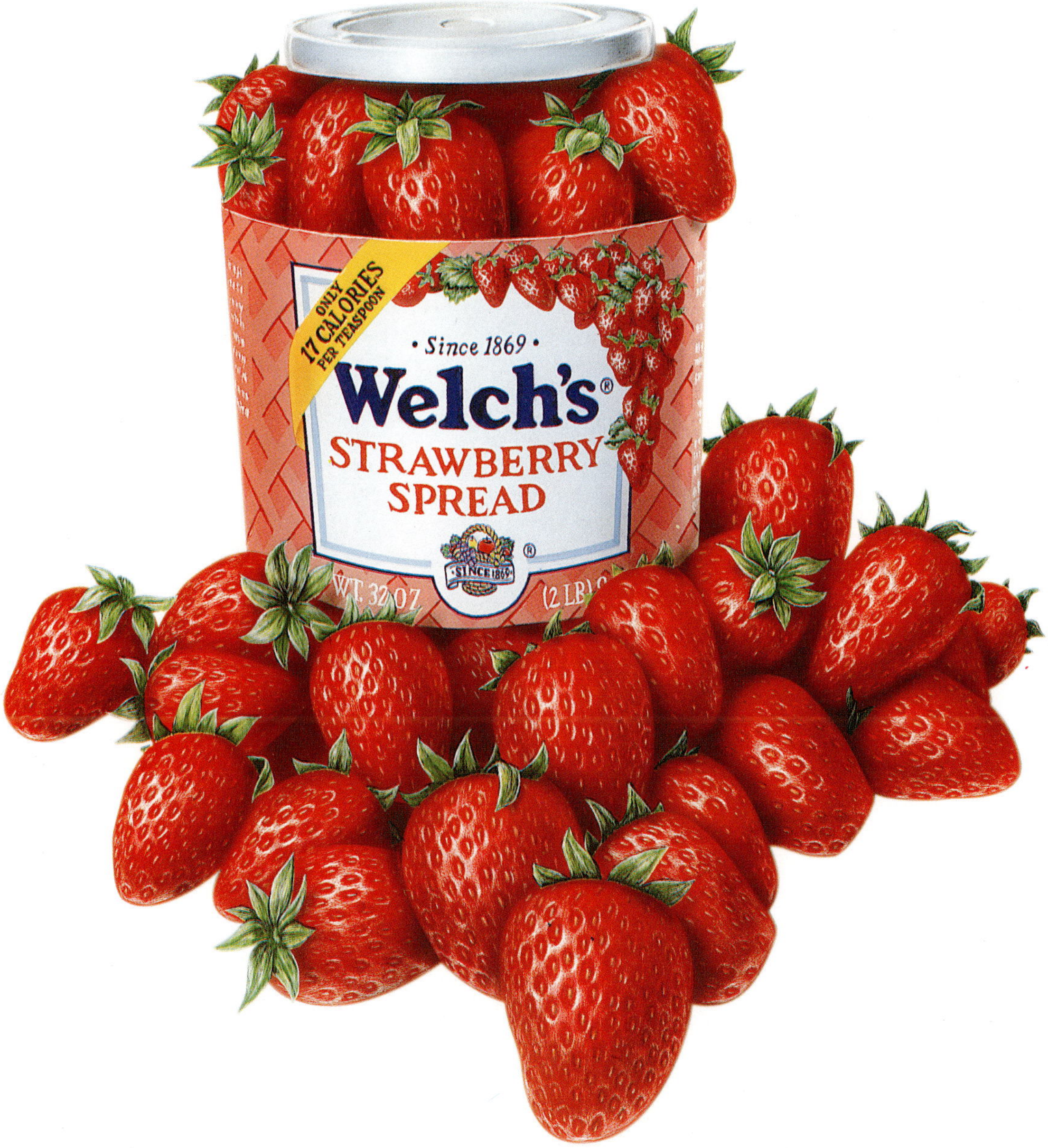

3

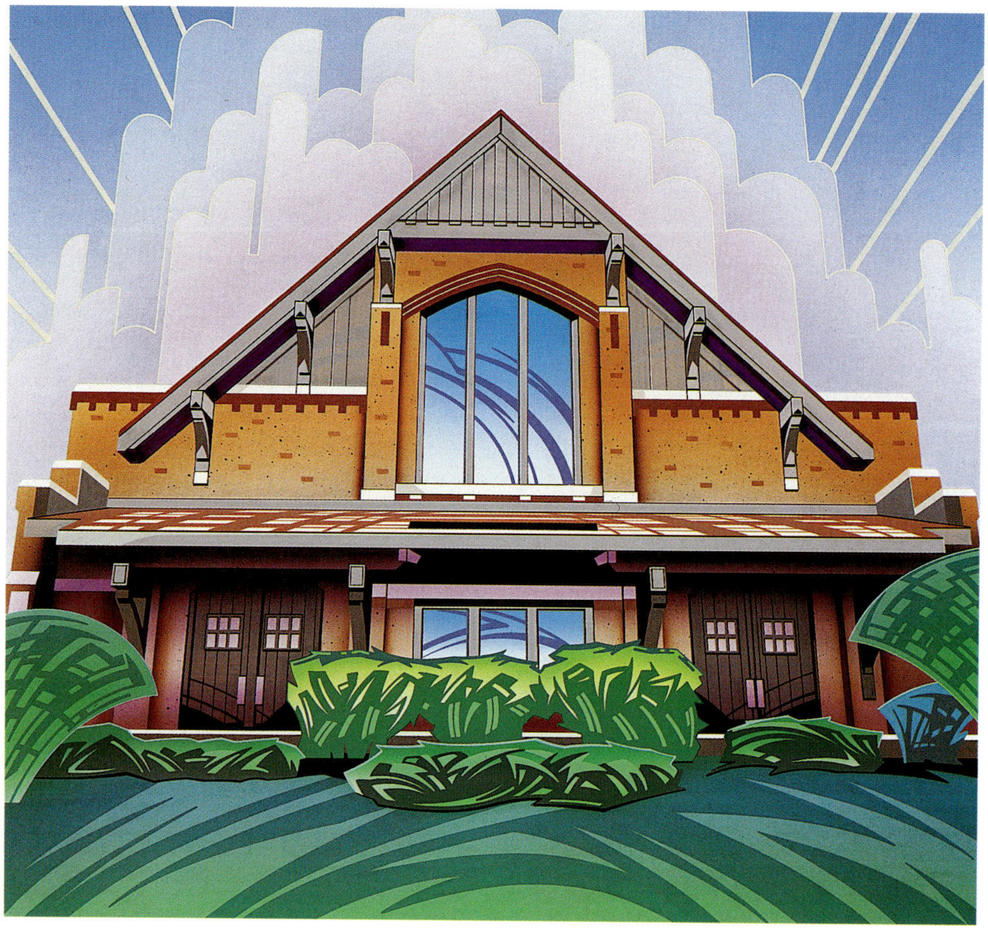

1

2

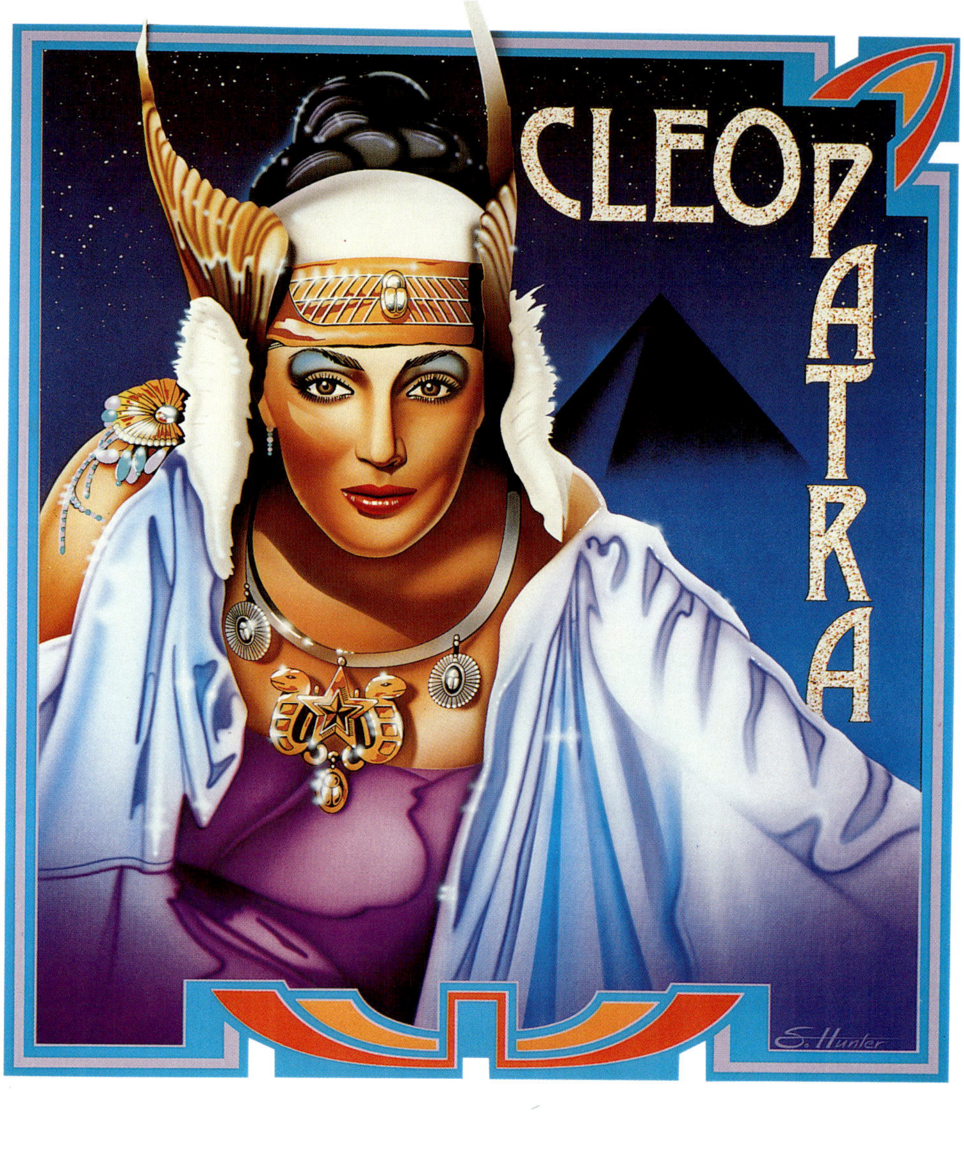

1
Illustrator **STEPHEN M. HUNTER**
Title **THE STUDIO**
Client **HELLMAN ASSOCIATES**
Art Director **STEPHEN M. HUNTER**
Usage **STUDIO PROMOTION**
Media Used **ACRYLIC**

2
Illustrator **STEPHEN M. HUNTER**
Title **CLEOPATRA**
Client **HELLMAN ASSOCIATES**
Usage **PROMOTIONAL CALENDAR**
Media Used **ACRYLIC**

3
Illustrator **STEPHEN M. HUNTER**
Title **ZEPPELIN**
Usage **SELF PROMOTION**
Media Used **ACRYLIC, INK**

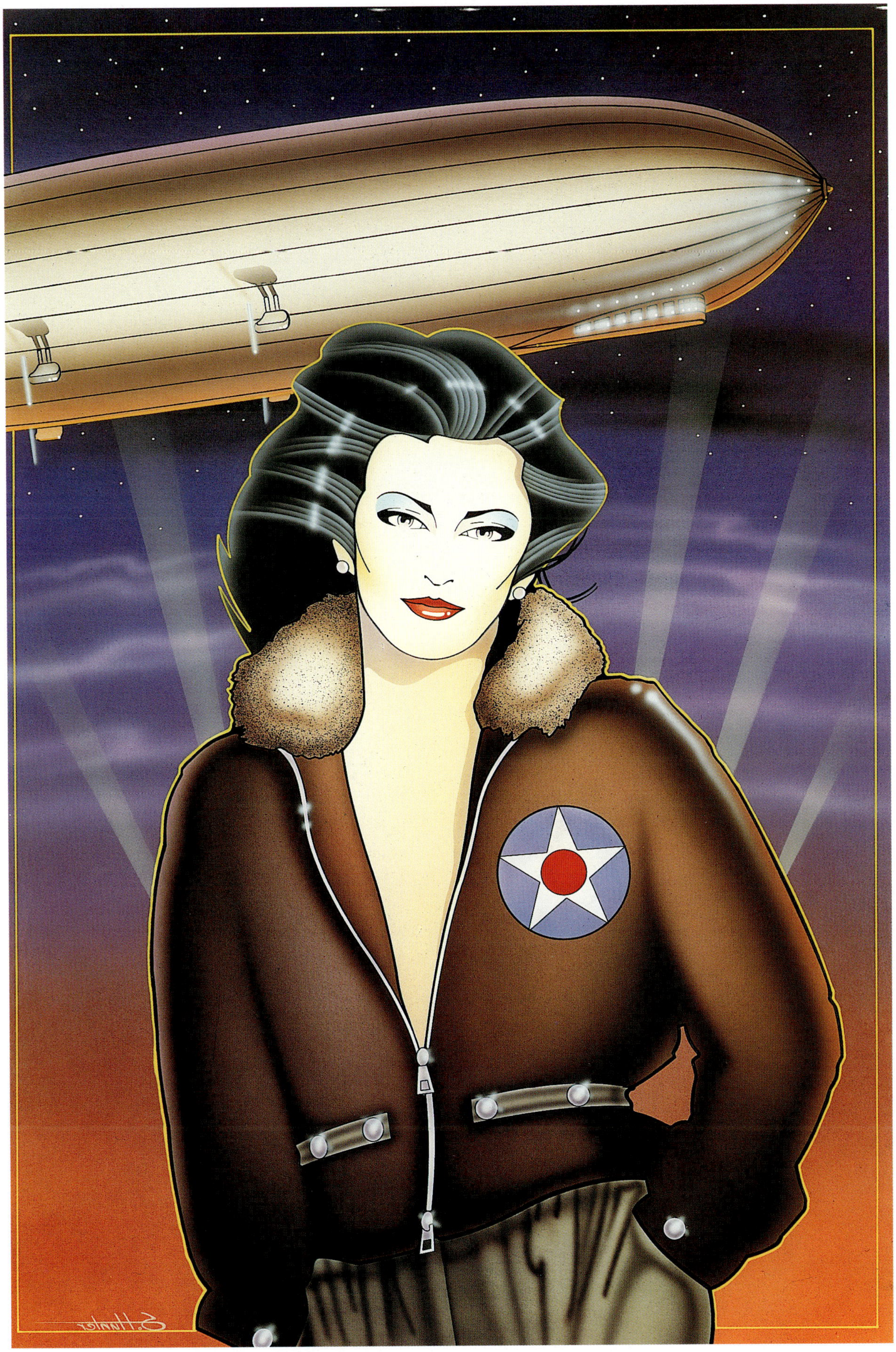

3

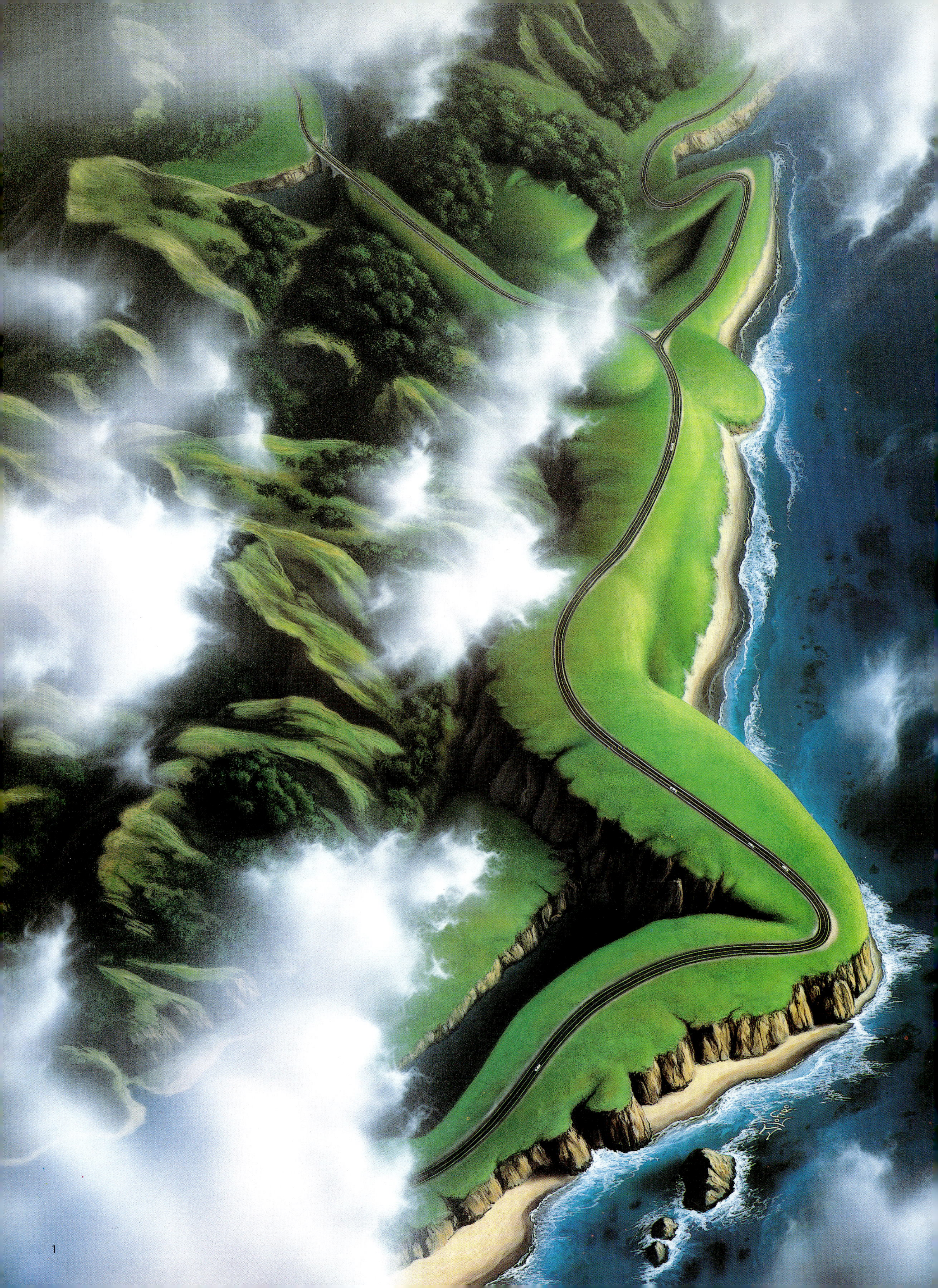

1

1
Illustrator **JERRY LOFARO**
Title **WORLD THE COLOR OF SALT**
Client **AVON BOOKS**
Usage **BOOK COVER**
Media Used **ACRYLIC**

2
Illustrator **JERRY LOFARO**
Title **SELF PROMOTION**
Media Used **ACRYLIC**

3
Illustrator **JERRY LOFARO**
Title **AUNT DIMITY'S DEATH**
Client **VIKING PENGUIN**
Art Director **NEIL STUART**
Usage **BOOK COVER**
Media Used **ACRYLIC**

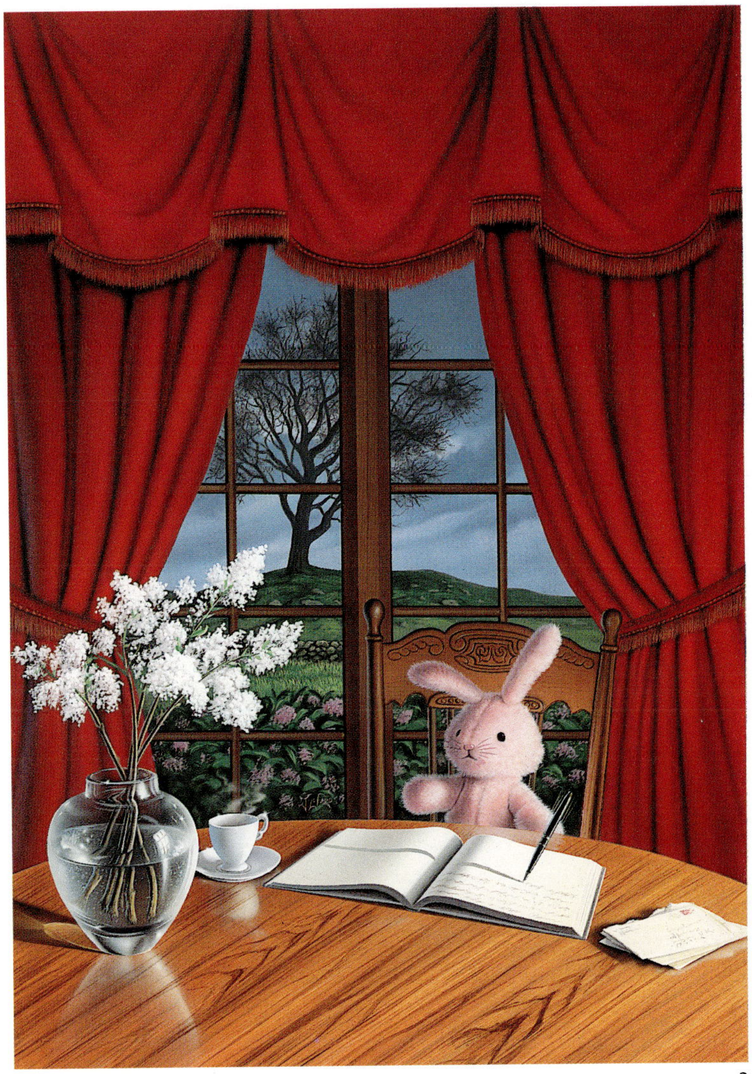

3

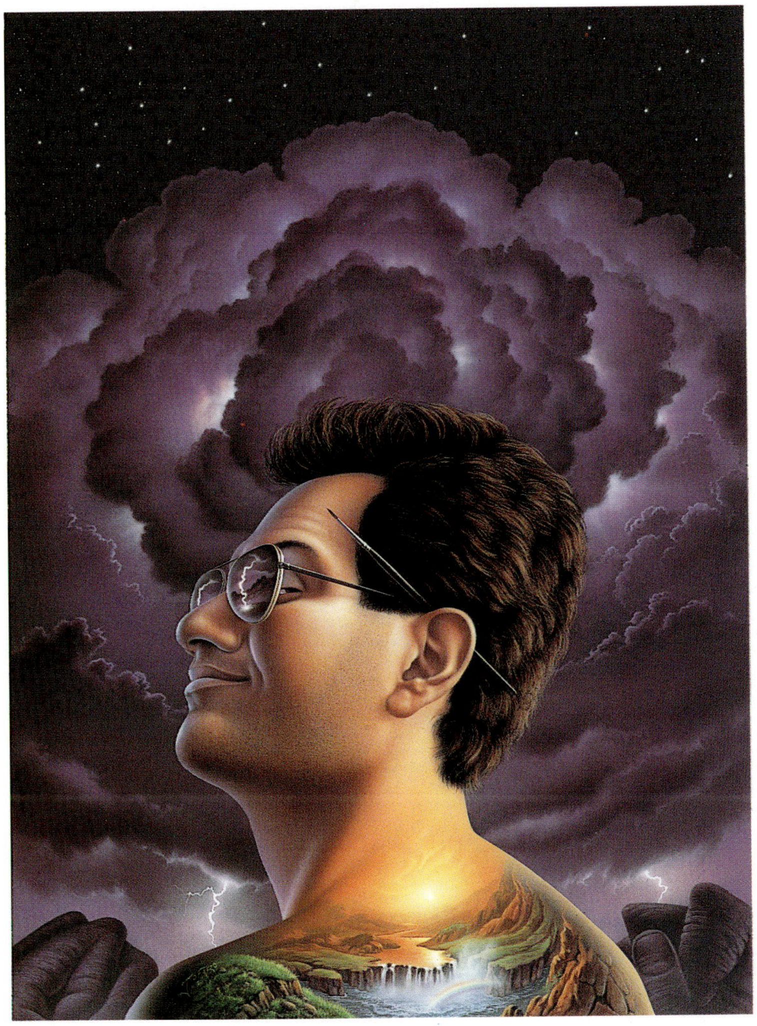

2

1
Illustrator **BILL MAYER**
Title **TILLES CENTER FOR PERFORMING ARTS**
Client **TILLES CENTER**
Art Director **JOHN PETERSON**
Usage **POSTER**
Media Used **GOUACHE, DYES**

2
Illustrator **BILL MAYER**
Title **FRED MARTINS**
Usage **ADVERTISING**
Media Used **GOUACHE, DYES**

3
Illustrator **BILL MAYER**
Title **THEY'RE BACK**
Client **WOODRIDGE MALL**
Art Director **SHIRLEY FEE**
Usage **POSTER**
Media Used **GOUACHE, DYES**

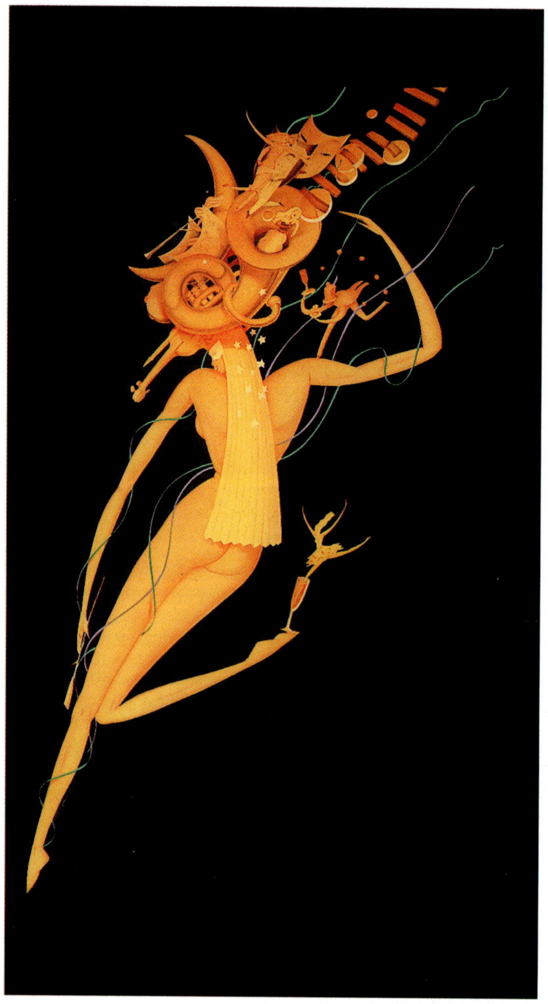
1

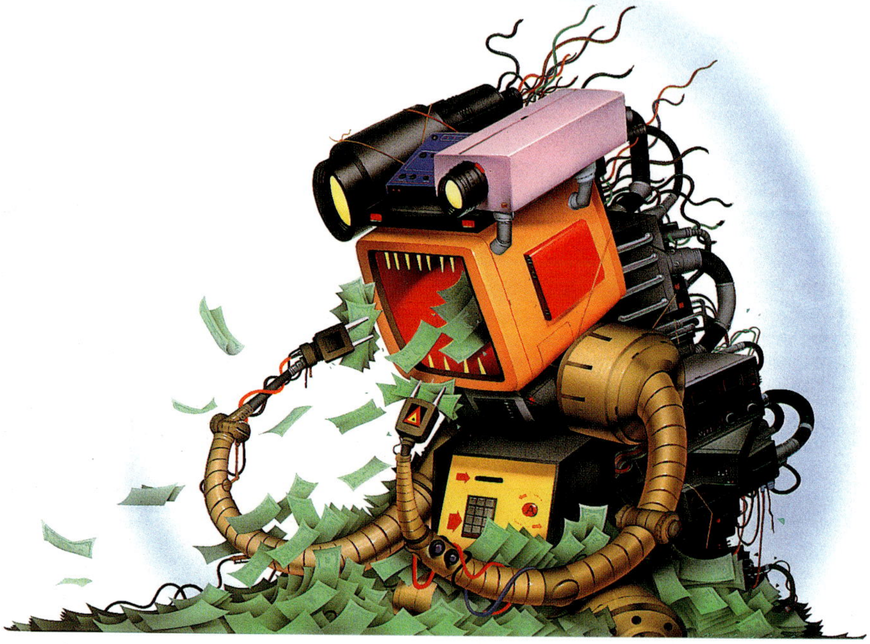
2

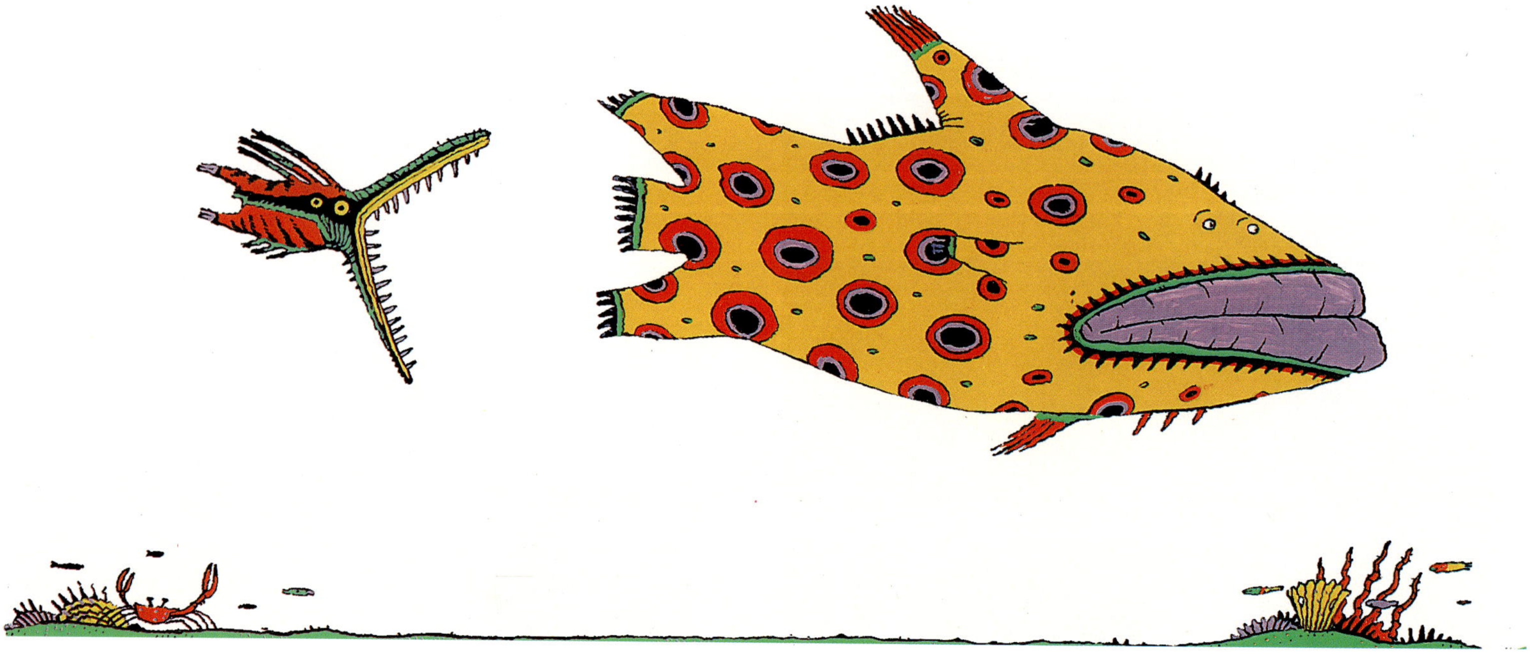
3

1
Illustrator **BILL MAYER**
Client **BOSTON CHILDREN'S MUSEUM**
Art Director **LARRY BOWDISH**
Usage **OUTDOOR & ADVERTISEMENT**
Media Used **GOUACHE, DYES**

2
Illustrator **BILL MAYER**
Title **SELF PORTRAIT**
Client **FRISK ARTIST MATERIALS**
Art Director **STEVE ROUSEAU**
Usage **ADVERTISEMENT**
Media Used **GOUACHE, DYES**

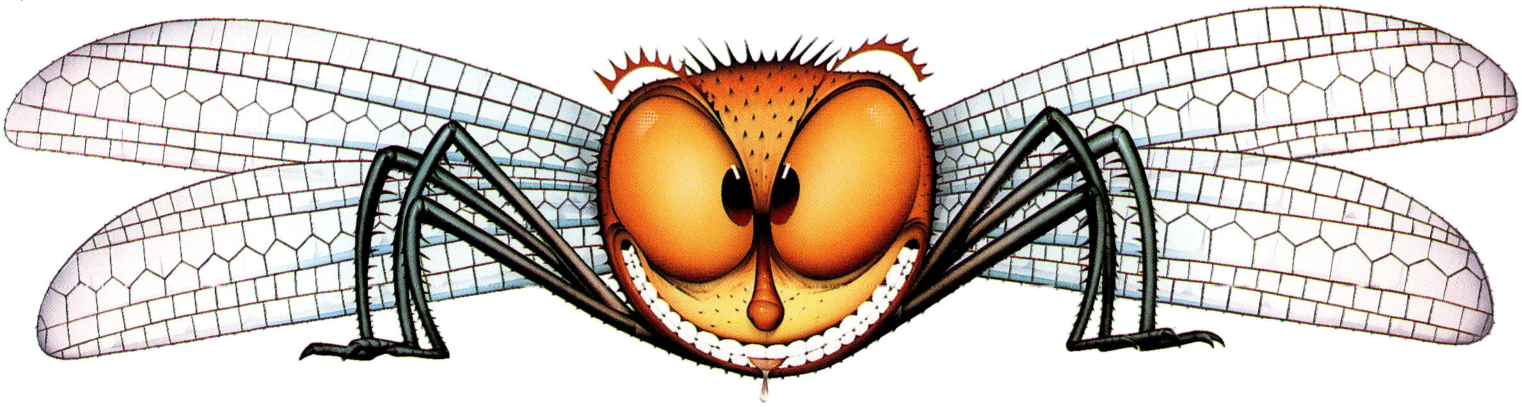

1

2

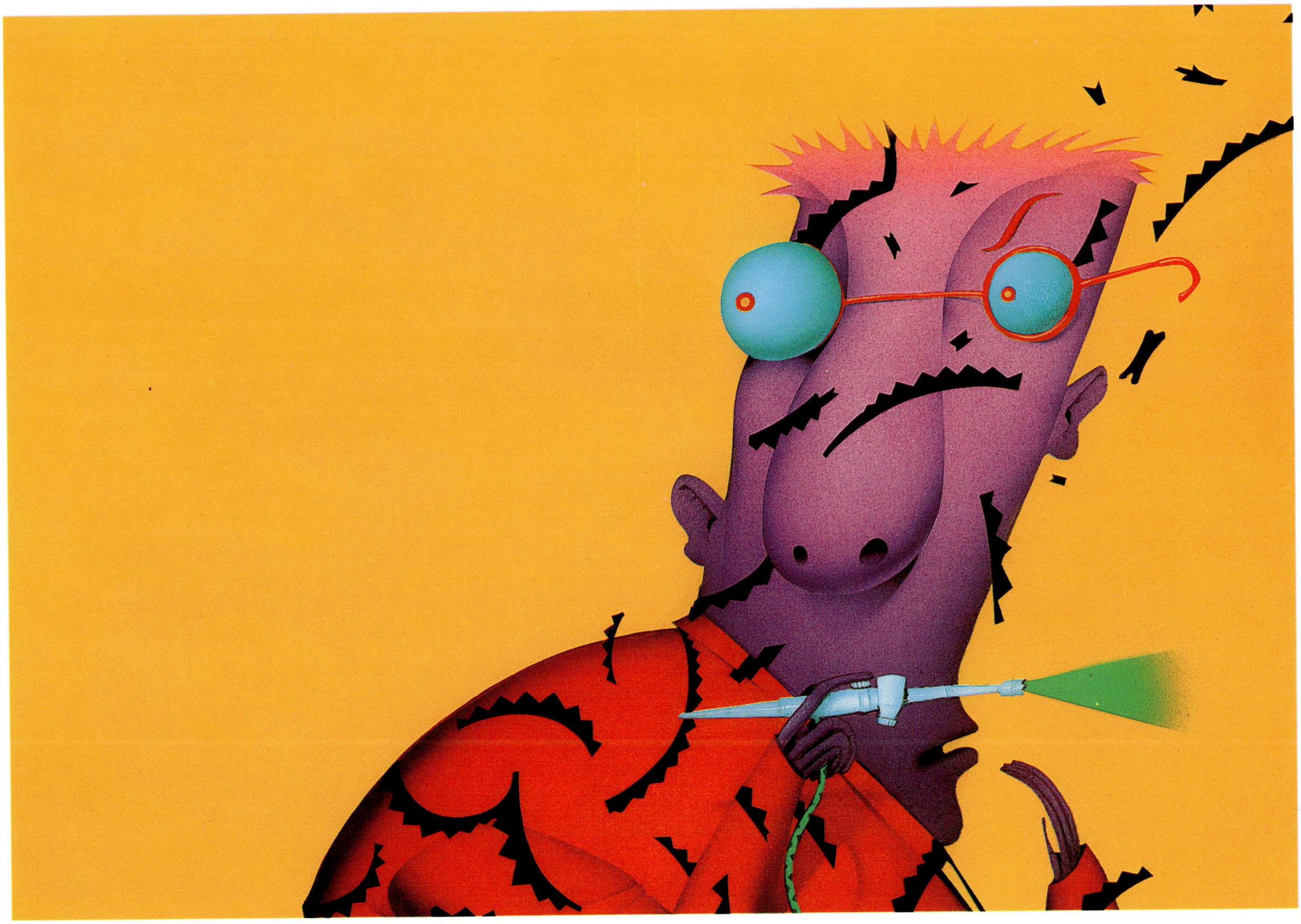

1
Illustrator **BILL MAYER**
Title **CURVES AHEAD**
Client **RIPPINGTONS/GRP RECORDS**
Art Director **ANDI BALTIMORE**
Usage **AUDIO FILE COVER**
Media Used **GOUACHE, DYES**

2
Illustrator **BILL MAYER**
Client **NFL PROPERTIES**
Art Director **VICTORIA EICHINGER**
Usage **POSTER**
Media Used **GOUACHE, DYES**

3
Illustrator **BILL MAYER**
Title **SOFTWARE MADE SIMPLE**
Client **BUSINESS WEEK**
Art Director **CYNTHIA FRIEDMAN**
Usage **COVER**
Media Used **GOUACHE, DYES**

4
Illustrator **BILL MAYER**
Title **BULL**
Client **WORD PERFECT**
Art Director **RON STUCKIE**
Usage **SPOT/MAGAZINE**
Media Used **GOUACHE, DYES**

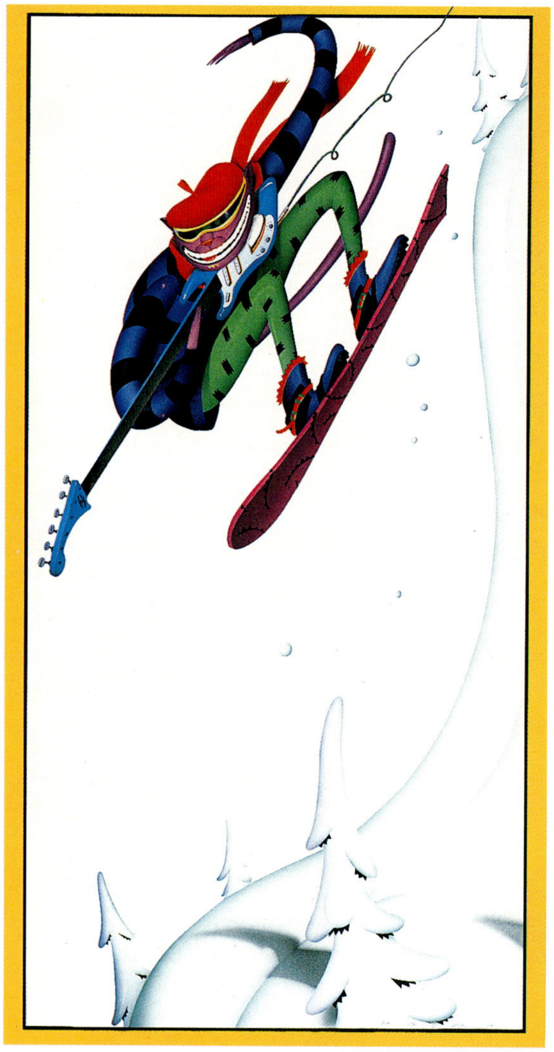

1

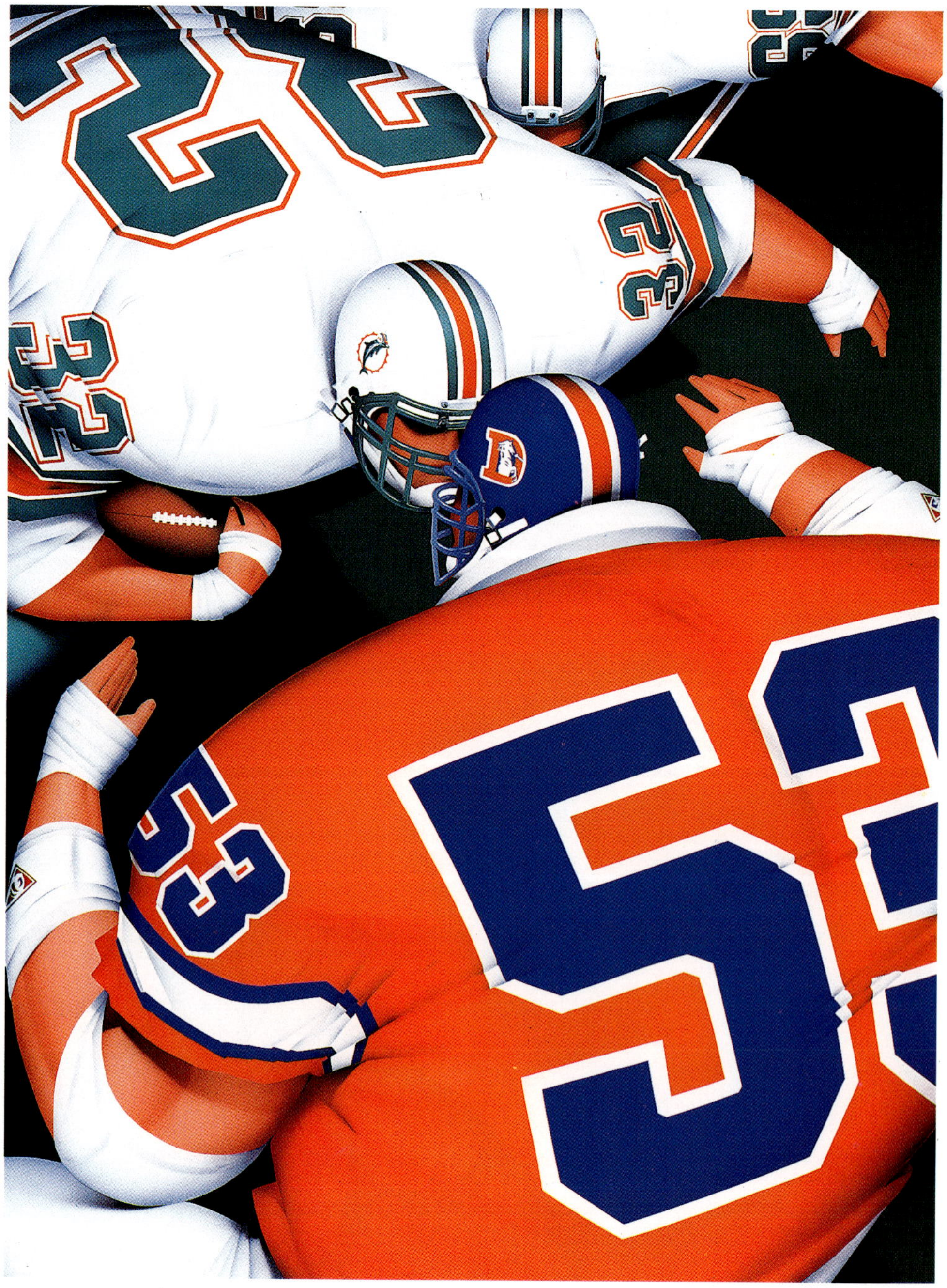

2

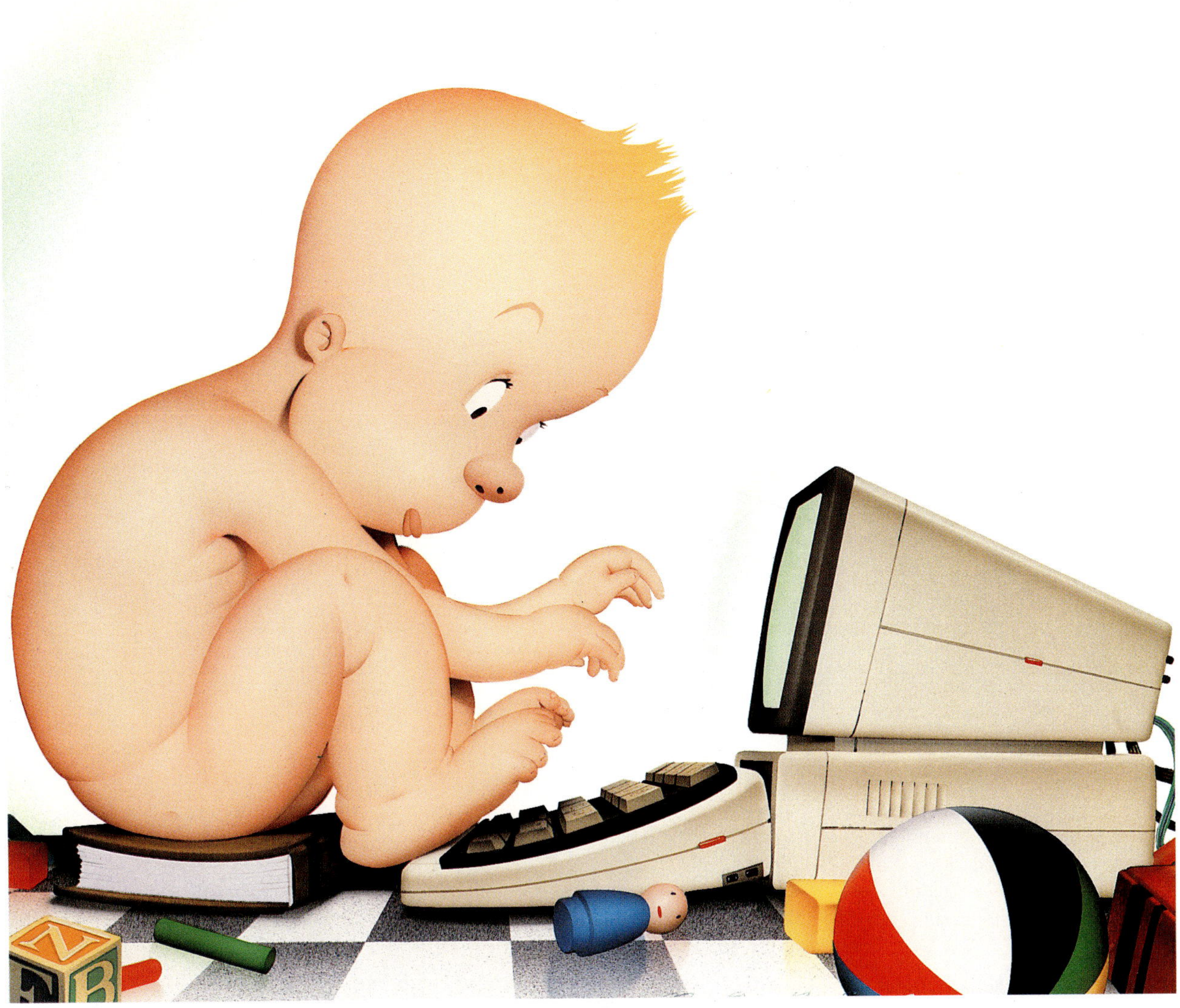

3

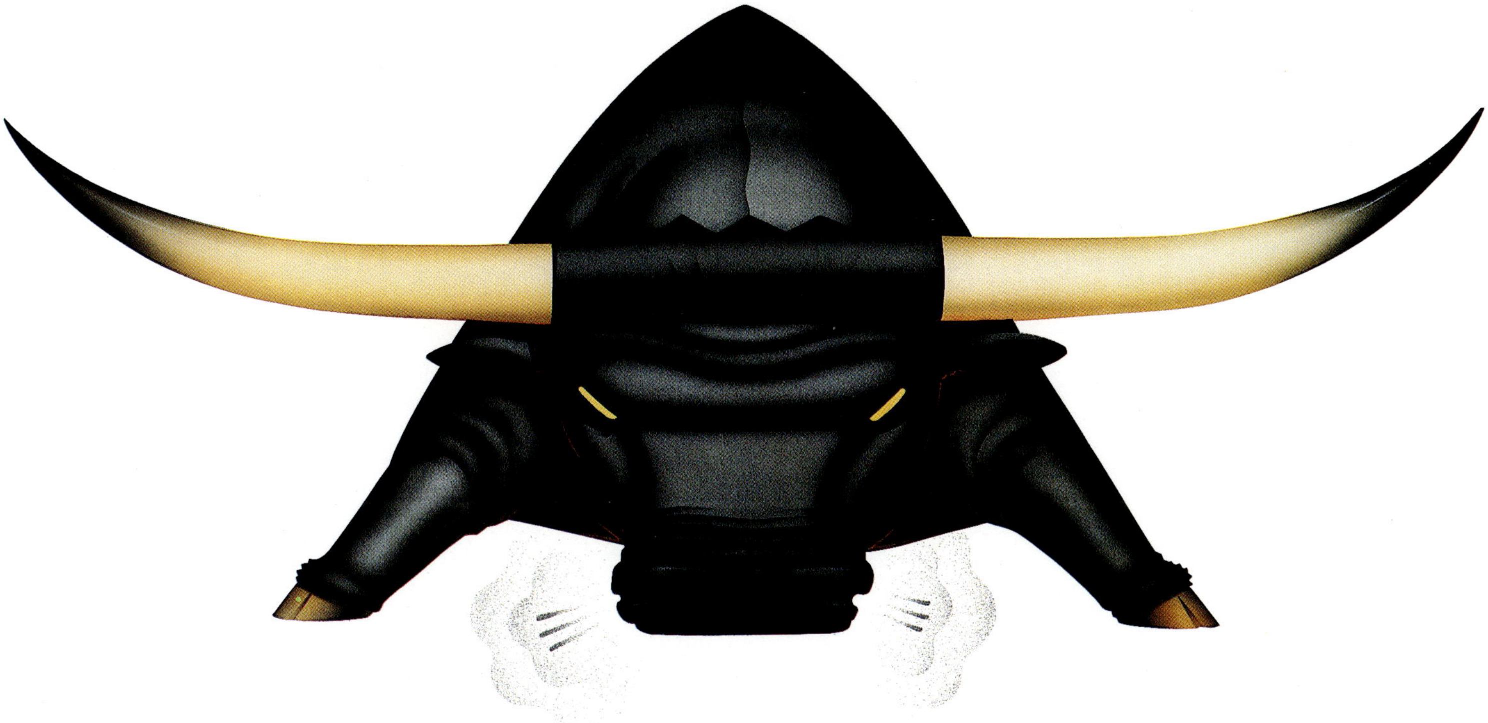

4

1
Illustrator **PEGGY MOZLEY**
Title **THE GIRL IN THE T-BIRD**
Usage **SELF PROMOTION**
Media Used **GOUACHE, DR. MARTIN INKS**

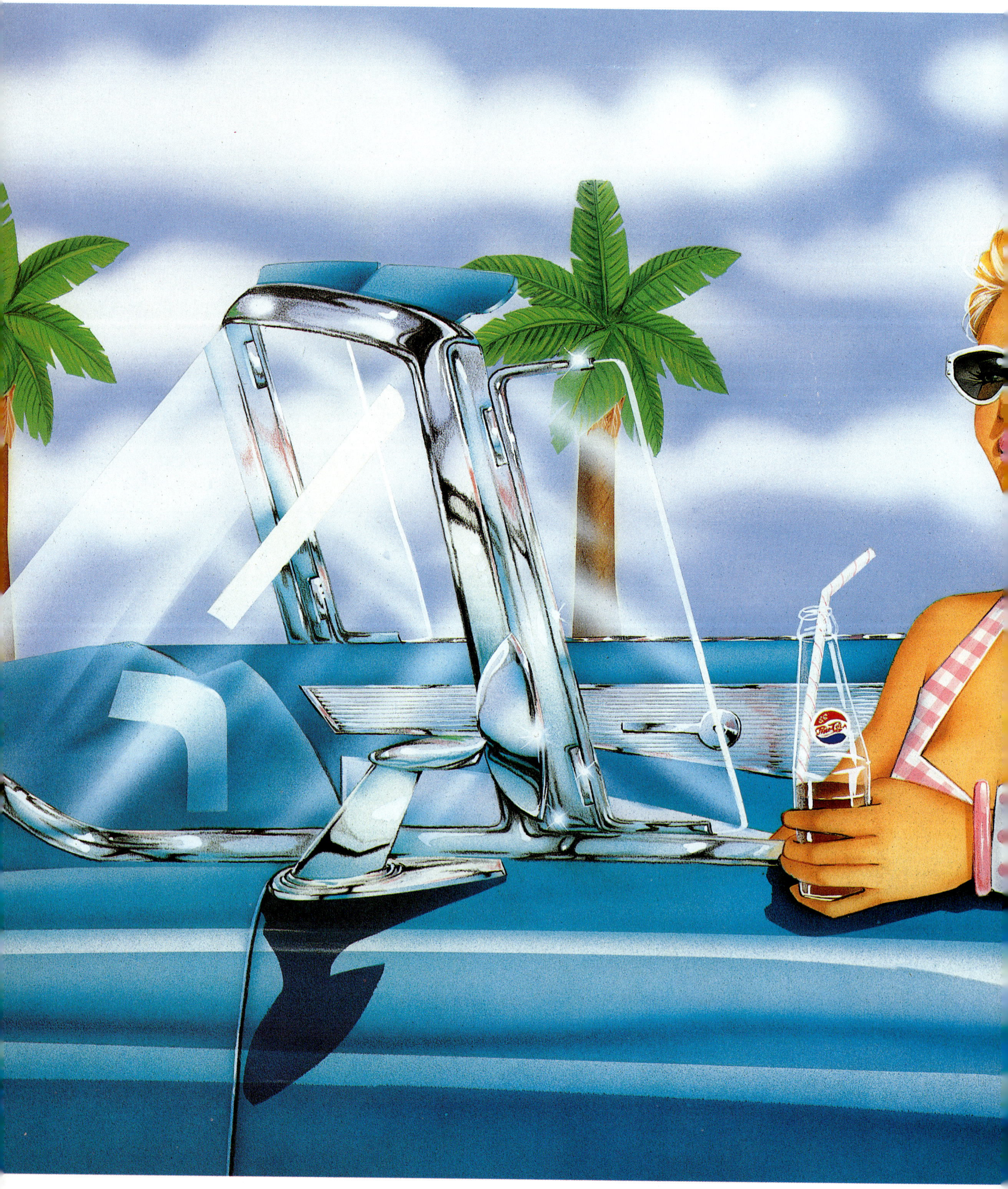

1

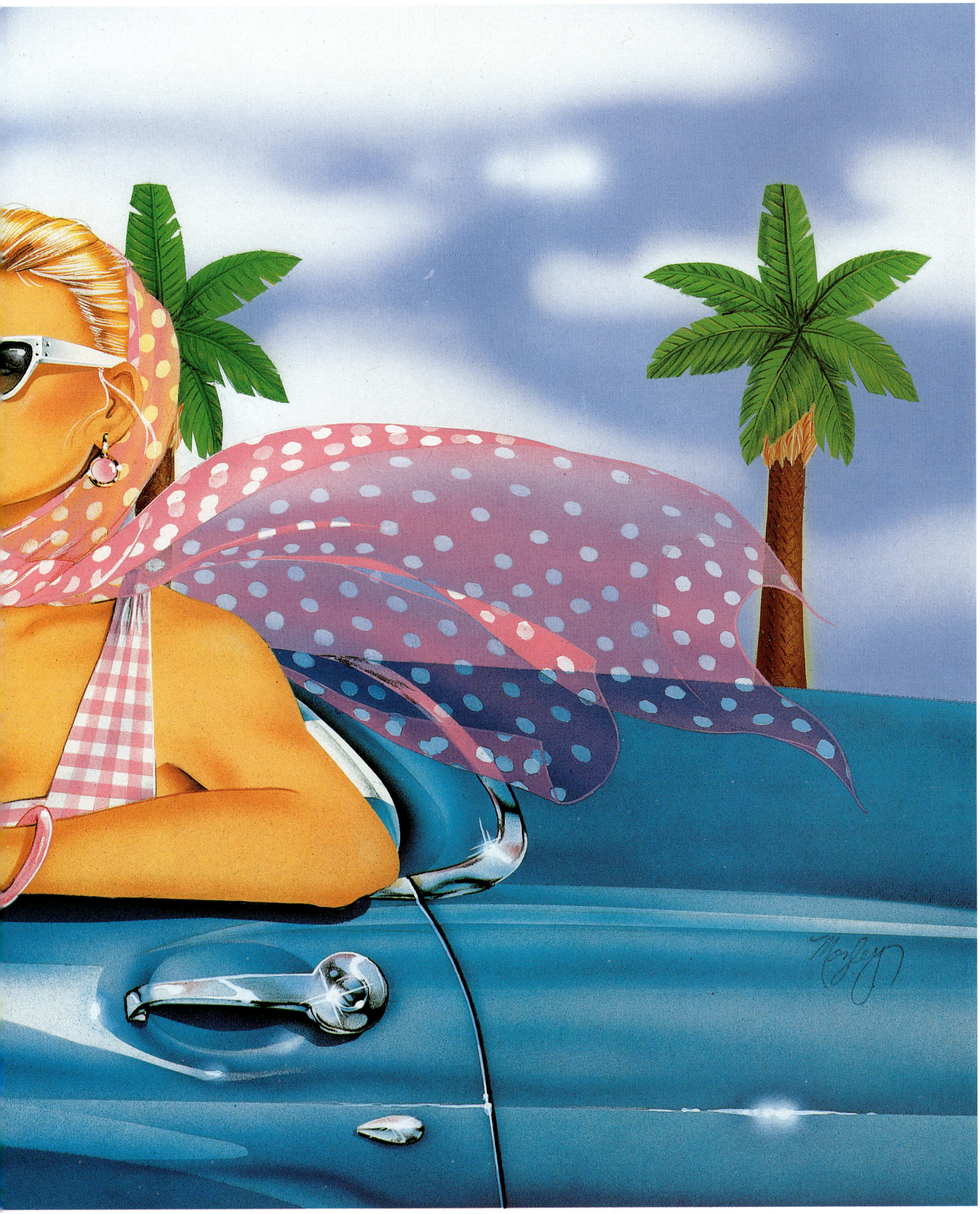

1
Illustrator **ROBERT REVELS**
Title **FATHER FIGURE**
Art Director **ACADEMY OF ART**
Usage **STUDENT ART**
Media Used **GOUACHE, ACRYLIC**

2
Illustrator **ROBERT REVELS**
Title **SPIKE**
Art Director **ACADEMY OF ART**
Usage **STUDENT ART**
Media Used **GOUACHE, ACRYLIC**

3
Illustrator **MARK V. ROBINSON**
Title **49 BUICK EIGHT**
Client **SELF PROMOTION**
Usage **COMMERCIAL ART**
Media Used **ACRYLIC**

1

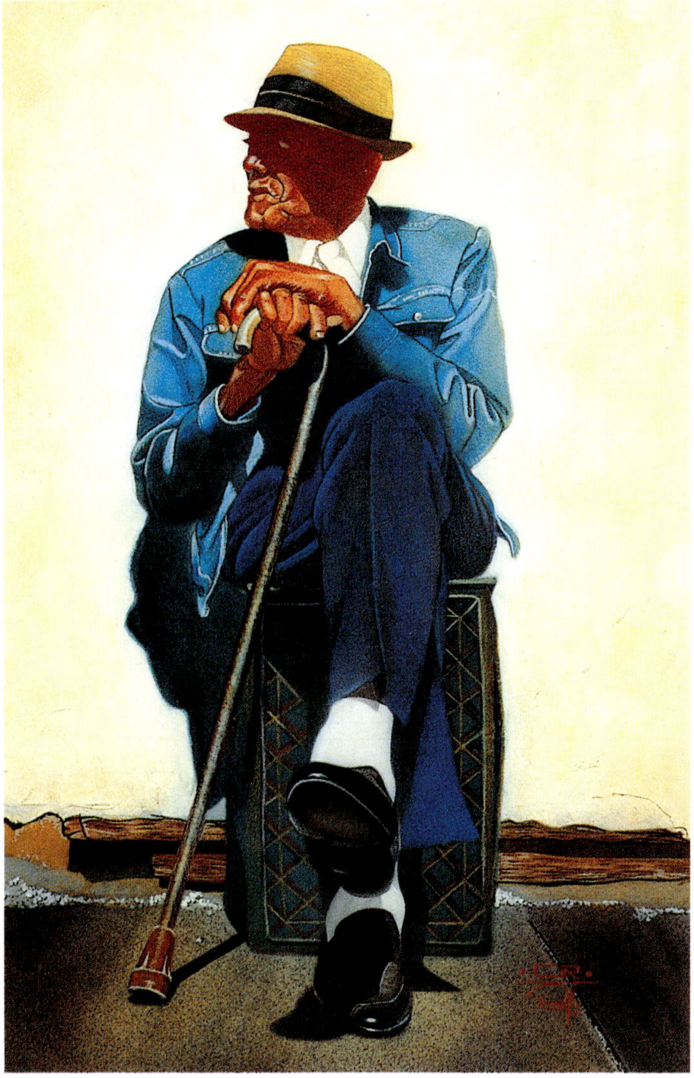

2

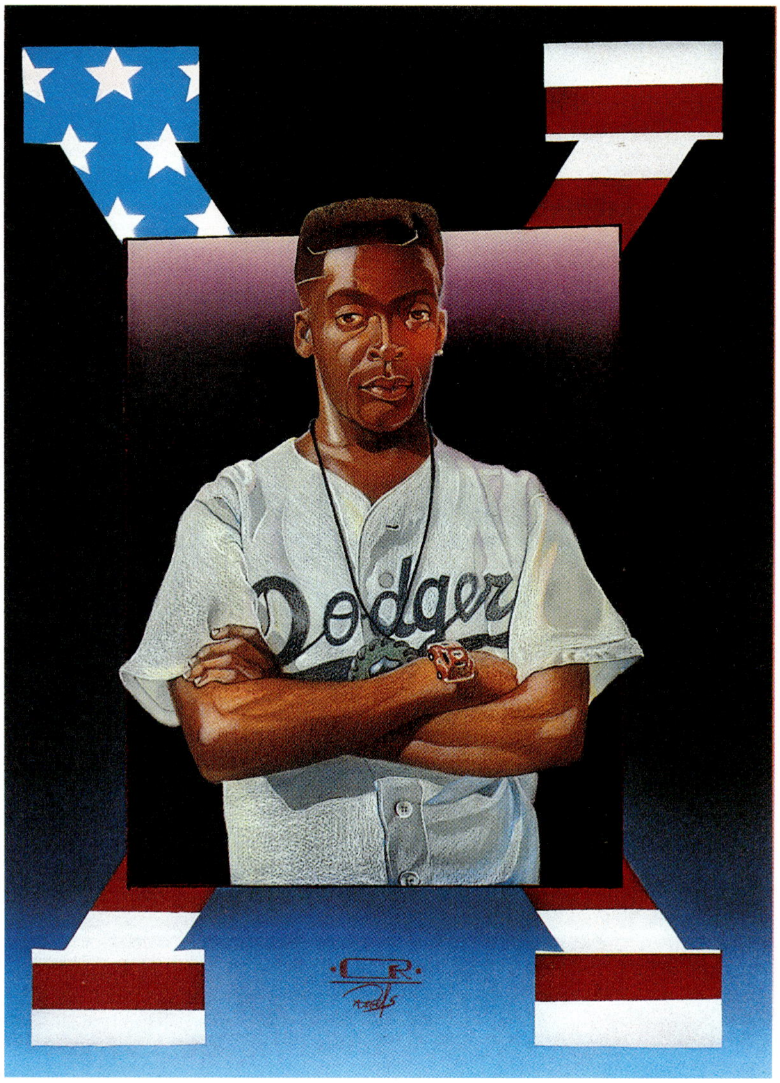

3

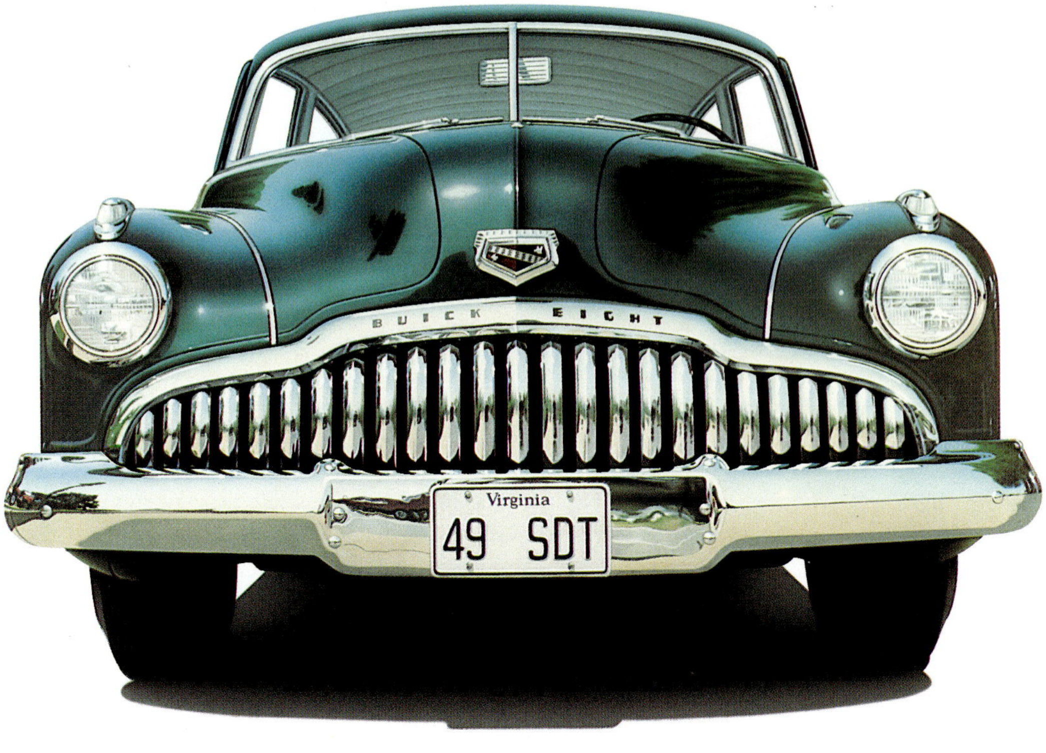

1
Illustrator **DAVID SALAZAR**
Usage **FINE ART**
Media Used **ACRYLIC**

2
Illustrator **SAMUEL SALFINO III**
Title **CHEVEROLET**
Client **MOORE SPORTS**
Usage **COMMERCIAL ART**
Media Used **ACRYLIC**

3
Illustrator **SAMUEL SALFINO III**
Title **"LIL" MISS MUFFET**
Client **SELF PROMOTION**
Usage **COMMERCIAL ART**
Media Used **ACRYLIC**

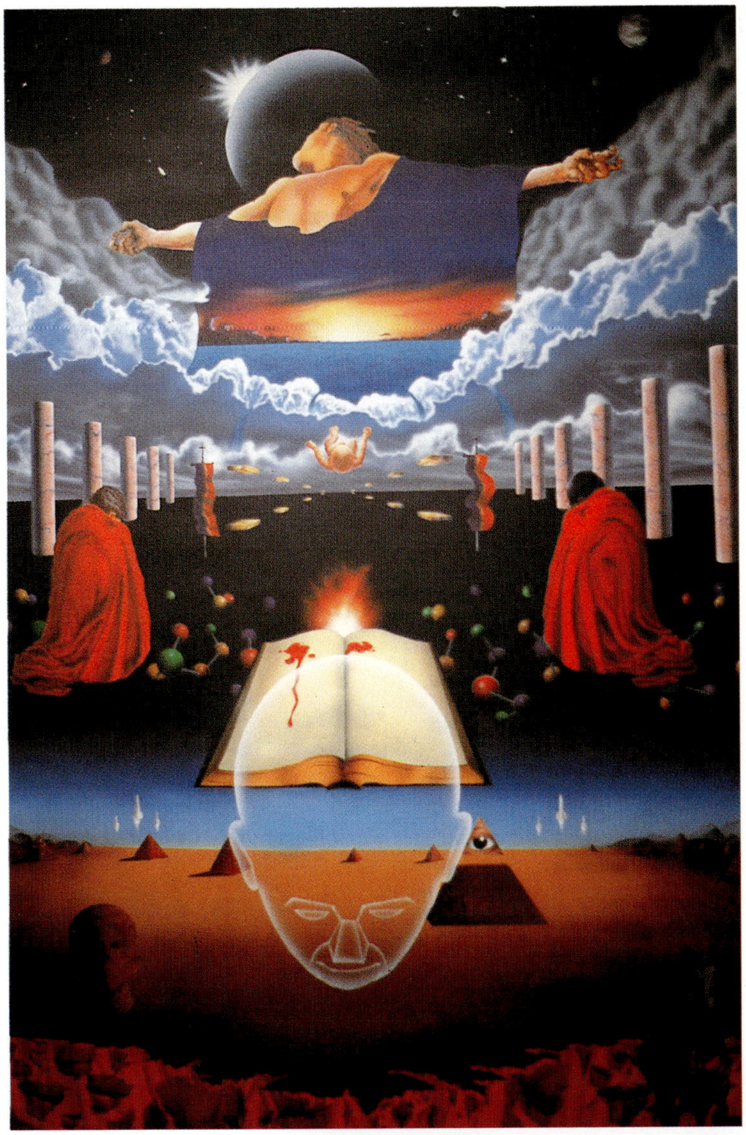
1

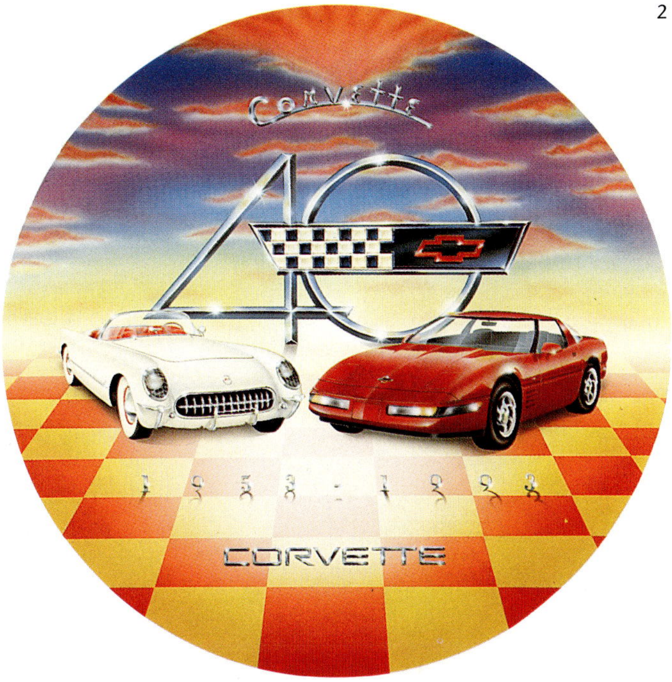

2

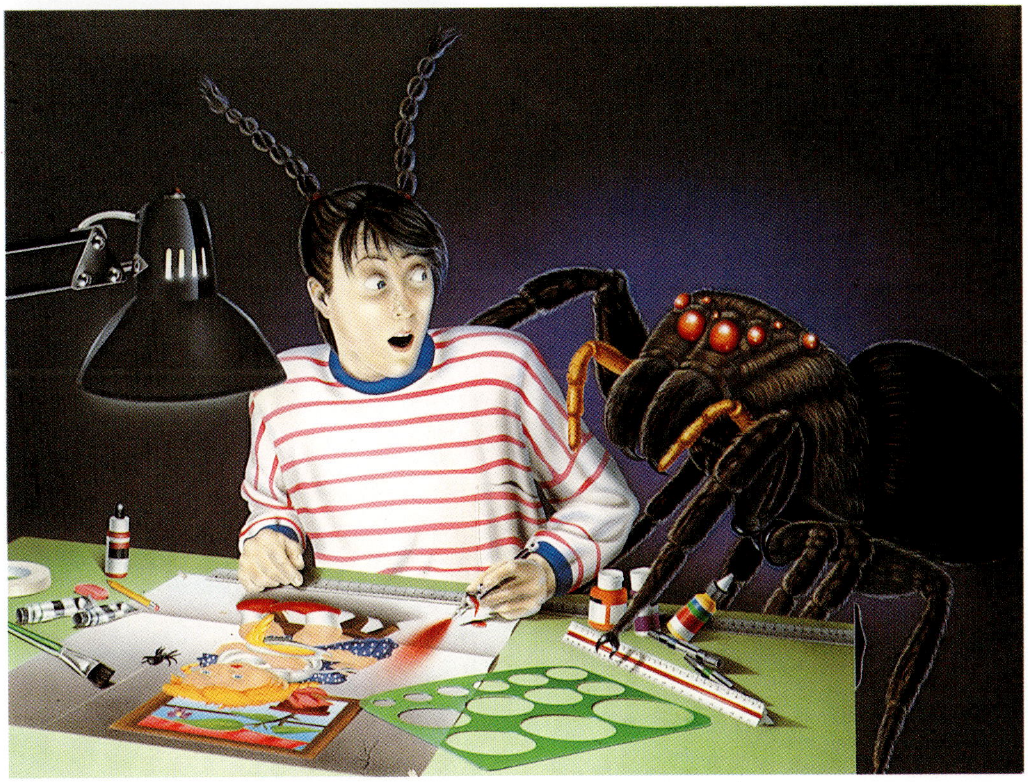
3

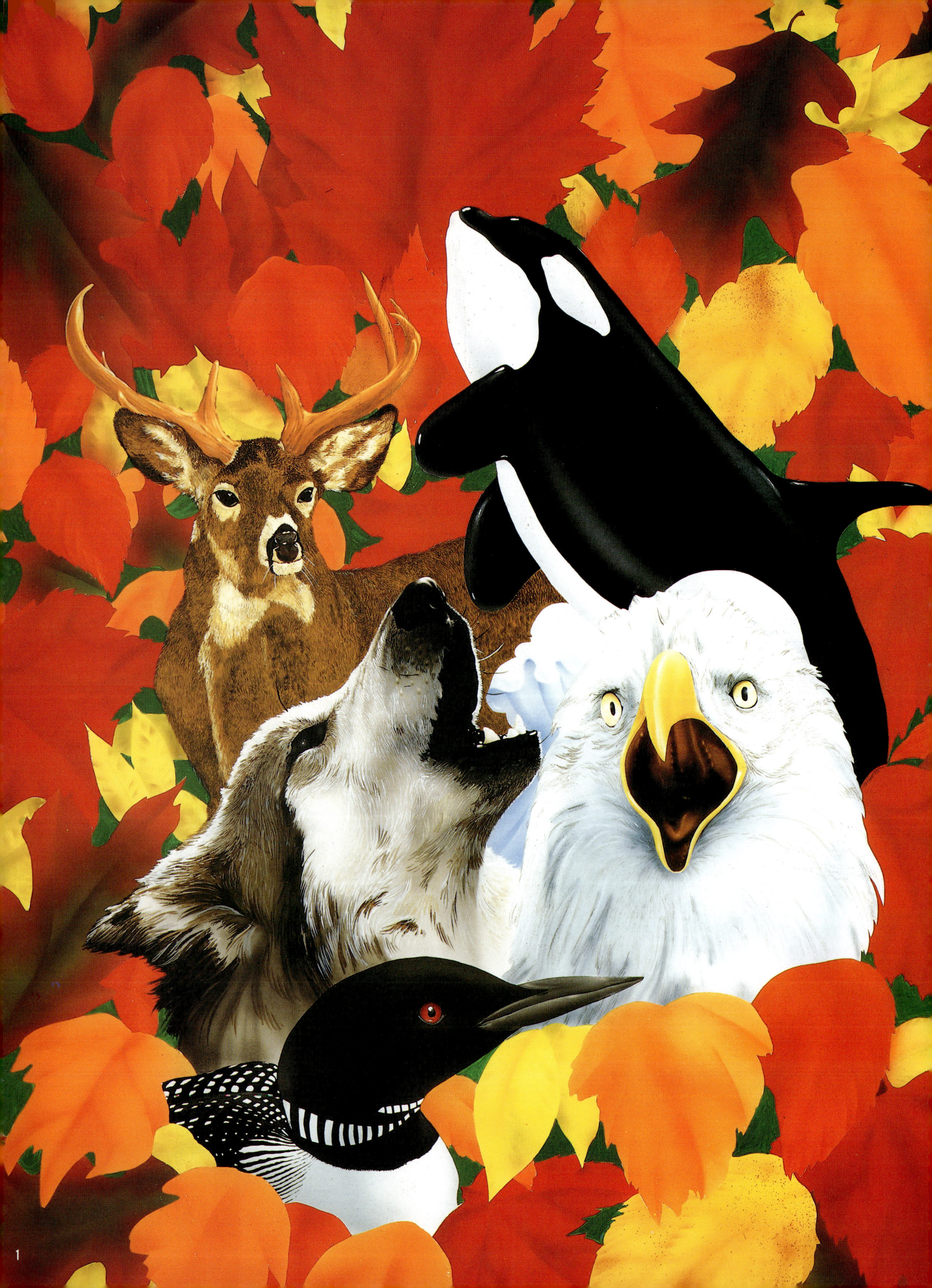

1
Illustrator **MARY A. SHAFER**
Title **WHERE THE WILD THINGS ARE**
Client **NORTHWORD PRESS, INC.**
Art Director **MARY A. SHAFER**
Usage **POINT OF SALE PROMOTION - NATURE BOOKS**
Media Used **GOUACHE, WATERCOLOR, INK**

2
Illustrator **STEVE SINGER**
Title **PARTNER**
Usage **STUDENT ART**
Media Used **MEDEA AIRBRUSH COLORS**

3
Illustrator **TIMOTHY STAFFORD**
Title **FLY TRAP**
Usage **STUDENT ART**
Media Used **ACRYLIC**

4
Illustrator **TIMOTHY STAFFORD**
Title **HAPPY PAINTING**
Usage **STUDENT ART**
Media Used **ACRYLIC**

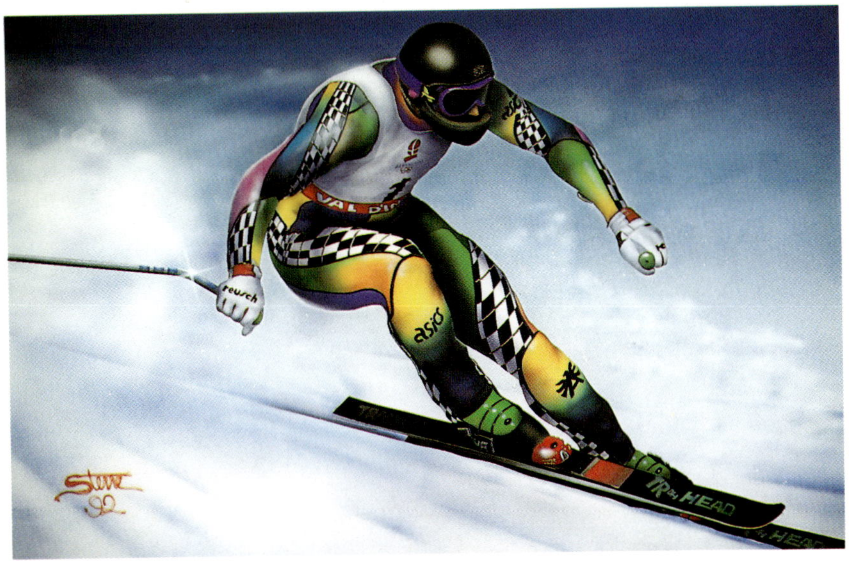

2

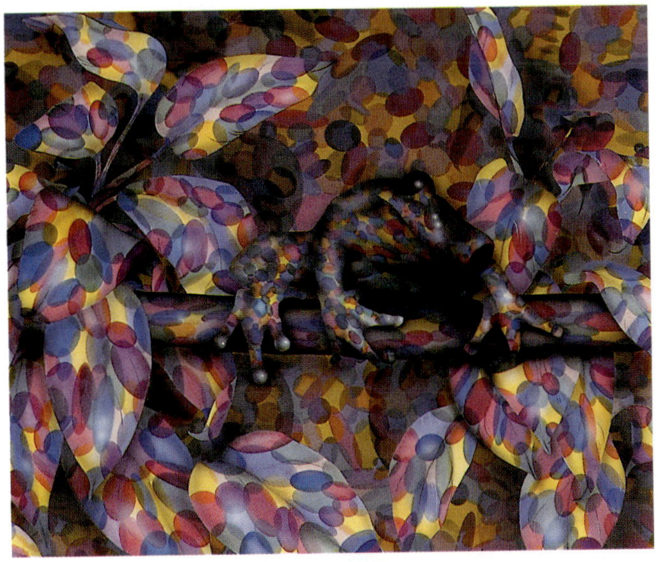
3

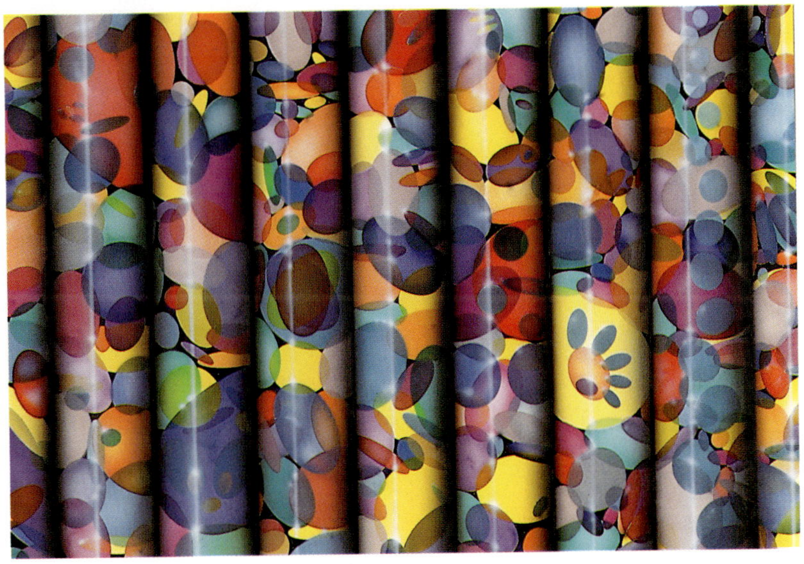
4

1
Illustrator **DANIEL K. TENNANT**
Title **STILL LIFE WITH PHILODENDRON**
Client **GALLERY HENOCH**
Gallery Director **GEORGE H. SHECHTMAN**
Usage **FINE ART**
Media Used **GOUACHE ON MUSEUM BOARD**

2
Illustrator **DANIEL K. TENNANT**
Title **STILL LIFE WITH BLUE CLOTH**
Client **GALLERY HENOCH**
Gallery Director **GEORGE H. SHECHTMAN**
Usage **FINE ART**
Media Used **GOUACHE ON MUSEUM BOARD**

3
Illustrator **DANIEL K. TENNANT**
Title **STILL LIFE IN A BOOK SHOP**
Client **GALLERY HENOCH**
Gallery Director **GEORGE H. SHECHTMAN**
Usage **FINE ART**
Media Used **GOUACHE ON MUSEUM BOARD**

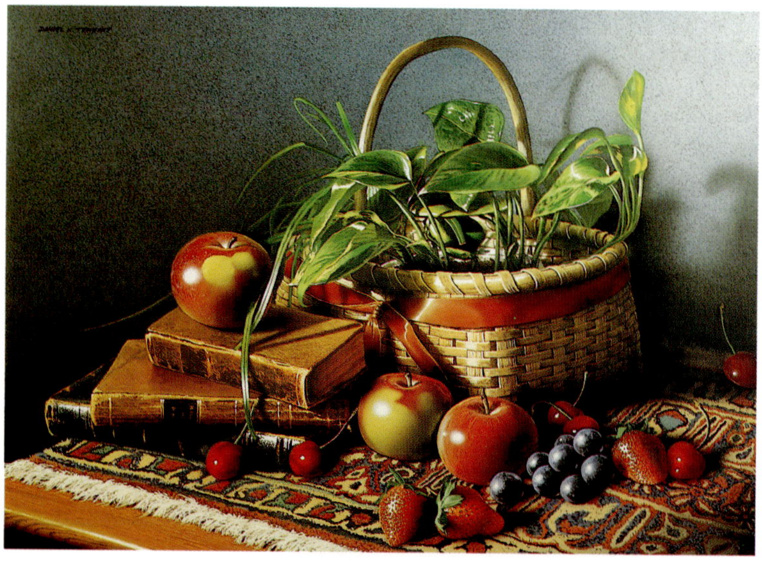

1

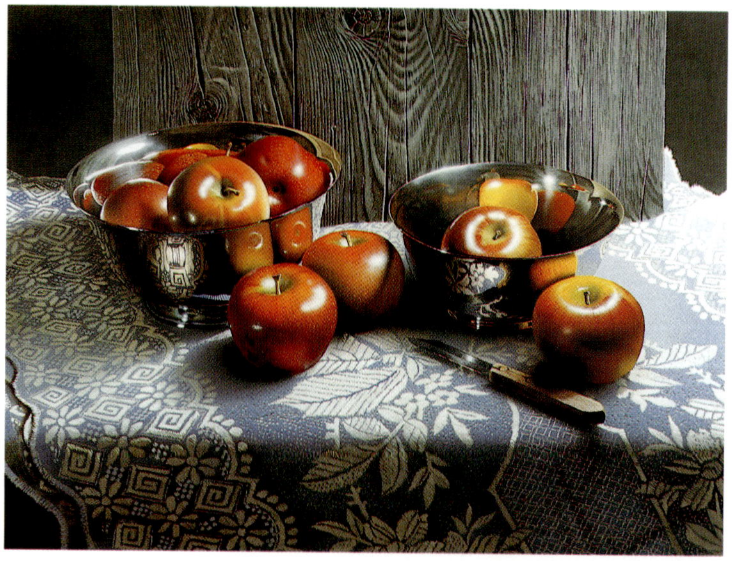

2

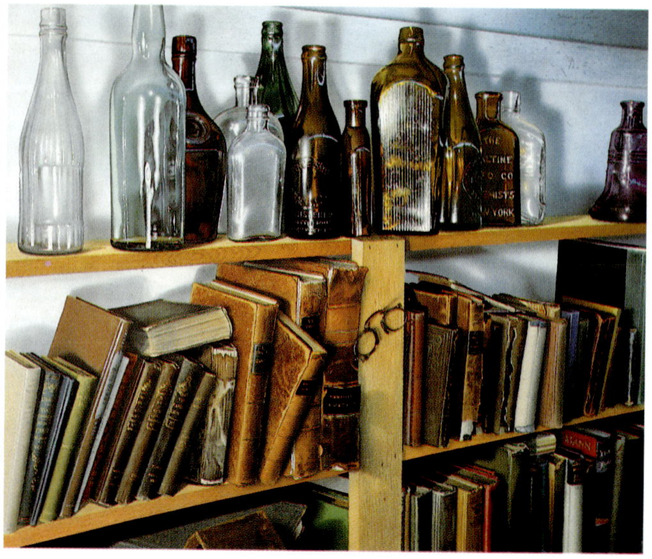

3

1
Illustrator **DANIEL K. TENNANT**
Title **STILL LIFE WITH SUNDROPS**
Client **GALLERY HENOCH**
Gallery Director **GEORGE H. SHECHTMAN**
Usage **FINE ART**
Media Used **GOUACHE ON MUSEUM BOARD**

2
Illustrator **DANIEL K. TENNANT**
Title **STILL LIFE WITH OPEN BOOK**
Client **GALLERY HENOCH**
Gallery Director **GEORGE H. SHECHTMAN**
Usage **FINE ART**
Media Used **GOUACHE ON MUSEUM BOARD**

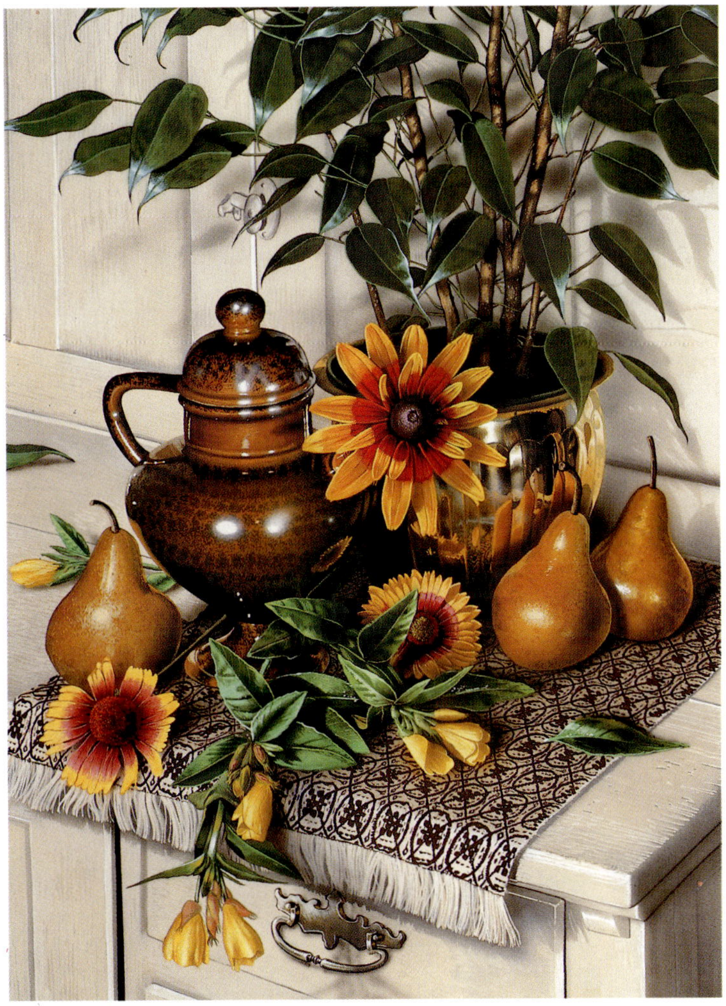
1

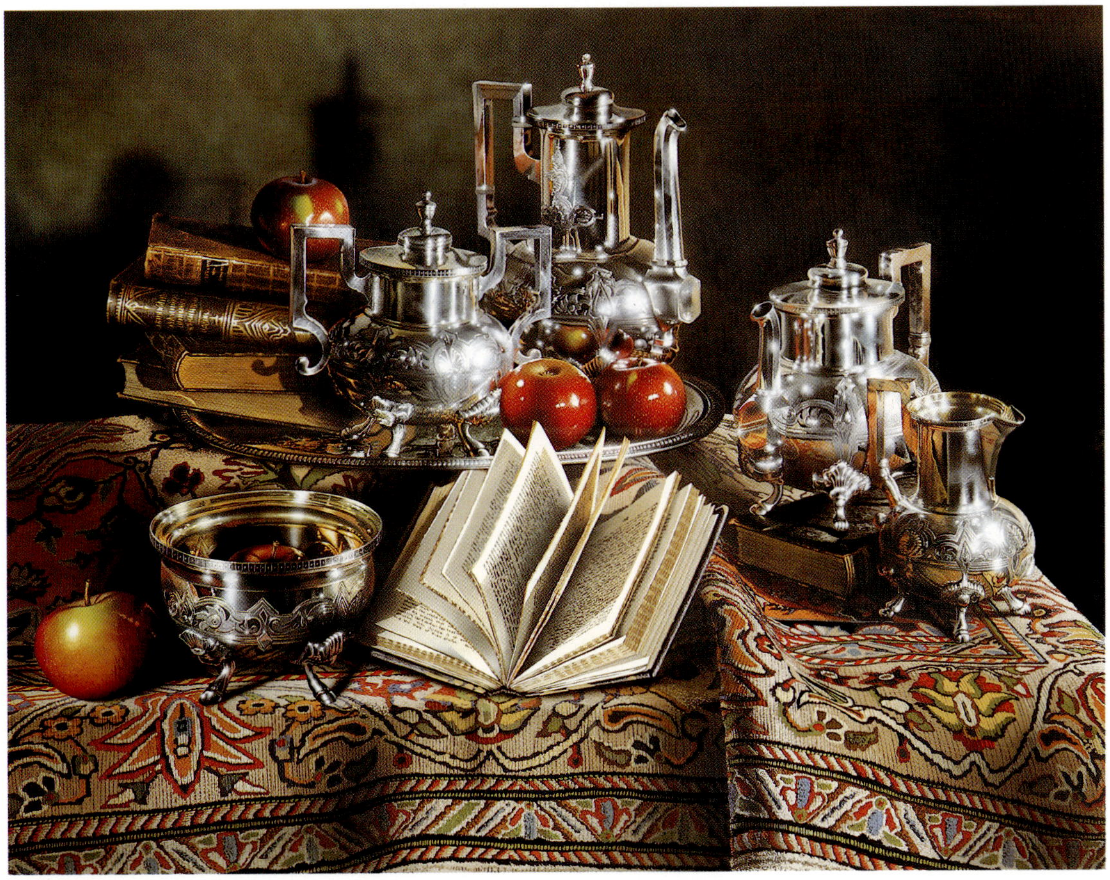
2

1
Illustrator PATRICK C. WANEBO
Client PATRICK C. WANEBO
Art Director PATRICK C. WANEBO
Usage STUDENT ART
Media Used ACRYLIC

2
Illustrator TOBIE WARREN
Title BOGIE
Client JOE KERNAN
Usage FINE ART
Media Used ACRYLIC

3
Illustrator TOBIE WARREN
Title BONO
Client SUE DONAHUE
Usage FINE ART
Media Used ACRYLIC

4
Illustrator TOBIE WARREN
Title STEVEN TYLER
Client GARRY WILLETS
Usage FINE ART
Media Used ACRYLIC

1

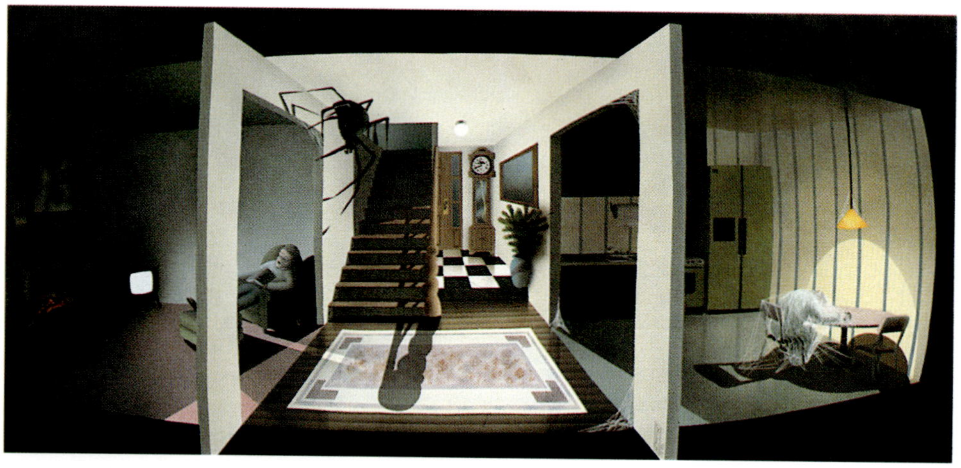

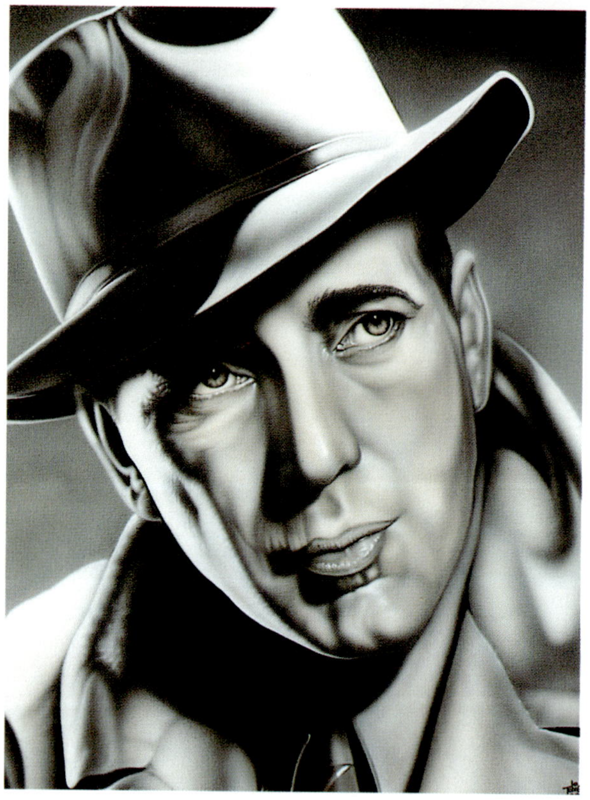

2

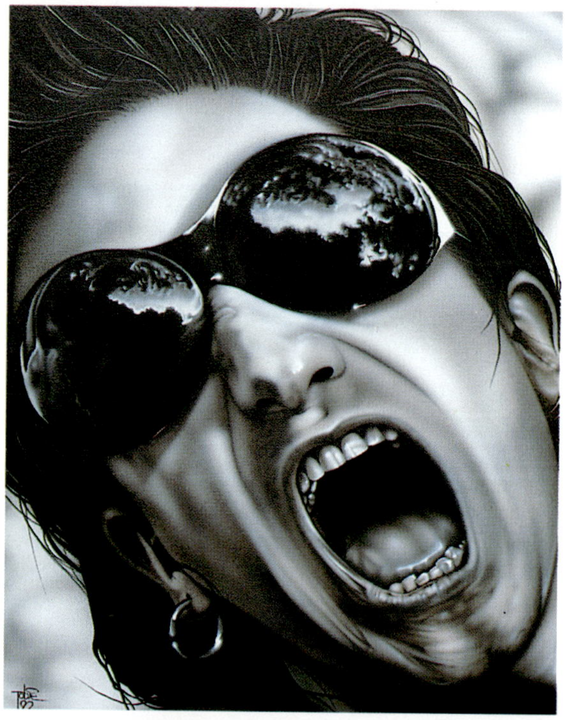

3

4

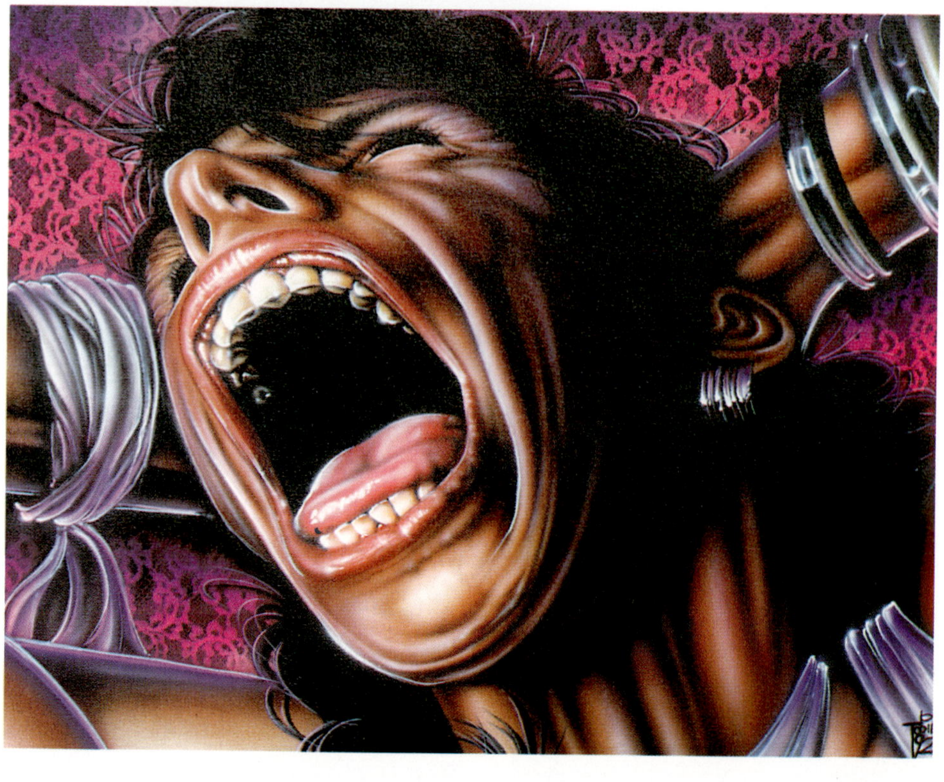

1
Illustrator **WAYNE WATFORD**
Client **LONG HAYMES & CARR/RJR**
Art Director **INGA BORGMEYER**
Usage **POSTER**
Media Used **ACRYLIC**

2
Illustrator **WAYNE WATFORD**
Client **BUSCH CREATIVE**
Art Director **MIKE IVESTER**
Usage **POSTER**
Media Used **ACRYLIC**

3
Illustrator **WAYNE WATFORD**
Usage **SELF PROMOTION**
Media Used **ACRYLIC**

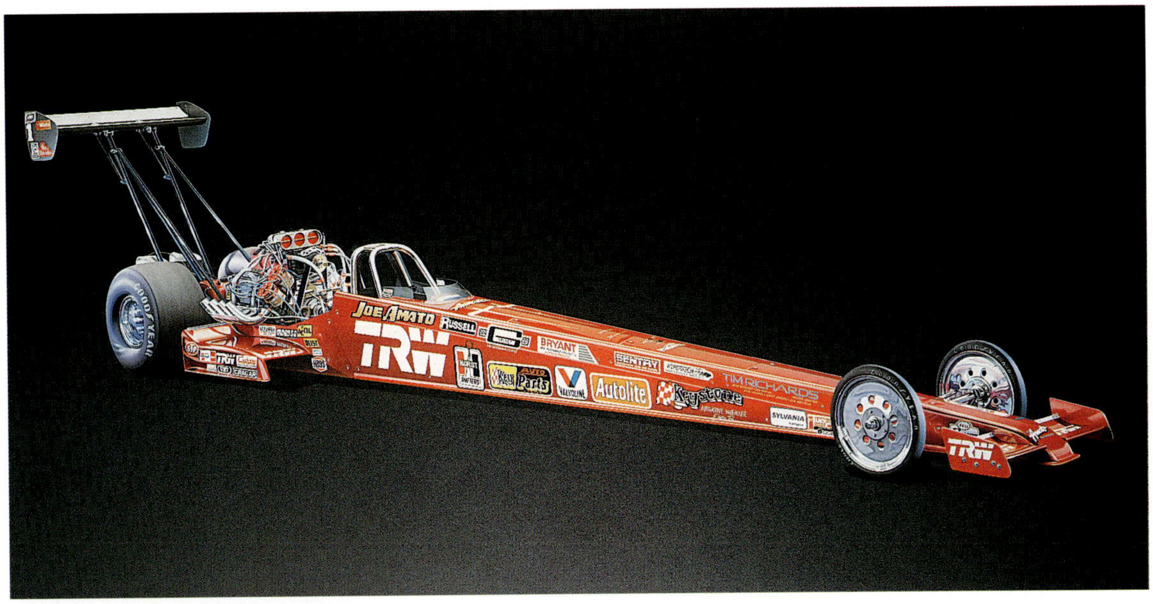

1

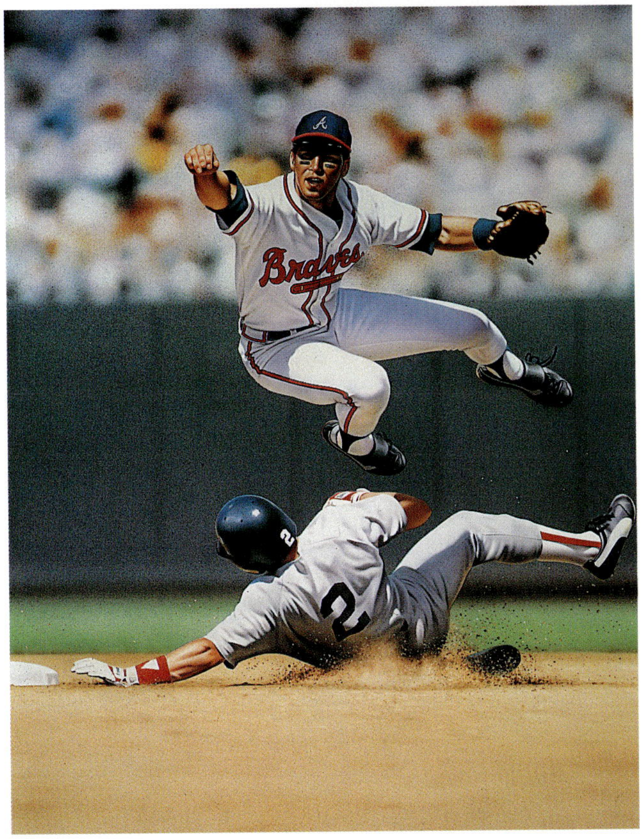

2

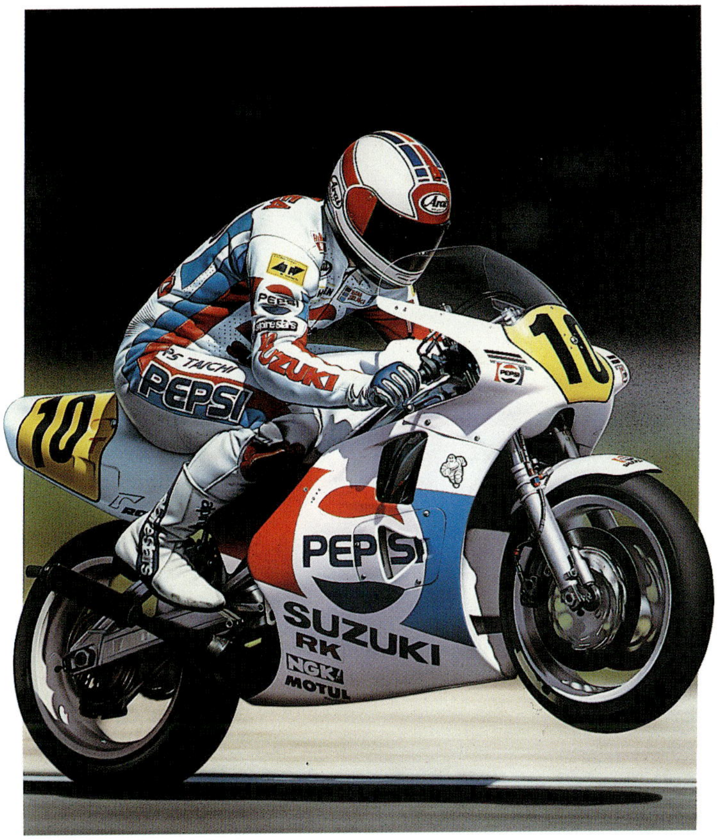

3